D0340153

Praise for *Evidence-Based Recruiting*

"In the NFL, the success (or failure) of a draft is manifest: teams receive swift unmistakable feedback about the quality of the players they selected *and* those they did *not*. (All nine teams who passed on Patrick Mahomes later got to see him play.) By contrast, businesses often fail to even *measure* the performance of the candidates they selected, much less compare that to the performance of those they rejected. As a result, terrible 'draft' strategies can persist, unchecked, for decades, guided by nothing but tradition and intuition. *Evidence-Based Recruiting* provides a needed wake-up call for companies who believe—but can rarely demonstrate—that their selection strategies 'work.' I recommend it to anyone who cares enough about doing better that they are willing to seriously assess how well they are currently doing."

—**Shane Frederick**, Professor of Marketing,
Yale School of Management

"Having selected CEOs and other senior executives for over 100 portfolio companies, it is clear that you can only produce extraordinary results if you hire extraordinary talent. In this book, Atta Tarki provides important insights and practical approaches to doing just that."

—**Jim Williams**, Senior Advisor and former Partner, TPG Global

"Talent will increasingly be the main competitive differentiation between companies. Hiring managers can improve their recruiting results by following the evidence-based methods presented in this book."

—**Marc Bitzer**, CEO, Whirlpool

"One of the most important ingredients to a successful business is recruiting the right talent. *Evidence-Based Recruiting* provides many important and helpful insights that can help you recruit, develop, and retain a winning team."

—**Ron Williams**, former Chairman and CEO, Aetna Inc., and
Chairman and CEO, RW2 Enterprises

"If you believe that human capital is the key differentiator in driving business success, then this transformational book is your path forward to secure optimal talent."

—**Kenneth Svendsen**, CEO, Entertainment Cruises

"Recruiting and retaining top talent is a critical part of my job. *Evidence-Based Recruiting* captures the key strategies I use, while also introducing new ones. An excellent read."

—**M-K O'Connell**, Managing Director, M2O

"The definitive book on recruiting."

—**Inanc Balci**, Cofounder of unicorn Lazada Group, the largest e-commerce company in Southeast Asia

EVIDENCE-BASED RECRUITING

EVIDENCE-BASED RECRUITING

HOW TO BUILD
A COMPANY
OF STAR PERFORMERS
THROUGH SYSTEMATIC
AND REPEATABLE
HIRING PRACTICES

ATTA TARKI

New York   Chicago   San Francisco   Athens   London
Madrid   Mexico City   Milan   New Delhi
Singapore   Sydney   Toronto

Copyright © 2020 by McGraw-Hill Education. All rights reserved. Printed
in the United States of America. Except as permitted under the United States
Copyright Act of 1976, no part of this publication may be reproduced or distributed in any form or by any means, or stored in a database or retrieval system, without the prior written permission of the publisher.

1 2 3 4 5 6 7 8 9   LCR   25 24 23 22 21 20

ISBN   978-1-260-46141-1
MHID   1-260-46141-6

e-ISBN   978-1-260-46142-8
e-MHID   1-260-46142-4

This publication is designed to provide accurate and authoritative information in
regard to the subject matter covered. It is sold with the understanding that neither
the author nor the publisher is engaged in rendering legal, accounting, securities
trading, or other professional services. If legal advice or other expert assistance is
required, the services of a competent professional person should be sought.

—*From a Declaration of Principles Jointly Adopted by*
a Committee of the American Bar Association
and a Committee of Publishers and Associations

McGraw-Hill Education books are available at special quantity discounts to
use as premiums and sales promotions or for use in corporate training
programs. To contact a representative, please visit the Contact Us pages at
www.mhprofessional.com.

To Ava, Kamran, and Kian—and to all other kids whose names are auto corrected. Stay unique!

Contents

Foreword

The first question every CEO should ask is, "How do I create more value for my customers?" The second question is, "How do I do that better than anyone else, while also maximizing value for shareholders?"

When discussing how to achieve these goals, traditional corporate playbooks emphasize focusing on those market segments in which you can create a sustainable competitive advantage by setting up barriers to market entry for your rivals. However, in a rapidly changing business environment, few such barriers remain—so the real question is, "How do I find a lasting competitive edge?"

The answer to this question is surprisingly simple: focus on your people. In the past, you could outperform your competition simply by relying on regulation, securing distribution channels, making large capital investments, or having a differentiated technology, or you might even be able to count on brand recognition—but these traditional strategies are no longer enough. In today's era, your team's talent and passion should be your competitive advantage.

As the CEO of DHL Express U.S., I've made it a priority for my team and me to focus on strategies to develop our people and provide them with the best possible work environment. Globally, we have about 100,000 employees in more than 220 countries and territories, so for a company of our size, these goals come with unique challenges. Yet as a result of our concerted efforts, in the past two years, DHL Express has been recognized as one of the top 10 companies on Fortune's annual list of the World's Best Workplaces.

Much of our success is the result of our efforts to identify and hire the best possible job candidates, and *Evidence-Based Recruiting* offers an easy-to-implement playbook on how to more consistently achieve better hiring outcomes for your own organization. The author illustrates how leading companies use measurable data to land top-tier talent, and how other hiring managers can do the same by implementing the novel—and practical—methods laid out in this book.

One of the hallmarks of a great business leader is the use of intuition to make good decisions. While the instincts of today's top executives are as good as they ever have been, the most successful leaders also recognize their limits and do not rely solely on their own intuition to make many decisions. Otherwise they could become the bottleneck, potentially preventing their firms from creating scalable, repeatable processes that can lead to consistent results.

Rather, the top business leaders are utilizing evidence-based techniques—fueled by a variety of technological innovations—to continually evaluate and improve performance across all business functions.

To find one of the clearest examples of how evidence-based techniques have transformed business practices, one can look to an area that, only two decades ago, relied on intuition perhaps more than any other function: marketing. Today it would be virtually unimaginable to run a marketing campaign without using evidence-based methods to evaluate its effectiveness. Yet 20 years ago, that was the norm.

Ironically, while talent acquisition is an element that is most critical to a company's success, it remains one of the key business processes in which evidence-based methods are least used to improve results. All too often, hiring managers still rely on their intuition and old industry habits to make critical personnel decisions. The recommendations in *Evidence-Based Recruiting* give hiring managers the tools to beneficially transform their practices, in much the same way that evidence-based methods have transformed other key strategic business processes.

Greg Hewitt, CEO, DHL Express U.S.

Introduction

The team with the best players wins.

—Jack Welch

CLASSIC SUSTAINABLE COMPETITIVE ADVANTAGES ARE NO LONGER SUSTAINABLE

Traditional ways of creating a "sustainable competitive advantage" are quickly eroding. The global economy is operating at a breakneck pace, and companies can no longer rely on traditional barriers of entry to preserve their market positions.

Even traditionally well-fortified barriers, such as monopolistic power, have been challenged in recent years. Just look at Uber. It upended the monopolistic hold on taxi cab licenses by classifying itself as a ride-sharing service; and by ignoring existing rules, Uber was able to rewrite the rules to its own advantage. In just two years, Uber overcame traditional barriers to entry that had protected taxis in New York City from any substantial competition for three-quarters of a century.

Another example that illustrates the changing rules of the game can be found in the entertainment sector. Around the year 2000, three years after its founding, Netflix offered Blockbuster the chance to acquire a majority stake in it for about $50 million. Famously, Blockbuster rejected the offer, and everyone knows what happened next: Blockbuster went bankrupt, while Netflix saw its market cap exceed $100 billion for the first time in 2018.

So why did Blockbuster, a company with $6 billion in revenue, get beaten by a tiny start-up?

What did Netflix have that Blockbuster lacked?

What's the key to maintaining sustainable advantage in today's economy?

In a word: *talent.*

The Old Barriers Don't Hold Up

Traditional business books have emphasized the importance of building barriers to entry to secure competitive position and maximize shareholder value. Businesses that do not have well-fortified barriers to market entry, such as monopolistic rights, can use softer barriers to entry, such as large capital investments, to defend their positions. The underlying, historical rationale has been that new and often by default smaller market entrants may be nimbler, but they cannot easily access huge piles of cash.

But times have changed. The investment information company, Crunchbase, estimated that global investors deployed $342 billion of venture capital investments in 2018, more than three times the volume of five years earlier.[1] Venture capitalists are not merely deploying money following the same old patterns—they are growing bolder, as exemplified by Ant Financials' $14 billion capital raise, the largest VC deal ever.

As these examples make clear, few business sectors are immune to having their business model fundamentally challenged. Taxi monopolies, real estate companies, video rental companies—countless businesses with large capital investments all thought to have "sustainable competitive advantages"—have had their business models challenged. The question therefore remains, "What barrier to market entry can help you keep the barbarians—or at least your competition—*outside* the gate?"

Let Your Spartans Be Your City Walls

Whirlpool's CEO, Marc Bitzer, highlights why the rapidly changing environment has increased the importance of building the right team: "Michael Porter's model for how to create a sustained competitive advantage is no longer fully sustainable. If you don't have a competitive edge in terms of talent, your market position will be difficult to defend."

Bitzer's conclusion brings to mind Agesilaus the Great, king of the legendary warrior city-state Sparta. When visitors would ask him why Sparta lacked protective city walls, Agesilaus would point to his citizens in full armor and say, "These are the Spartans' walls."

Agesilaus's message was clear: If anyone were foolish enough to attack Sparta, he had no intention to seek shelter behind any barriers or walls. He'd welcome the fight. Agesilaus knew that it was not the height of his city walls that would make the barbarians think twice about encroaching on Spartan territory, but rather the quality and might of his warriors.

Today's business leaders can learn from Agesilaus. Either they can play defense and spend their resources by building barriers to entry, or they can go on the offensive and let the quality of their talent—their Spartans—be their barriers to market entry.

The choice seems clear.

HOW WINNING COMPANIES INVEST IN THEIR TALENT

The common approach in attempting to build winning teams is to recruit slightly above-average talent and then invest in training, development, and mentorship for these individuals to bring the best out of them—let's call this *The Karate Kid* approach. But Google, Netflix, and a number of other winning companies are taking a starkly different approach. These companies shift their talent budgets to identifying star performers to begin with—let's call this the *Moneyball* approach. If talent is costlier to develop than it is to identify, massive investment in the selection process can pay off. Google and Netflix have demonstrated success using this approach and continue using this insight to create a sustainable advantage over their competitors.

Winning the War for Talent Using Evidence-Based Hiring

Isn't all hiring evidence-based? Unfortunately, no. The vast majority of hiring practices today are based on "the way it has always been done," standard channels in which talent is found, based upon gut feelings, intuition, emotions, subjective beliefs, and common misconceptions about what actually works.

If you are one of the few executives unfamiliar with the book *Moneyball: The Art of Winning an Unfair Game* by Michael Lewis, I highly recommend it. In brief, the book tells about how the Oakland Athletics baseball team, and its general manager, Billy Beane, used superior recruiting practices to take the team to the playoffs two years in a row despite having only well under half the budget of larger teams. While the New York Yankees won both playoffs, it had to spend $1.2 million per win that season. The

Oakland A's achieved nearly the same results but spent three times less per win. While nearly all other teams outspent the Oakland A's, the A's outperformed all the other teams but one. The lesson of this book is the same: you too can outperform organizations with deeper pockets than yours by utilizing superior hiring practices and committing to a razor-sharp focus on recruiting better talent.

Hundreds of companies have taken this lesson to heart and are building up their talent acquisition analytics teams to improve the accuracy of their hiring predictions. Each hire these companies make will have slightly higher odds of being a star performer and slightly lower odds of being a mis-hire. Like skilled poker players, these companies are slowly but surely tilting the odds in their favor without "showing their hand." And whether or not you know it, you are sitting at the same table as Google, Netflix, and the countless other companies obsessing about their talent strategies. While in the traditional sense, you should worry only about companies trying to compete for your *customers*, you must remember this: these companies are competing with you for the *talent* that will innovate even better ways to attract your customers.

EVIDENCE-BASED RECRUITING

In this book I have leveraged my extensive experience interviewing candidates and working with clients to observe and learn from their hiring practices, both good and bad. Through my work at ECA, a specialized executive search firm of which I'm the founder and CEO, I have been privy to the thought processes of senior executives at some of the most globally admired companies as they make their hiring decisions, and I have integrated these scenarios into this book.

I have also sought to summarize cutting-edge research with the most practical implications for hiring managers. To challenge my own understanding of the research, I asked Professor Shane Frederick of Yale University and three of my colleagues, Eli Castle, MaryAnn Kontonicolas, and Gustav Brown, who all hold PhD degrees from UCLA, to independently review and critique the claims made in this book. Any errors, of course, remain solely my responsibility.

I should clarify that I'm not just summarizing the scientific fact base. Nor do I argue that hiring managers should rely on purely quantitative candidate attributes or hiring methods. The strengths of quantitative methods are that you can measure, standardize, and replicate many of the outcomes. The strengths of qualitative methods are the richness and depth of the insights. My view is that *both* methods should be used as complementary tools when assessing candidates. I have therefore sought to augment the scientific fact base with qualitative feedback from CEOs and other thought leaders, as well as my own experience.

To this end, I humbly admit that I'm not a scientist. I have, however, made an honest attempt to distill the scientific fact base on recruiting methods and strategies. I feel that sometimes, we business professionals are so much in awe of the complexity and intellectual depth of scientific methods that we are afraid to opine even on science that pertains to our fields. The withdrawal of business professionals from the scientific debate leads to a divide that hurts both scientific progress and business results. Scientists and business professionals alike criticize each other for misunderstanding the other side's point of view and dismiss each other's perspectives, when both sides would benefit from a closer collaboration. I hope that my thoughts on this topic help increase the interest in both these communities working more closely together to find better hiring methods.

Evidence-Based Recruiting is my attempt at helping hiring managers who, like the Oakland A's, seek to create a competitive edge through a relentless focus on building a superior team. Let's call it *Moneyball* for recruiting. The core recommendations in this book can be applied by underdogs as well as by established organizations that have the luxury of large wallets. While some of the recommendations in this book require CEO buy-in, many of these techniques can be applied by any hiring manager, HR executive, or talent acquisition professional who seeks to build a strong team.

The evidence is clear. The key to maintaining a sustainable advantage in today's economy is talent. *Evidence-Based Recruiting* gives you the blueprint to create systematic, repeatable, and scalable best-in-class hiring practices—now and into the future.

Why Bother?

> Those who build great companies understand that the ultimate throttle on growth for any company is not markets, or technology, or competition, or products. It is one thing above all others: the ability to get and keep enough of the right people.
>
> —Jim Collins, *Good to Great*

THE PERFORMANCE ILLUSION

In my experience, most hiring managers think they can maximize the value their team produces by focusing on hiring "solid" performers. The majority of these hiring managers are wrong. They would have produced greater value by spending more resources on finding star performers.

The Müller-Lyer Illusion of Performance

The most common reason I hear hiring managers cite when focusing on "solid" (read "average") performers is that they feel most of the value is created by these slightly above-average performers. This view is often rooted in the *number* of average versus star performers. These hiring managers argue that star performers are so few that they only make up a small share of the entire value created. On the surface, this view seems to make sense.

One of the key concepts I want readers of this book to walk away with is this: The number of average versus star performers follows a normal distribution. The value created by these individuals follows a power distribution.

Let's look at the valuation of unicorns, VC-backed companies valued at $1 billion or higher.[1] Most people think about unicorns in terms of Figure 1.1. You'll notice that the vast majority of unicorns are valued at $5 billion or less. One might therefore conclude that a wise investment strategy is to discover unicorns in this bucket. If a company happens to be valued above, that's great too. However, there is no need to spend resources on finding the companies valued above $5 billion since there are so few.

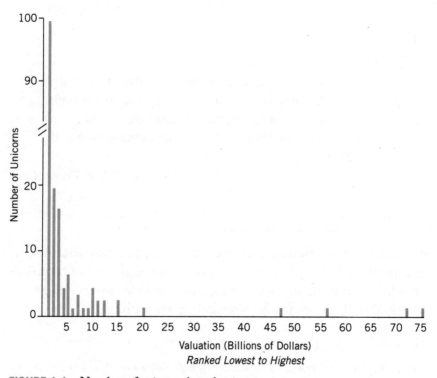

FIGURE 1.1   Number of unicorns by valuation.
Based on data from CB Insights, April 2019.

The issue with "the number of performers" way of viewing performance is that it often misses where the bulk of the *value* is created. The top 10 percent of unicorns, companies valued roughly at $5.5 billion and above, composed roughly 52 percent of the total value generated by all unicorns. The value of these unicorns by their rank is illustrated in Figure 1.2.

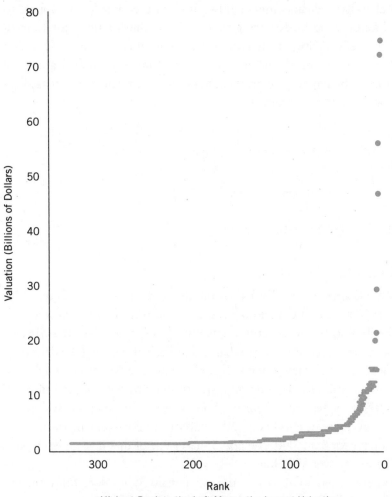

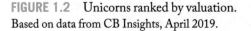
Rank
Highest Rank to the Left Means the Lowest Valuation

FIGURE 1.2 Unicorns ranked by valuation.
Based on data from CB Insights, April 2019.

Viewed from this perspective, it becomes clear that an investor would be better off targeting one of the thirty-three companies in the top 10 percent with an average valuation of $17 billion, rather than making, say, five investments in the bottom 70 percent of unicorns with a valuation of $1 billion to $2 billion each.

This is, of course, much easier said than done. It can be compared with the Müller-Lyer illusion, in which two lines of the same length appear to be of different lengths. Knowing that this is an illusion does not seem to dampen its effect. Every time I look at the lines, there is a part of me that asks, "Are you *sure* one of the lines isn't longer?" Similarly, the facts about the value created by star performers seem to perplex hiring managers regardless of the proof in front of them.

FIGURE 1.3   The Müller-Lyer illusion.

The Power Law of Performance

In his book *Zero to One,* PayPal cofounder and VC investor Peter Thiel describes how most VC investors assume their returns will follow a normal distribution, when the returns actually follow a power law. These investors therefore underestimate to what extent their success will be driven by their most successful investments. These VC investors "spray and pray" their investments. Thiel follows the opposite strategy by focusing his time on finding the very best opportunities. Following this strategy, he was one of the first investors in Facebook and secured a 10.2 percent investment in the company for $500,000. The nondiluted value of that investment would today be worth over $50 billion.

It's nice to use VC investments as an analogy, but does this apply to strategies that hiring managers should follow? In a word: yes.

It's difficult to measure the value created by each role at each company since many roles do not have quantitative measures of how much value they produce, and since there are also a number of intangibles that are difficult to track. For example, one person may be good at motivating her coworkers, but not as productive in other aspects of her job.

In a number of professions, however, the dollar value produced by each person can be precisely tracked. Looking at as many of these dollar values as possible can show us if the power law is unique to top performers in the VC world or if it also applies to other professions.

I therefore analyzed the lifetime prize money won by over 450,000 poker players (Figure 1.4) and over 24,000 ATP tennis players (Figure 1.5). Since these data sets are quite large, they are more likely to be representative of the real-world differences of value produced by thousands of individuals in each profession. I also analyzed the lifetime prize money won by over 1,600 top UFC fighters (Figure 1.6) and over 600 top golf players (Figure 1.7).

Just as in VC investments, the *number* of average versus star performers may follow a normal distribution. The *value* created by these individuals follows a power distribution.

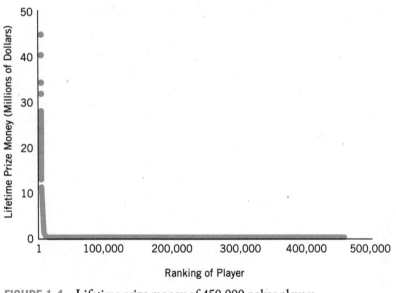

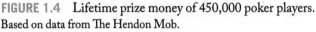

FIGURE 1.4   Lifetime prize money of 450,000 poker players.
Based on data from The Hendon Mob.

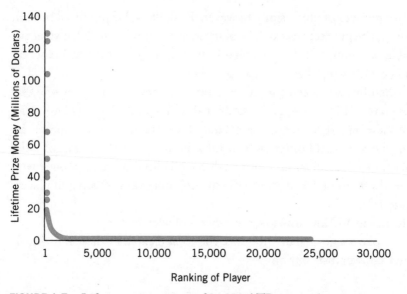

FIGURE 1.5 Lifetime prize money of 24,000 ATP tennis players. Based on data from Pro Tennis Live.

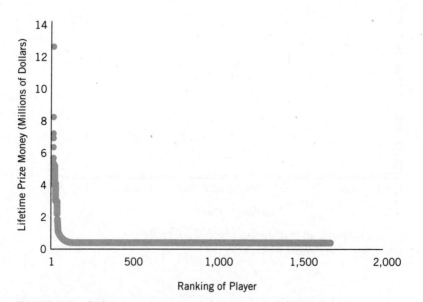

FIGURE 1.6 Lifetime prize money of the top 1,600 UFC fighters. Based on data from The Sports Daily.

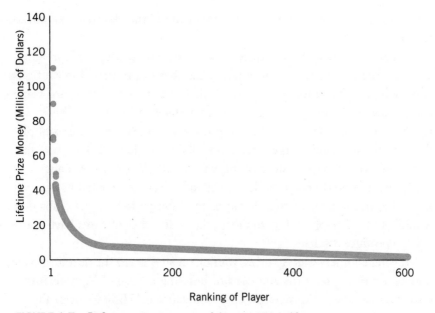

FIGURE 1.7   Lifetime prize money of the top 600 golfers.
Based on data from PGA Tour.

Researchers O'Boyle and Aguinis examined the performance of over 600,000 professionals across 198 samples in order to see if the long-held assumption that performance follows a normal distribution is correct.[2] Their conclusion was clear: "Results are remarkably consistent across industries, types of jobs, types of performance measures, and time frames and indicate that individual performance is not normally distributed—instead if follows a Paretian (power law) distribution."

That Sounds Great in Practice, but Does It Work in Theory?

As discussed above, Thiel utilized his insight about the power law to become successful in VC investing. The same principles apply to recruiting. In her book *Blockbusters*, Harvard Business School professor Anita Elberse describes how bigger bets on talent strategies have changed the landscape in movie studios, record companies, book publishers, sports teams, and even nightclubs. "A Spanish businessman single-handedly raised the bar for investments in A-list talent in the world of soccer," Elberse explains. "Bringing a show-business mentality to his renowned soccer club, Real Madrid's president, Florentino Pérez, started pursuing what he called his 'galácticos' strategy, a reference to the star power of the players he sought to recruit."

Elberse contrasts this with the more cautious strategy of spreading around smaller investments in a larger number of projects. The cautious approach is "a recipe for mediocrity," which may be satisfactory for some companies but is not sustainable in winner-takes-all markets. This is not to say that companies cannot develop their own talent. Elberse exemplifies how the legendary Argentine soccer club Boca Juniors does just that. However, the strategy of developing your own talent requires enormous discipline and bold bets in building the infrastructure needed to succeed deploying this strategy. After all, out of the thousands of soccer clubs that would like to develop their own talent, only a few dozen teams have managed to produce results.

If you genuinely want to bring your talent strategy to the next level, you may be weighing the pros and cons of building a team of high performers versus average performers. You may ask yourself, "Have we been able to consistently attract or develop high performers in the past? If so, what has worked? Can we do more of that?" Saying a few inspirational words to your HR team and hoping that it will work this time around is not enough. If you want significantly different results, you will need to significantly change your approach. And you may need to make significant investments in your talent acquisition team and the budget you allocate per recruit. Simply "trying harder" without investing more resources rarely works. To borrow a line from Nextdoor CEO Sarah Friar, "You never increment your way to greatness."

One CEO who has taken the rule about the power distribution of performance to heart is Inanc Balci, who cofounded the unicorn Lazada, often called the Amazon of Southeast Asia. Inanc recently led the sale of a majority stake in Lazada to the Alibaba Group for $1.5 billion. Inanc explained his hiring philosophy to me: "Most hiring managers try to avoid hiring poor performers. I focus most of my effort on making sure that I don't turn down any star performers. I'm therefore more cautious in turning down candidates who display signs of having the potential to be a star."

Recalling this simple rule can help you invest your time wisely in recruiting star performers as opposed to hiring 10 times more average performers. Taking this simple principle to heart, Apple rolled out its operating system, iOS 10, within two years from the time the project begun, using

600 engineers; Microsoft used 10,000 engineers over five years to release (and then retract) Vista. Which recruiting model do you prefer?

UNDERSTAND THE VALUE OF YOUR HIGH PERFORMERS

> Intellectual, scientific, and artistic activities belong to the province of Extremistan, where there is a severe concentration of success with a very small number of winners claiming a large share of the pot.
>
> —Nassim Taleb, *The Black Swan*

We have all worked with top performers who are much more productive than average performers. But how much more productive are they?

In a presentation made publicly available, Netflix explains why it cares so much about hiring the very best performers. Netflix's view is that these performers are 2 times better than average for procedural work and fully *10* times better than average for creative and inventive work.

And Google's former CEO, Eric Schmidt, was often heard by other employees to say that top performers are 10 times more productive than average performers.

Netflix and Google are not alone in understanding that top performers are not just marginally more productive than "replacement" performers but are multiple times more productive. Much like Mike Trout and Cody Bellinger, they simply deliver many more wins for their teams.

Hunter, Schmidt, and Judiesch, studying over 21,000 professionals across 7 samples, found top performers to be 225 percent as productive as average performers in high-complexity jobs (see Figure 1.8).[3] O'Boyle and Aguinis, examining the performance of over 600,000 professionals across 198 samples, estimated top performers to be about 500 percent as productive as average performers in high-complexity jobs.[4] McKinsey & Company, in a separate study, estimated high performers to be 900 percent as productive as average performers in high-complexity jobs, such as managerial roles and software development roles.[5]

Hiring a head of sales, operations, marketing, engineering, or CEO who is "good" rather than "one of the best" in the field will have a material impact. This ratio, of course, varies by company and profession. If performance at your firm is more similar to the firms in the Hunter, Schmidt,

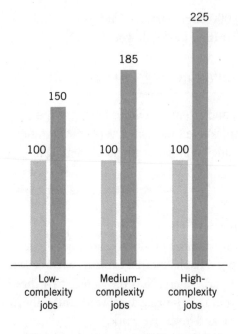

FIGURE 1.8 Relative productivity of average versus top performers.
Based on data from Hunter, Schmidt, and Judiesch, 1990.

and Judiesch study, a top performer produces 2.25 times better results than an average performer. If your company has more in common with Netflix, Google, or the firms studied by McKinsey & Company, a top performer produces *9 to 10 times* better results than an average performer. If performance at your firm is more similar to the lifetime prize money of golf, tennis, and poker pros, the difference would be even more material as the top pros in each field earned thousands of times more money than the average player in their field.

UNDERSTAND THE COST OF BAD HIRES

The Direct Costs of Bad Hires

Making better hiring decisions can involve two things: (1) hiring more top performers and (2) making fewer hiring mistakes. It's just as important to reduce hiring mistakes as it is to hire more top performers, the reason being that hiring mistakes can be costly (see Figure 1.9).

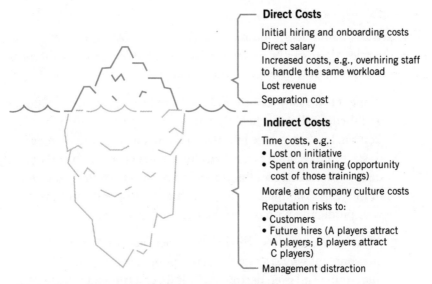

Direct Costs

Initial hiring and onboarding costs
Direct salary
Increased costs, e.g., overhiring staff to handle the same workload
Lost revenue
Separation cost

Indirect Costs

Time costs, e.g.:
• Lost on initiative
• Spent on training (opportunity cost of those trainings)

Morale and company culture costs

Reputation risks to:
• Customers
• Future hires (A players attract A players; B players attract C players)

Management distraction

FIGURE 1.9 Direct versus indirect costs of mis-hire.
Based on data from Appelbaum and Milkman (2006); *Society for Human Resource Management*; Smart, *Topgrading*; Watkins, *The First 90 Days*; U.S. Dept. of Labor Statistics.

The direct costs of hiring mistakes can include:

- **Hiring and onboarding costs.** These include the costs of job ads, potential fees to recruiters or salaries of your in-house recruiters, and the time paid for people's salaries while onboarding them.

- **Increased cost of overhiring.** For example, costs rise if you need to overhire to manage the same workload.

- **Lost revenue opportunities.** For example:

  - Worse decisions by management lead to lost revenue.

  - Clients deprioritize your firm because of lower-quality products or service.

  - Lower productivity leads to lost revenue.

- **Separation costs.** These include severance packages and potential legal fees.

Indirect Costs of Bad Hires

There are also a number of indirect costs associated with hiring mistakes. For some roles, these can be as dangerous as the hidden part of an iceberg and greatly exceed the direct costs. They include:

- **Time.** How many months did it take to hire a person, train him, and then, finally, conclude that he was not able to do the job? You can lose six to nine months on the wrong hire and then need to start from scratch again. Will the members of your board of directors be understanding, or will they expect results by the end of the year? Another big-time expense is the opportunity cost of your productive employees who train the mis-hire.

- **Morale.** Most people who have experienced a toxic work environment would agree that a few poor performers can undermine and even destroy the culture of a company, while strong performers have the opposite effect. If an employer fires a bottom performer, company morale will often also suffer. High-performing colleagues of the fired employee are not robots; they may have developed an affinity for the individual getting fired, especially if the company culture doesn't support the practice of asking poor performers to leave.

- **Reputation risks.** Mis-hires may embarrass you in front of a client. They can also make it more difficult to attract good talent. Indeed, in the era of social media, this is truer today than ever before. Bottom performers are more likely to be dissatisfied with their work. When they turn to Glassdoor to tell other prospective hires about how it is to work at your firm, you are likely to end up with a negative review.

- **Management distraction.** In many organizations, bottom performers are not only a distraction to those training them; they also take up a significant amount of management's time.

CEO Estimates of the Cost of a Bad Hire

Which costs are higher for a mis-hire, direct or indirect? This will, of course, vary by type of position, company, duration of stay, and the performance of each hire. However, the consensus among both researchers and executives is that the more senior a position, the higher the costs, even when compared with the employee's salary.

In his book *Topgrading*, Bradford Smart describes how one of his clients estimated the costs of mis-hires for a client company's sales roles. While one-third of the cost for this role was direct costs, two-thirds were indirect (see Figure 1.10).

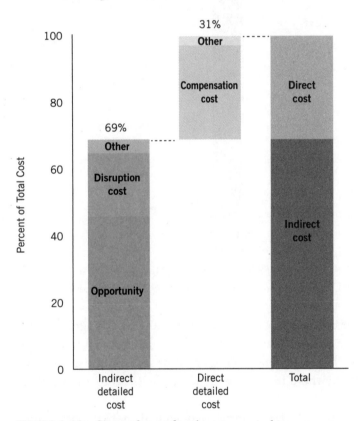

FIGURE 1.10 Share of cost of a salesperson mis-hire.
Based on data from Smart, *Topgrading*.

Experts vary in their estimates of the cost of a bad hire for a senior-level position. The U.S. Department of Labor estimates the cost at five times the annual salary of the executive. Dr. Michael Watkins, author of the best-seller *The First 90 Days*, estimates the cost at 15 times the annual salary. The CEOs we interviewed stated the cost at an average of 7 times the annual salary of a senior-level executive (see Figure 1.11).

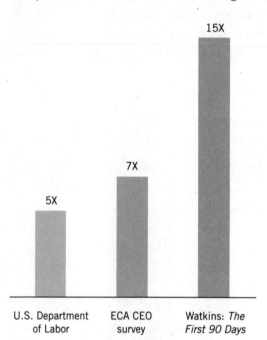

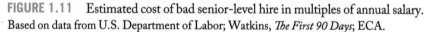

FIGURE 1.11   Estimated cost of bad senior-level hire in multiples of annual salary. Based on data from U.S. Department of Labor; Watkins, *The First 90 Days*; ECA.

While these estimates span a broad range, most experts agree that the cost of a bad hire *at least* equals the position's annual salary for senior-level hires. Given the high compensation of executives, a mis-hire at this level could cost you anywhere from a few hundred thousand to a few million dollars.

A number of the CEOs we interviewed pointed out that most companies underestimate this cost.

WHAT WE SAY VERSUS WHAT WE DO

If making better hiring decisions can have real monetary benefits, why don't more companies take advantage of this opportunity? Summarizing findings from tech consulting firm PwC's 2018 global CEO survey, Carol Stubbings, global leader for people and organization, wrote that the ability of companies to capitalize on their growth prospects is "as much about talent as technology, if not more so. People, not systems, drive innovation and realize its full commercial potential."

Companies typically report such tendencies as:

"Hiring and retaining great people is our priority."
"Our employees are the true force behind our success."
"Our employees are our most important asset."

Table 1.1 presents some more statements—and their relationship to reality.

TABLE 1.1　Vision Statements Versus Reality

Typical Vision Statements	Reality
Our competitive advantage is our people.	Most companies don't really care if their best people are assigned to recruiting or not.
We take our hiring process very seriously.	Management rarely "obsesses" about recruiting.
Our success comes from our people, not our products or technology.	Most organizations don't do anything different to attract or evaluate above-average talent.
I only hire people who are smarter than I am.	Best hires come from a random series of events that happen to come together, not from a systematic process that leads to repeatable success.

These statements were made by Frontier Communications, Sears, and Hertz, respectively. They have one thing in common: based on ratings and reviews on Glassdoor, they made it onto the same prestigious list, 24/7 Wall Street's "Worst Companies to Work For."

If a company's employees really are their biggest asset and most important drivers of success, shouldn't companies focus more resources on improving their talent acquisition and employee satisfaction?

Companies That Walk the Talk

A hard focus on the quality of hires should not apply only to billion-dollar companies. In fact, it is likely that smaller companies should focus even more on this area, since each hire has a relatively bigger impact on their overall success.

Why are some companies saying one thing about their talent acquisition strategies but doing another? For three main reasons:

1. They think it is more effective to hire average performers and train them to become top performers. Even if companies rarely admit this, it is often how they actually operate.

2. They simply don't believe that poor hiring decisions are all that costly.

3. They don't know how to operate otherwise. That is, even if they understand that poor hiring decisions can be extremely costly, they still don't believe they can appreciably improve their hiring results, so they see little value in trying.

Or maybe it is like what Forbes CEO Mike Federle expressed in an interview with me: "Like a lot of things in life, there is the way you want to be and there is the way you are." Recognizing this discrepancy is a necessary first step. "Most companies have good intentions," continued Federle, "but achieving your goals requires a lot of concerted efforts."

Learn from *Moneyball*, Not *The Karate Kid*

In 2011, American technology reporter Steven Levy got a rare opportunity to share Google's origins and philosophies in his book *In the Plex*. Levy describes how, in its early days, Google discovered that "getting more computers was no problem. Google needed brain power."

Google was not alone in reaching this conclusion. What set the company apart, though, was its ability and discipline to positively implement this vision. Within a year of its founding, Google had recruited some of the most brilliant minds in the world in their fields (see Table 1.2). The company has remained true to this vision to this day.

TABLE 1.2 Select Google Hires in the First Year of Business
Based on data from *In the Plex*

Name	Previous Organization and Title	Description
Marissa Mayer	Stanford student	Superstar in AI
Urs Hölzle	Professor of computer science at UC Santa Barbara	Invented fundamental techniques used in most of today's leading Java compilers
Louis Monier	Researcher and consultant	Technical advisor at Context Scout (aimed to improve web search technology)
Jeffrey Deane	Software designer and developer	Worked on profiling tools, microprocessor architecture, and information retrieval
Krishna Bharat	Georgia Tech, research scientist	Created Google News, opened research and development center in India
Anurag Wadehra	Board member of iMerit Technology	Specialties in executive and business management, product management, and product launch
Ben Gomes	Worked at ICSI under AI group leader	"Guru" of the search engine
Amit Singhal	Member of technical staff at AT&T	"Master" of Google's ranking algorithm
Omid Kordestani	VP of BD and Sales at Netscape	Was being courted by "The Wizard of Cupertino," Steve Jobs, for high-level role at Apple

As noted earlier, many companies seem to follow the mantra that it is more effective to hire average performers and then train them to become top performers than hire a top performer to begin with. This strategy is not always explicitly stated, but it is what many companies do.

How they actually operate is reflected in where they spend their resources. The average U.S. company spends about $600 on training each employee and $450 on recruiting each employee (see Figure 1.12).

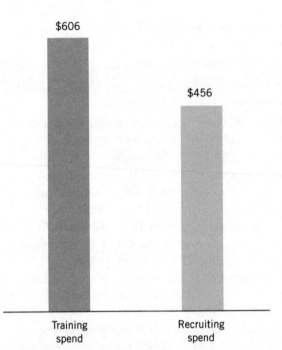

$606

$456

Training
spend

Recruiting
spend

FIGURE 1.12   Average spend per employee at U.S. companies.
Based on data from Bock, *Work Rules!*.

There is little wrong with this strategy per se. The question is, does
it work? In his book *Work Rules!*, Laszlo Bock, who once ran all recruiting and people operations at Google, argues forcefully against the practice of allocating more resources on training than recruiting. He argues that
the vast majority of corporate training programs are a waste of time and
money, because they are incapable of significantly improving the skills of
the employees who participate. Instead, he argues, companies should spend
their training budgets on better recruiting.

Imagine you are the coach of a college basketball team. Would you have
a greater chance of winning if you recruit average-skilled players and try to
train them up or if you recruit the very best players available?

Michael Lewis's classic book *Moneyball* provides invaluable perspective on this question. The central insight of the book is how the Oakland
A's went about identifying and hiring the best-performing athletes they
could afford. This approach should not be confused with the storyline of
the movie *The Karate Kid*. In this movie a superior coach, Mr. Miyagi,

unrealistically turns a kid who is a subpar performer into a superstar in nearly no time at all. (Apologies to any practitioners of karate who feel I'm being too generous to the kid.)

The question is, do you think you can be more successful emulating Billy Beane in *Moneyball* or Mr. Miyagi in *The Karate Kid*? In other words, can you drive more success by deploying evidence-based practices to hire top performers or by hiring average performers and trying to use your Miyagi-esque coaching skills to miraculously transform them into asskicking black belts?

Regardless of your answer, is your hiring strategy reflected in your actions? Do they reflect how you spend your time and energy? Does your hiring budget exceed your training budget or vice versa? Do you even know how much these budgets amount to? Are you obsessing about your hiring strategy? Or is it more of a vague hope or ambition?

BELIEVE YOUR OWN NUMBERS

Are Poor Hiring Methods Costing You Real Money?

One person who is following his own advice to spend more time hiring topnotch employees, as opposed to coaching up pretty good ones, is DoorDash CEO Tony Xu. In a 2017 interview he described how he sees recruiting as the most productive activity he can spend his time on, saying, "I spend 50%+ of my time in recruiting, as I find it has the highest output to input ratio."[6]

As noted earlier, one reason that many companies fail to adhere to their stated recruitment ideals is that they ultimately don't believe that poor hiring methods are as costly as their own calculations show them to be. Many of the companies might be willing to stipulate that poor hiring methods are expensive, and yet their hiring tactics prove otherwise. Few appreciate this tendency better than Thompson Barton, who writes in his book *Please Lie to Me*, "How I really know what I want is by noticing what I have. The rest is just what I say I want."

For some companies, the assumption that mediocre hiring methods are not always terribly expensive may in fact be correct. Such companies might be better off reducing their hiring costs than trying to improve their results. This frees up a great deal of management's time and other resources.

Most companies, however, don't fall into this category. Poor hiring methods *are* costing them serious money. And in many cases, the executives of these firms admit this is true. Yet when it comes to where they actually spend the organization's time and money, their decisions indicate they don't really appreciate the steep costs of substandard hiring methods.

David Kong, CEO of Best Western Hotels & Resorts, has an alternative explanation: "It's the easy thing to do. Doing something else than the norm requires effort. But it's easy to say that hiring is important. And it's easy to use the same hiring process and screening questions as everyone else."

Google, contrary to many of the companies described above, wholeheartedly believes that it can make money by hiring better people. It therefore acts as if there is money to be made by finding and identifying better hires. As described earlier, Google's CEO personally approved all of the 6,000 to 10,000 hires the company makes in a year.

Tony Hsieh, the CEO of the online clothing company Zappos and the author of the bestselling business book *Delivering Happiness*, is another example of a leader who believes that poor hiring decisions waste a startling amount of his company's money. In an interview with *Inc.* magazine, Hsieh shared that Zappos's "biggest category of mistakes is definitely in the hiring process" and estimated that these mistakes have cost the firm "well over $100M."[7] These are not just empty statements. Zappos has spent years trying out an array of hiring methods, many of which go against conventional wisdom.

How Much of a Company's Success Can Be Attributed to the Quality of the Management?

A number of private equity firms I have interviewed have mentioned that it's difficult for them to estimate the value of a great CEO compared with an average one since they have too few data points in order to make the distinction. I therefore turned to Jim Williams, partner at leading private equity firm TPG. Jim oversees human capital initiatives across TPG's entire portfolio and has over the years been personally involved in more than 200 CEO hiring decisions, including most recently the hiring of Uber's CEO. Jim told me he had given this topic quite a bit of thought:

> We regularly study how much a great CEO is worth. In our 25-year history we have noticed that the two most important fac-

tors impacting our internal rate of return on an investment are (a) buying the right business at the right price and (b) quality of the management team. The difference in ROI between top-quartile deals and lower-quartile deals is about 20–25 percentage points. You could surmise that up to half of that difference is because of the CEO and management team. Five percentage points of IRR for a great CEO is a lot, and that's why we pay well. It also depends on the business. Are we swinging hard and going for a home run, or is this a stable business that just needs small changes?

Given that TPG has over $100 billion under management, a 5-percentage-point difference in the internal rate of return would amount to billions of dollars in higher returns. No wonder TPG prides itself on how well it pays its executives.

Sample Calculation of the Value of Better Hires

Improving your recruiting methods often starts with understanding how much it would be worth to you (see Table 1.3). When going through this exercise, keep these simple rules in mind:

- If your calculations don't show that you can create more value than what you would need to spend to get there, you are better off focusing on other activities.

- Keep the calculation simple, and use modest, realistic assumptions. If you and other executives ultimately don't believe the numbers, you will not try to change your methods.

- After going through the exercise, if you (or other decision makers in your firm) are still not willing to invest in achieving these results, it most likely means that you don't truly believe that your assumptions are realistic. Redo the exercise until you are willing to believe your own numbers. A good sign is that you are willing to act on your own estimates and believe that it is sensible to invest the amounts your calculations are yielding to achieve better hiring results.

TABLE 1.3 Total Value Analysis by Better Hiring Practices

Questions	Sample Responses	Calculation
Who are my best performers?	Ella, Prince, and Lenny	
Who are my average performers?	Adam, Ferdinand, and Lisa	
Who are my bottom performers?	Karl, Tom, and Riley	
How much more value are my top performers creating for the company than my average performers? (No need to over-complicate this. If you don't have detailed data on this, go with a rough guess.)	7X	700%
How much value does an average performer create for the company?	$100K (e.g., total profit produced by a division divided by total number of employees in that division)	$100,000
Value created by each top performer	$100K x 700% (note: the math here isn't quite precise, but this is a high-level estimate, not a precise calculation)	$700,000
Number of annual hires at the company (or in your division)	100	
Share of current hires that turn out to be top performers	10%	
Share that could be top performers with more time and resources spent on improving hiring quality	15%	
Incremental number of employees better hiring processes can lead to	5% (15% – 10%) x 100 annual hires	5
Value better hiring processes can create in year 1 by hiring more top performers	5 incremental top performer hires x $700K value created by each top performer	$3,500,000

Many organizations that fail to improve their hiring methods do not do so because of a lack of sophistication in how they run these estimates. More often, they fail because they do not take a step back and make sure they get these basic points right.

Chapter Summary and Conclusion

Context:

- Most hiring managers believe performance follows a normal distribution. This is not correct for managerial and creative roles. While the number of performers may correspond to a normal distribution, the *value* created by these individuals follows a power distribution.
- Likewise, mis-hires are costlier than most hiring managers believe them to be.
- Leading organizations take the two points above seriously and obsess about hiring stars.

What you can do about it:

- Do the math to truly understand how much star performers are worth to you and how much mis-hires cost you.
  - If you are not willing to act upon your own numbers, it's a good sign that you don't truly believe in them. Use more realistic assumptions and redo the math until you do.
  - If star performers produce most of the value, instead of focusing on recruiting average performers and hoping a few of the hires will turn into stars, set up a recruiting strategy that produces more stars and reduces chances of mis-hires.
- Decide if your talent strategy will more resemble the *Moneyball* approach, in which you recruit high performers right out of the gate, or the modus operandi of *The Karate Kid*, hoping to turn mediocre performers into stars through training and development.
- Stick to your plan. Whichever strategy you choose, follow it. Paying lip service does not produce results.
- Make larger bets on talent strategies that work for you; don't just try to "increment your way to greatness," to paraphrase Nextdoor CEO Sarah Friar.

2

Why Now: The New Era of Talent Acquisition

Vision without execution is hallucination.

—Thomas Edison

THE DEATH OF THE ROLODEX

The era of the specialized Rolodex as the main way to differentiate recruiters is over. LinkedIn killed it.

Does this mean that you are wasting your time expecting more of your recruiting team? No; on the contrary. In a *Harvard Business Review* piece titled "How Recruiters Can Stay Relevant in the Age of LinkedIn,"[1] ECA's president Ken Kanara and I highlight how technological change has made it possible for recruiters to make themselves more critical to organizations than ever before. Recruiters, however, need to adapt and focus their value proposition on areas that can clearly add value. Clinging to old methods will at best produce mediocre results.

Recruiting can be defined fairly broadly. We will therefore initially focus on active talent acquisition via inbound and outbound recruiting activities. Inbound recruiting is when candidates come to you; outbound recruiting is when your company reaches out to candidates.

Inbound recruiters have been responsible primarily for attracting and screening talent through job ads, college campus recruiting, and job fairs.

Some inbound recruiters have also partnered with external agencies, which in turn use either inbound or outbound methods.

Historically, most positions were recruited through inbound methods. When an outbound method was used, it was typically through referrals or the use of an external specialized outbound recruiting firm.

The main value proposition of outbound recruiters was their network of professionals in a certain niche, such as a specific industry (e.g., automotive professionals), position (e.g., CFOs), geography, or all of the above.

This specialization was highly valuable. Before the internet, and more specifically, social media, it was very costly to find specific professionals. If the CEO of a company wanted to hire a VP of engineering to set up a new factory, it would have been time consuming for the in-house recruiting team to research, find, and connect with a sufficient number of engineering professionals who had the appropriate skill set and were willing to accept the job. Most CEOs in this situation therefore preferred to use an external outbound recruiter who had already built a specialized Rolodex (Figure 2.1) and who, ideally, focused on engineers setting up new factories.

FIGURE 2.1   The good old Rolodex.

The specialized Rolodex certainly added value in the past. These outbound recruiters would significantly reduce the transaction cost for companies by finding them specialized executives.

The reason that finding the right executives prior to the advent of social media was so costly is illustrated by my first job out of college in 2004. I would cold-call companies all day long to find executives relevant to market research studies. One of my challenges was that many of the companies used automated phone systems, and I didn't know the name of the executives. In some cases, companies had a policy that they would not connect a caller unless the caller knew the person's name or specific title. A successful day meant that I got hold of one to three executives.

As these methods were costly, few firms had any significant in-house outbound talent acquisition teams, especially for management-level hires. Since companies did not have a frequent need for this level of hire, it was not economical for them to develop a Rolodex of such professionals for when they did need someone with that skill set, which might be as seldom as once or twice a decade. But the main value proposition of outbound talent acquisition professionals has changed tremendously over the past decade.

WHY TECHNOLOGICAL CHANGE HAS MADE THE OLD VALUE PROPOSITION OF RECRUITERS OBSOLETE

In 2003, the social media platform LinkedIn launched. By 2010, LinkedIn reported 90 million users. By 2017, the platform had passed the 500 million user mark. LinkedIn's current goal is to get to 3 billion users globally (Figure 2.2). Today's recruiters can now find information using LinkedIn and other information platforms in minutes that would have taken them days or weeks to find a decade or two ago.

The New Value Proposition of Recruiters

Top-tier talent used to be equally inaccessible to all companies, but now those who ignore technological change are not competing on a level playing field. Top-tier talent is much more reachable by companies that embrace innovative technologies and practices.

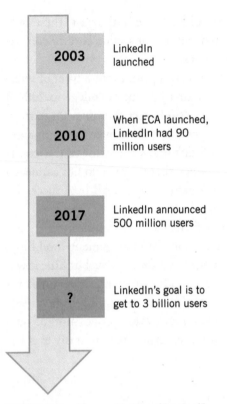

FIGURE 2.2 The evolution of LinkedIn.

This is not to say that recruiters no longer have a role to play in acquiring such talent. The new value proposition of recruiters should be organized around the five steps described here and in Table 2.1.

TABLE 2.1 The New Value Proposition of Recruiters

Strategy	Help hiring managers define the correct search strategy
Candidate sourcing	Identify and engage candidates
Predicting on-the-job success	Screening techniques
Offer management	Help hiring managers get candidates over the finish line
Evaluating and reiterating the process	Continually evaluate and improve steps above

Step 1: Help Hiring Managers Define the Correct Search Strategy

Asking insightful questions is essential in defining the ideal strategy. Strong recruiters will play a crucial role as thought partners in conversations with hiring managers, even if that means breaking the time-worn transactional recruiter relationship.

In a recent Talent Acquisition Summit, Nellie Peshkov, Netflix's vice president of talent acquisition, explained, "Our value in talent acquisition is really about coaching, guiding, providing creative thinking and strategies for that hiring manager."

Michael Orozco, a Netflix recruiter, added that while some recruiters ask their hiring manager, "What do you want?," Netflix recruiters ask questions such as, "Why are you looking for them?" and "How will they make an impact?"

Asking insightful questions is essential to defining the correct search strategy. Strong recruiters will play a crucial role in these conversations.

Recruiters often receive frantic calls from hiring managers looking to fill roles. Strong recruiters have learned that convincing hiring managers to take a step back can be difficult but valuable. For example, one of our clients recently asked us to urgently recruit a VP of new retail to support the large number of new stores his company planned to open. "Find me someone who did this at Starbucks," he told us. Since the coffee chain had also rapidly opened new stores, our client believed a candidate with experience there would have the right skill set to manage a large number of building contractors while recruiting and training staff for the new stores.

Instead of leaping off into a search for executives at Starbucks or similar chains, we asked him to describe the main challenges his company's new stores typically face. The discussion helped our client realize that contrary to his original belief, attracting sufficient foot traffic due to his company's weak brand recognition was the primary challenge. It took him a minute or so, but he ultimately concluded that a background at Starbucks was likely to be the absolute *wrong* profile he needed. A few minutes invested up front in such discussions will allow recruiters to focus their efforts from the beginning of a search, target more ideal profiles, and land better-suited candidates faster.

This is exactly what happened in our case. Helping our client to more closely define what he was looking for enabled him to focus his efforts at the beginning of a search and ultimately hire a better profile.

Step 2: Get the Best Candidates to Apply

The value proposition of recruiters includes being highly efficient at using the correct platforms and methods to identify and engage candidates who are most likely to perform well in the role.

A 2016 SilkRoad study of 13 million applicants and 300,000 hires at 1,200 companies revealed that the "post-and-pray" strategy remains a surprisingly common method for hiring candidates.[2] That is, four times more hires came from posting roles on job boards and company websites than through recruiter-sourced candidates.

While job postings have some benefits, hoping that star performers will fall into your lap is hardly advisable. Successful recruiters help organizations by building a repeatable and a scalable formula for finding and engaging star performers. Recruiters can do this by experimenting with and increasing the efficiency of other sourcing channels.

Step 3: Select the Best of the Best

The next step is to help hiring managers better understand how to predict job performance. Based on this information, recruiters can more efficiently help hiring managers select the best fits among the pool of high-potential candidates who have already applied.

Google's recruiting team is perhaps the best in the world at this: the team helps hiring managers understand what categories of questions they should ask candidates and even provides hiring managers with sample questions they can ask.

Step 4: Get Candidates Over the Finish Line

Strong recruiters will help hiring managers get candidates over the finish line by helping their companies create a positive candidate experience as well as organizing and managing the interview and offer process. One candidate we spoke with who had recently declined an offer cited how she had originally been excited by the company's pitch about being entrepreneurial and fast moving, but started doubting that this was true when the interview process dragged on for three months.

Step 5: Evaluate and Reiterate the Process

Talent acquisition teams should follow up on their hiring practices and apply an iterative process to continually improve their methods. Without establishing this critical step, it is difficult to determine what is working and what isn't.

Some organizations will blindly apply solutions that seem to make sense, or at least sound good to them, without following up to see if these are working. This is because if something feels as if it should work, many of us convince ourselves that it does. Others apply solutions outlined in a report without testing to see whether these are effective in a particular setting. For instance, job knowledge tests may be predictive of job performance at Google, but a while after you implement them at your organization, wouldn't it be useful to know if the tests you are using have improved the accuracy of your hiring predictions? After all, Google has spent years developing and evaluating the success of its tests. Surely it has scrapped a few ineffective tests along the way.

Our own continual evaluation underscores this point: methods that were highly effective two years ago no longer work. One simple example is that by putting a candidate's first name in the e-mail subject line, we used to get up to twice as many candidates to engage in our searches. Now, perhaps because this tactic has been overused, we have abandoned this approach, as it no longer increases candidate engagement.

CEOs who position their recruiting teams to follow these five steps will gain a significant advantage in attracting the right candidates in the new era of talent acquisition, and, as Jack Welch says, "win."

THE "MONEYBALL" OF RECRUITING

People often ask me, "What is the *Moneyball* of recruiting?" When I ask what they mean by this question, they often respond along the lines of, "What is the one question I need to ask candidates in order to hire better performers?"

My key takeaways from *Moneyball* are:

- Identifying talent is much more important to winning than developing talent.

- A data-driven method is far superior to an intuitive approach to identifying talent.

- Applying a data-driven method needs to be done thoughtfully to ensure that the relevant issues are being measured. This is much easier said than done, and it can only be accomplished by testing and retesting your criteria for a specific position. Billy Beane understood that no single variable was relevant for all baseball positions. Assessing candidates for all your positions based on one interview question would be as counterproductive as relying on the same criterion when hiring both a pitcher and a leadoff hitter.

- Focus on what's necessary for each job and discourage procedures that create noise in the candidate-selection process.

The One-Question Candidate Screening Test

I decided to find out if there was one question all employers could ask to predict any candidate's future job performance. I began by arranging an interview with Shane Frederick, a professor at the Yale School of Management. Frederick has coauthored a number of peer-reviewed academic papers with Nobel Laureate Daniel Kahneman, who held up the CRT (cognitive reflection test) as a prime example of this override tendency in his bestselling book *Thinking, Fast and Slow*. Frederick's own research focuses on decision making under uncertainty, that is, choosing actions based on imperfect information and how impulsive thinking and "keen intuition" can boost decision makers' confidence in answers that are demonstrably wrong. Frederick created the CRT, a three-question test that measured the tendency to override one's "system 1" gut reaction and come up with a more accurate "system 2" response.

Rumor has it that Frederick had also developed a one-question test to predict outcomes for MBA students. If there were one person who could intellectually defend the single silver bullet approach, he would be the one.

To my surprise, Frederick refuted the notion that employers should try to predict job performance, or even specific candidate traits such as general mental ability, with a single question. "Why would you limit yourself to one question?" he asked me.

"It's very context specific," he continued. "It's unlikely that the same variable works across multiple industries, or even for multiple roles in the same company. While you could develop one variable that can predict success for a role fairly well, it's very difficult, and most people are likely to get it wrong."

Employers today have far more tools than ever before to use in assessing candidates before making them a job offer (see Table 2.2). Yet even with the new smorgasbord of hiring tools, many hiring managers revert to thinking that they can predict job performance from one or two questions. Instead of finding their silver bullet, Frederick said, "Most people are shooting a rubber bullet from a musket when more modern tools are at their disposal." My advice is to stop believing in the chimera of a silver bullet, a single magic question that will improve your hiring results.

TABLE 2.2   Smorgasbord of Tools Available for Assessing a Candidate

Relevance of past titles and job functions
Relevance of past job duties
Impressiveness of accomplishments

Career path:
   Job-hopping
   Fast-track promotions
   Stagnation in a job

Education pedigree
GPA or SAT scores
Behavioral interviews
Situational interviews

Assessments of soft traits:
   General personality
   Conscientiousness

Assessments of hard skills:
   Cognitive ability
   Work-related tasks

Combined assessments:
   Typing tests that link data to personality traits
   Reference checks

Background checks
Drug tests

By now you can see where I'm coming from: be strategic, use proven tools and methods, and don't follow old paths or new fads. In other words, the *Moneyball* of recruiting is to heed the lessons of *Moneyball*: develop a comprehensive, strategic, and evidence-based system for evaluating talent.

The One Big Idea

Many hiring managers look for superficial solutions when they screen candidates, but better results can be achieved by applying a more thoughtful, evidence-based process that seeks out hidden talent.

That being said, most interviewers also have their own "One Big Idea" that they believe will help them predict on-the-job success for candidates. I am no exception to this rule, even though I try hard to resist the temptation to use it by itself.

We think that our One Big Idea is the best predictor of future success when assessing a candidate, but why do we do this? Because none of the available methods are entirely able to predict on-the-job success, we are tempted to think that nothing works. One reason for this is that our brains aren't very good at understanding statistical truths. Even if something is true 70 percent of the time, our brains may take note of one instance when it's not true and write off the whole hypothesis as false.

One way of combating this tendency to rely on your One Big Idea is to consciously acknowledge it in the evaluation process. Go ahead and put it in your evaluation spreadsheet for every applicant. If your One Big Idea is that you can tell if a candidate will be a good "cultural fit" for your firm in the first two minutes of an interview, immediately give the candidate a high numerical rating. Once you've done this, make a conscious effort to not overly value the One Big Idea against your other metrics. This is because your gut instinct might indeed have some value—it is based, after all, on your years of experience evaluating recruits—but it is not necessarily the best measure of a candidate and should be supplemented with other criteria.

"So You Are Telling Me There Is a Chance?"

Fad diets have long fascinated me. These diets are often the subject of ridicule. Yet, they keep appearing on supermarket magazine covers, issue after issue, year after year. It almost feels as though the editors of these magazines have a secret bet to see how often they can make claims of new miracle diet pills and come up with ridiculous diet ideas, such as the "pizza diet." How far back does this scam go? Hard to say, but at least a hundred years. Do a Google search for magazines from the early 1900s, and you'll find ads for fat-burning soap, tapeworm diets, and many other creative ideas. The fact that simplistic solutions to lose weight haven't worked for the past hundred years hasn't stopped them from being popular. And while many of the world's discoveries are elegant in their simplicity, simplistic solutions nearly always fail to work.

Stanford professor Christopher Gardner points out that going back to the basics to lose weight gives better results (see Table 2.3). This is true for recruiters as well. They need to stick to the basic methods that have worked for decades and not overcomplicate them. When you add too much complexity to a predictive method, you are likely to fall into a fad diet–type trap and reduce your predictive power instead of increasing it.

TABLE 2.3 Why We Keep Using Fad Diets

Reason	Hard to distinguish credible theories from quackery
	A lot of noise (too much information)
Resulting Behavior	Dismiss the experts: "These experts can't make up their minds, so I'm not going to believe them."
Solution	1. Go back to the basics: *[The] key to weight loss has changed little in the last 50 years: eat balanced, nutritious meals while cutting calories, and exercise daily.* —Christopher Gardner, Assistant Professor of Medicine at Stanford
	2. Improve your knowledge base so that you can evaluate what is true and what is not.

If, like me, you can't resist the temptation to constantly seek new and more accurate ways to extrapolate from data to performance, be sure to skeptically evaluate any new screening tools to determine if they actually add value.

No doubt there are factors we can't yet explain or measure that still lead candidates to be successful in their jobs. But make sure you first learn how to "stress-test" them before deploying them in your interview process.

WE ALL KNOW WHAT GOOD LOOKS LIKE, OR DO WE?

Wishing you could measure a variable isn't enough. Spend some time researching whether the traits you want to assess have been successfully measured in the past. If so, have they been linked to job performance? You can try to measure these traits if you think they're important; after all, key insights don't often appear in the rearview mirror. Test your hypotheses as often as possible and take pride in following through on your stress test. But first ...

To measure success, you need to define it. A lot of organizations set out to improve their recruiting results without defining what "good," "outstanding," or "star" would look like. A year later, either they're convinced by a manager pointing to a few anecdotal data and declaring that things are great, or they're disappointed that their newfangled process had convinced them to hire a substandard teammate.

Few methods work 100 percent of the time, but without clearly defined expectations many of us tend to go back to a fad diet–type logic in determining what might or might not work. My uncle, a smoker in his earlier days, would occasionally fire back at family and friends telling him how harmful cigarettes were. He'd remind us that our great-grandmother smoked at least a pack a day and still lived past 80, outlasting all of her non-smoking siblings. He refused to admit that this wasn't evidence that smoking was good for your health.

How "Good" in Talent Acquisition Compares with "Good" in Other Fields

No recruiting tool will be able to predict recruiting outcomes 100% of the time. So what rate of accurate predictions is considered "good" in recruiting? To answer this question, it might be helpful to compare the correlation of talent identification tools and job performance with that of a number of other variables.

> As a rule of thumb most social sciences consider correlations of .30 and above as noteworthy and potentially helpful in explaining the relationship between two variables [see Figure 2.3]. The correlation between smoking and developing lung cancer is .04 for former smokers and .13 for current smokers;[3] the correlation between bypass surgery and reduced risk of death is .14;[4] the correlation between Ibuprofen consumption and pain reduction is .37.[5] The correlation between scientifically robust talent identification tools and job performance is around .78. [This will be discussed in more detail in Chapter 4.]

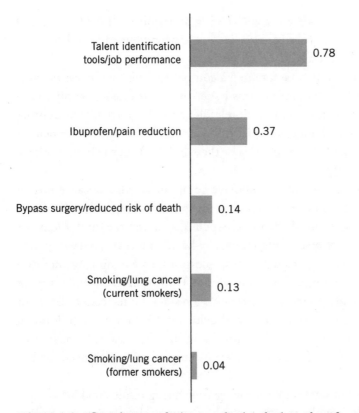

FIGURE 2.3 Correlations of robust medical and talent identification methods. Based on data from Eldridge, Mar. 15, 2019; Kraft, Apr. 5, 2011; Domino, Feb. 22, 2019.

IMPROVING TALENT ACQUISITION STARTS WITH GIVING UP THE BELIEF IN QUICK FIXES

Designing measurably better talent acquisition models is difficult. There are no quick fixes, and nothing works *all the time*. But some methods are significantly more effective than others. Discovering these methods requires specific expertise from someone who understands how to design and evaluate them. Such expertise can in turn be costly to find and correctly evaluate. There is no shortage of people who sincerely believe they have the right expertise, but how many actually do? Even when you find and hire a real expert, it will take that person a fair amount of time to design and implement better models for you. Doing so requires a lot of effort and patience. Yet the alternative is to keep repeating your old methods and expecting different results.

Google and Netflix have gained a competitive edge by investing considerable time and resources in this issue. They've learned to apply rigorous standards that aim to improve their talent acquisition, while most other companies stick with more simplistic procedures. It's an understatement to say that the investments in this area by these Silicon Valley behemoths have paid off abundantly.

They have not gained this massive competitive edge because one of their interviewers came up with an ingenious screening question. Nor have they taken hiring seriously by merely spending more time on it. Plenty of companies try to reverse hiring failures by having more interviews, spending more time writing evaluative test questions, or having lengthier discussions on which candidates to hire or not. Unfortunately, spending more time is not enough to produce better hiring results. Time needs to be spent on a more rigorous, disciplined, and evidence-based approach. Google and Netflix have improved their results in part because they have precisely tracked which of their efforts are paying off and which need further fine-tuning.

Despite the obstacles to improving your hiring results, making it happen starts with carefully tracking which of your efforts are paying off. This requires clearly defined measures of success before you start retooling your hiring methods. Without clear metrics, not only will achieving success seem impossible, but it most likely will be.

Chapter Summary and Conclusion

Context:

- The Rolodex is dead. LinkedIn killed it.
- While technological change has made the old value proposition of recruiters obsolete, recruiters can today add more value to their organizations than ever before.
- The *Moneyball* of recruiting is not about finding One Big Idea that always works.

- Some hiring managers keep randomly switching from one candidate screening tool to another in the same way others keep trying new diet fads. Neither method works.
- A lack of clarity about what "good" means can hamper the ability of talent acquisition teams to add value.

What you can do about it:

- Technological change has made it possible for recruiters to add more value than ever before:
  - Help hiring managers define the correct search strategy.
  - Get the best candidates to apply by moving away from post and pray and learning the most efficient methods of engaging these candidates directly.
  - Select the best of the best by helping hiring managers better understand how to predict job performance.
  - Get candidates over the finish line by creating a positive candidate experience.
  - Continually evaluate and fine-tune your process.
- Organizations with winning talent strategies rather than trying to find the One Big Idea recognize that:
  - Identifying talent is more important to winning than developing talent.
  - A data-driven method is far superior to an intuitive approach to identifying talent.
  - Data-driven methods need to be applied thoughtfully to ensure that the right thing is being quantified.
  - Discouraging any procedures that create noise in the candidate selection process allows you to focus on what matters.
- Improving talent acquisition means helping hiring managers understand what "good" hiring results mean in the context of various areas of your company.

3

How to Improve On-the-Job Success Predictions

CHANGING THE IMPOSSIBLE—HOW GOOGLE MEASURES THE UNMEASURABLE

Around the turn of the twentieth century, department store magnate John Wanamaker said, "Half the money I spend on advertising is wasted; the trouble is, I don't know which half." A century later, his statement was truer than ever. William Bernbach, one of the giants of American advertising in the 1960s and 1970s, observed, "Advertising is fundamentally persuasion and persuasion happens to be not a science, but an art." And for many years, his philosophy influenced how advertisers viewed marketing investments, or to use the more telling industry term, "marketing spend."

At the time Google was founded, advertisers were still fiercely clinging to the notion that marketing effectiveness should be evaluated as an art, not a science. This practice deeply clashed with the core of what Google stood for. Google was built on a foundation of data, so it was obvious to its leaders that they should apply this core principle to the online ads they sold. For instance, Google was willing to turn away revenue and cut off ads that were underperforming, arguing that it would improve customer experience. Ad buyers, who were not used to having the money refused by ad sellers, were naturally upset by this practice.

In his book *In the Plex*, tech reporter Steven Levy writes that angry customers would exclaim, "Who the hell is Google to tell me the success of my ads? I've been in advertising for fifty years—I know what a bad ad is, and this isn't it!" Tim Armstrong, a Google head of sales, would respond, "Yes they are, and here's the data." The company's philosophy went strongly against how the marketing world believed advertising worked.

Advertisers had shifted a great deal of their spend to online ads, but they still wanted to pay for the number of impressions. The common argument was that it was more important to build up the brand image by having as many individuals as possible see an ad than it was to track how many people actually clicked on the ad. After all, the millions of people who were viewing but not clicking on the ads could still buy the products from other channels.

The introduction of click-counting technology hardly changed the mindset of advertisers. The ad industry was, and many wanted it to remain, an unquantifiable mystery. Maybe this was because advertisers didn't know any better. Or maybe it was because given the old paradigm that marketing is an art, those who agreed most with that philosophy were those being promoted to senior roles, controlling advertising spend. Still, maybe it was because top-ranking advertising executives felt that as long as the success of their work remained a mystery, they could use the same charisma they had used to get their current roles to convince their employers they were doing a good job—but if they were to rely on an external objective source to define success, their future would be much less in their own control.

Redefining Success

The main problem wasn't that advertisers were resistant to adapting to more quantitative methods; it was that they were giving up on the idea that such methods were even worth their time. In 2005, David C. Court, Jonathan W. Gordon, and Jesko Perrey wrote in a *McKinsey Quarterly* article, "Many marketers have observed a declining level of discipline in the way the potential impact of advertising is tested, and its actual impact reviewed."[1]

Salar Kamangar, Google's ninth employee, was set on changing this paradigm in the marketing world. Kamangar's impact on the world can be compared with that of Billy Beane's on baseball. Reading *Moneyball*, we saw that Beane did not just use better evaluation techniques to hire superior players according to the existing criteria of success in Major League Baseball. He completely redefined the criteria for success and *on top of that* used better techniques to hire better players. That is, Beane did not merely introduce the notion that teams should pay more attention to a player's stats and less to anecdotal data. Instead of using statistical metrics of player success, such as home runs, batting average, and runs batted in, Beane focused on good on-base and slugging percentages stats, which he argued were more predictive of team wins than the old stats.

Kamangar had seen what AdWords could accomplish with a simpler, scalable, self-service platform using credit cards instead of the traditional method of deploying a sales team. He assembled a new kind of marketing team, one that drove a number of innovations launched under AdWords Select in 2002, 14 years after Google was founded:

- Advertisers would pay per click, not for impressions.

- Keywords would be sold based on auction, with higher-paying clients getting better exposure higher up on the page.

- An ad's placement would be determined only partly by the auction price; the ad's performance would determine the rest. Lower-performing ads with fewer clicks would receive less prominent placement or even be discontinued.

All this would serve the interest of the users, who would be much more likely to see the ads they were interested in.

A Painful Switch

Meanwhile, the VCs were growing impatient with Google and wanted to see it making some money. In 2001 Google CEO Eric Schmidt instituted a policy to cut back on spending: new expenditures would only be considered for approval if presented to him at 10 a.m. on Fridays.

Kamangar made the case that in order for Google to infuse cash into the businesses, it needed to double down on AdWords. He argued that Google's salesforce should stop selling premium ads and switch to an entirely auction-based pay-per-click model. This was not an easy decision for Google's management team. Google was reaping $300 million in annual revenue for impression-based ads. If it followed Kamangar's advice, Google would have to replace that entire revenue stream.

As Levy writes in *In the Plex*, Schmidt would later recall that "people were extremely upset, because this was a material change in the way they were doing business." Google's sales reps would "day after day [go] to advertisers who told us we were wrong," sales head Tim Armstrong noted. A senior executive in the marketing department, Jeff Levick, recalled that one of the clients "told us to go fuck ourselves." However, Google continued to do what it believed in, standing firm on a full transition to Kamangar's vision.

Changing an Industry Norm

Over the next few years, Google took additional steps that changed the industry paradigm from paying for impressions to paying for the value created by those impressions. Sometime in late 2004 or early 2005, Google acquired Urchin, a web analytics firm, which established the foundation for what came to be known as Google Analytics, which went live in November 2005. It provided instant statistics on websites—for free! This led Schmidt to later call the launch "Google's most successful disaster," as it caused all of Google's servers to crash.

In 2007 the company took the additional step of launching Conversion Optimizer, a feature that aimed to prove the value of Google AdWords. It showed customers how their investments in AdWords were generating clicks as well as how many sales those clicks were delivering.

In just a few years, Google had managed to shift a hundred-year-old paradigm in advertising. Statements that would have been shrugged off or laughed at just a few years earlier were becoming the industry norm. Before this shift, you had to spend money without being able to track that spend to outcomes. The new norm enabled everything to be measured, proved, and improved. Levy quotes Armstrong: "It was really bringing science to the art of advertising and being able to scale the art of advertising through science."

The question, then, is, why would you not apply the same quantitative rigor to your recruiting?

BEFORE YOU DO ANYTHING ELSE, START MEASURING—*TODAY*

As a CEO, a hiring manager, or a leader of a talent organization, you can utilize the following tools to help your organization apply a more granular quantitative recruiting strategy:

- Create a feedback loop.

- Conduct tests in more controlled environments to help your team focus on improving one success lever at a time.

- Diligently measure and track activities that lead to success.

Let's look at two hypothetical examples of applying these tools. In the first, you will use them to develop a new skill set in one of two sports: throwing darts or fishing. In the second, you and a friend will take different approaches to coaching two middle school soccer teams.

Which of the two sports, throwing darts or fishing, do you think you could most improve your skill set through 20 hours of practice without any external instruction? Why?

My guess is that you would most improve your skills in throwing darts for reasons I will further explain below.

Now let's look at the second example: practice regimens for team sports. You and a friend have decided to coach two separate middle school soccer teams. Both teams have an equal number of practice hours, and the players, on average, have comparable skills at the beginning of the season. At each practice, your team always practices one skill at a time, such as how to pass the ball, shoot, play defense, etc. At the end of each practice, the team has an internal soccer match. Your friend believes in a more free-form approach, and his team always scrimmages against itself for the entire practice time. At the end of the season, the two teams play one another. Which team is more likely to win? Why?

I believe your soccer team is more likely to win than your friend's.

Has either of my guesses been scientifically proven? No. However, the two main reasons I would bet on throwing darts and on your soccer team are (1) a shorter feedback loop between efforts and results and (2) a more controlled environment.

CONTROLLED ENVIRONMENT

Throwing darts happens in a fairly well controlled environment. Unless you are practicing outdoors, you don't have to worry about wind, rain, or other external factors.

When fishing, you may get lucky and catch a fish, even if you use the wrong bait and lower it to the wrong depth, because a school of fish might swim by where you happened to cast your bait. The first time I went deep sea fishing, I caught (and released) a shark, a Pacific spiny dogfish to be specific. My friends have been patiently waiting ever since for me to catch something remotely as impressive.

Most novice fishermen struggle with disentangling the numerous variables that led to their original success or failure, so fishing for them usually involves waiting for the right conditions to randomly come together. Similarly, your friend's team members are attacking or defending with little skill or structure, while your team members are focusing on improving one offensive or defensive skill set at a time.

Controlled Environments in Talent Acquisition

Employers have many tools available with which to assess a candidate (as discussed in Chapter 2), so why is it that despite having all these new tools at their disposal, most employers are not improving their predictions for on-the-job success? The answer is because most employers do not check on how they performed during "target practice."

According to a survey that the Society for Human Resource Management conducted with more than 2,000 HR professionals, only 23 percent of organizations measure the quality of their hires (see Figure 3.1). I can only assume that even fewer employers measure the quality of their recruiting tools, since measuring the quality of their hires is an important prerequisite for that.

Aiming for the Right Target

Even organizations that do assess the quality of their hires struggle to come up with the appropriate metrics. One of the most common measures used to assess hiring quality is retention. While retention could be related to performance, I would argue that below-expected retention could be indicative of the recruiting team doing an extraordinarily poor job, although high retention does not necessarily indicate that the recruiting team hired more high performers. Even then, so much depends on the context. Low retention could be excellent if one of your core values is to counsel out poor fits early on, as opposed to trying to force a fit once a hiring mismatch becomes evident. Patty McCord, the former chief talent officer of Netflix and the

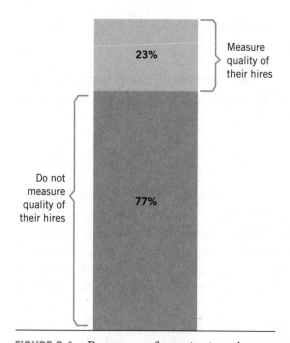

FIGURE 3.1   Percentage of organizations that measure the quality of their hires. Based on data from the website of the Society for Human Resource Management.

author of *Powerful,* explained that "retention is a terrible measure for quality of hires. You won't build a high performing team if you incentivize your recruiting team to hire for retention." McCord continued to describe how too many companies have a simplistic view of hires and retention:

> If someone is determined to be a star they should be retained for life. If they are not retained, it's either recruiting's fault for not discovering this in the hiring process, the HR team's fault for not stocking the company fridge with four flavors of water or their manager's fault for not motivating the employee enough. What if it is no longer a good fit? We had a brilliant employee who became in awe with Facebook's dominance in social media. He kept arguing that we should invest heavily in integrating a lot of our features with Facebook. These were not the right strategies for us at the time. In the end I sat down with him and asked him "are you sure you don't want to join Facebook?" He eventually

did join Facebook. I'm sure he was both happier and more productive there.

Management consulting firms, investment banks, many large tech firms, and high-performing PE funds have all accepted attrition as a necessary reality that comes with building high-performing teams.

CREATING A FEEDBACK LOOP IN TALENT ACQUISITION

Every time you throw a dart, you immediately know whether you did a good job or not, which allows you to try to adjust your next throw. With fishing, the feedback loop is significantly slower. Similarly, when your soccer team members repeatedly practice one skill, such as passing, they immediately see if the ball lands where they intended. If not, they will adjust their next pass. Your friend's coaching style provided his team members with less frequent feedback, if any.

The legendary coach John Wooden, who led the UCLA Bruins men's basketball team to 10 NCAA national championships in 12 years, kept his tongue well in cheek when he listed his eight laws of learning:

1. Explanation

2. Demonstration

3. Imitation

4. Repetition

5. Repetition

6. Repetition

7. Repetition

8. Repetition

Challenges with Feedback Loops in Talent Acquisition

One reason for the generally modest effort put into measuring hiring success and creating a feedback loop is that it is much easier said than done. It requires an organization to painstakingly sift through and overcome all the following issues:

- **Defining success.** You would need to quantify measurable definitions of success.

- **Investing time and effort up front.** Designing structured interviews and tests that yield valuable data requires a lot of time and effort.

- **Overcoming measurement difficulties.** Many qualities critical to on-the-job success are difficult to measure. One would need to overcome such difficulties, e.g., "Which measure of a candidate's intelligence is best?," to achieve meaningful results.

- **Overcoming test-design challenges associated with candidate interviews.** For instance, it is easy for a person to fake being reliable during the interview and first week on the job. It is almost impossible to fake reliability a year into the job.

- **Reaching a deep understanding of how to overcome assessment challenges.** It is always good to remember that correlation is not causation. And disentangling the effect of each screening tool when you have dozens of initiatives running at any given point in time is not easy.

- **Compensating for small sample sizes.** For every new idea you want to test, you have to muster a sufficient number of samples.

- **Being disciplined.** It's easy to follow all these steps for a few days, even for a couple of weeks, but it's hard to stay disciplined month after month, year after year.

- **Maintaining patience.** This is maybe the hardest thing of all for an organization. It can take a long time to determine who is or isn't successful. You may need to wait months, even years, to figure out whether your screening criteria were effective.

Is Anyone Creating a Feedback Loop in Recruiting?

As described above, fixing the feedback loop can be almost insanely difficult. That's exactly why no one does it. Well, almost no one. Amazon has created a skills-based assessment that does precisely what I have described. One of the assessments designed for Amazon's engineering candidates consists of coding and writing components. Candidates for nonengineering managerial positions receive a separate test, one carefully designed like a case-based interview, in which candidates need to make strategic choices based on various scenarios. However, the secret sauce of the tests is not in how well designed they were to begin with. It's the feedback loop that makes and keeps the tests effective.

Amazon regularly checks the performance of its hires via their test scores. If Amazon notices that candidates who scored better on a certain part of a test do well on the job, Amazon starts giving more weight to that part of the test. If Amazon notices that certain components of a test tend not to predict on-the-job-success, it eliminates those parts. One former Amazon executive I spoke with cited how these tests did have their limits, for instance in failing to highlight the very best candidates. However, he found the tests invaluable in screening out bottom performers. The tests might not be perfect, but they allow Amazon to effectively screen over 10,000 candidates a year and continue to get better at making good hiring decisions.

At our firm, ECA, we had our own "aha!" moment when we analyzed our internal data, discovering that certain candidate traits strongly correlated with job performance. It turned out that we were not always assigning these criteria enough weight in our process of evaluation.

Not all organizations have the discipline and resources to create a feedback loop like the one at Amazon. It's often easier to hand over responsibilities to someone who confidently proclaims to know how to screen candidates, rather than trying to understand more precisely how to screen more effectively. Unfortunately, what's easy does not always work.

If you truly want to make a difference in the quality of your hiring decisions, you have to have the discipline to tackle shortcomings in the feedback loop.

If your goal is to improve your talent acquisition, then before you do anything else, start measuring.

Today.

PAINFUL SWITCHES IN RECRUITING STRATEGIES

As discussed earlier, Google had to go through a painful switch when doubling down on AdWords. The company had to replace $300 million in revenues while upsetting a good number of its large accounts. Google believed, however, that the pay-per-click model was the right way of doing the business and decided to rip off the Band-Aid by switching its business model entirely away from impression-based ads.

I have seen a number of organizations that feel stuck with recruiting strategies set years, if not decades, ago. For instance, I once spoke with a company that knew it was paying below-market salaries. The HR leader explained that the company didn't mind paying new employees market salaries, but it didn't want to increase its cost for existing employees. The company realized that having two different salary systems would cause an uproar among existing employees, so it felt that its only option was to keep looking for employees willing to accept the existing compensation package. How long should this company wait before it starts paying market salaries? When it loses 10 percent of its existing workers? Or 50 percent? Or 90 percent? At what point will the company decide to pay market salary to attract back the workers who left? How about for workers who may or may not be as effective as their current employees?

Chapter Summary and Conclusion

Context:

- The secret sauce in any candidate screening recipe is not how well designed these tests and interview questions are to begin with. It's the feedback loop that makes the testing effective.
- A feedback loop is only possible if you measure interview performance and later compare it with the quality of people you hire. Amazingly, only 23 percent of organizations measure the quality of their hires.
- One reason for the minimal effort put into improving candidate screening techniques is that it's not easy. For example:
  - Organizations must overcome a number of test-design and execution challenges in order to get meaningful results.
  - They also need to be patient.
  - They can't improve what they don't measure.
- Sometimes it's painful to change how things are done, but change is necessary to achieve significantly better results, as

is demonstrated by Google's transformation of the advertising industry.

What you can do about it:

- If your goal is to improve your talent acquisition results, then before you do anything else, start measuring and creating a feedback loop. When? Today.
- Don't be afraid of measuring what's nearly unmeasurable and believing in your numbers.
  - Google's big breakthrough, AdWords Select, came after a ton of trial-and-error efforts 14 years after the company was founded.
  - This required a great deal of courage on the part of the Google executives to believe in what the numbers were telling them and then educating their skeptical clients and entirely changing their business model.
- The best ways to dramatically improve your results are unlikely to be the easiest ones:
  - The best solutions may not only cost time and money; they may also destroy the value, albeit limited, created by old solutions.
  - Regardless, if you want significantly better results, you may need to rip off the Band-Aid by fundamentally altering the way you do business.

4

What Do We Know Works?

Hire well, manage little.

—Warren Buffett

COMPLEX JOBS REQUIRE LEADERS WHO CAN LEARN AND ADAPT

If you spend just 10 minutes researching hiring techniques, you'll end up with more advice than you could realistically ever apply. A fair amount of this advice will be anecdotal and draw large conclusions based on dubious reasoning and indicators. One *New York Times* article, "How to Hire the Right Person," suggested you should pay attention to whether or not the candidate looks people in the eye.[1] An *Inc.* magazine article, titled "2 Easy Ways to Know Whether You're Hiring the Right Person," highlights the power of the "beer test."[2] The author argues that asking "Would I enjoy grabbing a beer with this person?" leads to better hiring decisions. Netflix's Patty McCord refutes such techniques and asked me, "What if the job is not about drinking beer?" These kinds of anecdotal interview techniques remind me of Barry Blitt's illustration "The Big Short" for the cover of *The New Yorker* (see Figure 4.1). Although Blitt is clearly referring to examples of self-promotion by a certain flaxen-haired politician, the picture also reminds me of how fortune-tellers claim to read their clients' character traits by studying the lines in their palms.

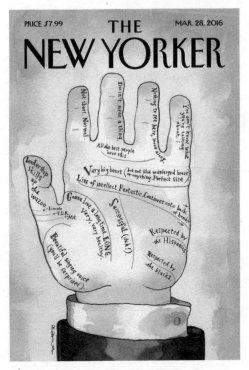

FIGURE 4.1 Barry Blitt's "The Big Short."
The New Yorker, Courtesy of Barry Blitt.

Likewise, many hiring managers look for signs and omens in a candidate that they believe are predictive of job success or failure. Which, of course, begets the question, is there a better way?

WHAT 100 YEARS OF RESEARCH TELLS US

The key to deciding which techniques to deploy is an accurate evaluation of the quality of the evidence presented in their favor (see Chapter 9). Scientific studies typically go through a rigorous process of testing to ensure the quality of the evidence supporting their claims; however, scientific studies do not always agree with each other. The scientific community addresses this issue in part by reviewing the evidence on all sides and coming to a consensus view, formed over time by the experts in each field.

One method that could eliminate potential measurement errors in individual studies is to combine data from multiple studies that aim to measure comparable effects. Frank Schmidt and John Hunter did just that in a 1998 study that summarized 100 years of research on hiring, evaluating 19 studies and their unique data sets in predicting job performance.[3] The study was updated by Schmidt, In-Sue Oh, and Jonathan Shaffer in 2016 for 31 unique data sets.[4] It's safe to say that this study represents our best understanding of what candidate evaluation techniques work in predicting on-the-job success.

In this section, I will rely heavily on the Schmidt, Oh, and Schaffer 2016 study, along with additional studies that present strong evidence but were not included in their study.

Why GMA Is the Strongest Predictor of Job Performance

The general mental ability (GMA) test assesses a candidate's ability to learn, understand instructions, and solve problems. This test is the single best predictor of job performance when using only one technique (see Figure 4.2). There are multiple reasons for this:

- Candidates with a high GMA score will pick up new job-related skills faster and more thoroughly than other candidates.

- Candidates with a high GMA score have greater success in complex jobs. A complex job is one that requires a candidate to learn a number of different skills, handle a lot of ambiguity, and/or learn new skills on an ongoing basis. It's perhaps for this reason that Warren Buffett in Berkshire Hathaway's 2011 report wrote, "Our trust is in people rather than process." In other words, capable leaders can figure out solutions to complex challenges.

- The techniques developed to measure GMA are far superior to techniques that measure any other candidate attributes. Thousands of scientific studies have been performed on GMA tests, and billions of GMA tests have been performed and evaluated over the past hundred years. As a result, our knowledge of how to construct and evaluate these tests is superior to what we know about handling other tests.

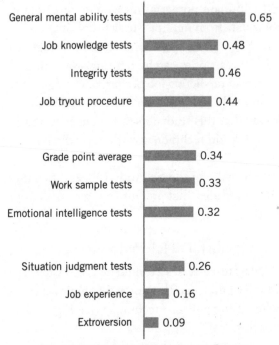

Correlation with Predicting On-the-Job Success

FIGURE 4.2 Predictive validity for job performance when using one measurement. Based on data from Schmidt, Oh, and Shaffer, 2016.

GMA correlates 65 percent with a hire's performance. This does not mean these results are causal, but for practical purposes, a high correlation (also referred to as R) is a pretty good indicator of which variables matter most. For example, a lot of people who suffer from chronic headaches take Advil. This obviously doesn't mean that taking Advil causes headaches; but looking at people who take Advil on a regular basis is a reasonably good way of coming up with a list of people who may suffer from chronic headaches. My purpose with this book is not to take you back to Statistics 101, but for some of my further thoughts on this topic please see sidebar "R^2 Versus R."

Following an evidence-based approach is the best way to consistently improve your hiring results. Suppose your office does a fantasy poker draft every year. Each of your colleagues has unique criteria for selecting the poker players, who will compete in a small tournament. Your own single criterion is to select the players with the highest GMAs. Your boss picks the players with the highest GPAs, and your buddy picks the most charismatic players (those with the highest extroversion). Year after year, your approach has been far superior to that of your colleagues. Sixty-five percent of your draft picks have reached the final table. Thirty-four percent of your boss's and only nine percent of your buddy's picks have made it that far. Before your next draft you read an article suggesting that the best players can intuit when their opponent is bluffing. The article even includes a list of the players who have supposedly developed the latest and best techniques for "reading" that an opponent is bluffing. Would you rather pick players from this new list or stick to your old technique?

Any hiring managers who give up the proven method of hiring for GMA and turn to the new technique will soon discover it is less efficient than hiring based on GMA.

We should also remember that for managerial roles, GMA is especially effective, correlating 74 percent with job performance, while for unskilled jobs, GMA "only" correlates 39 percent with performance.

Other Strong Predictors of Job Performance

Other strong individual techniques include job knowledge tests, integrity tests, and tryout stints such as internships. These measures correlate between 44 and 48 percent with performance.

GPAs, work sample tests (hands-on simulations of part or all of the job to be performed), and emotional intelligence tests each correlate between 23 and 34 percent with performance.

Situational judgment tests, job experience, and extroversion each correlate between 26 and 9 percent with performance. I find these stats particularly interesting because many hiring managers rely so heavily on oral situational interview questions, i.e., asking candidates what they would do if X happened or how many years of relevant experience they have. They also ask whether they "click with the candidate," which I believe tends to be highly correlated with extroversion.

Limitations of GMA and Other Hiring Assessments

In a CNBC interview, Google recruiter Lisa Stern Haynes explained that the company highly values GMA because the duties of many positions are constantly shifting. "If you think about how quickly Google changes, if you just hire someone to do one specific job but then our company needs change, we need to be rest assured that that person is going to find something else to do at Google," she said, adding, "That comes back to hiring smart generalists."

There are also downsides to the GMA test. Despite its usefulness, it tells only part of the story of a candidate's potential. Most employers utilizing it can recall candidates who scored low on the GMA but turned out to be superb employees. Another issue is that some candidates find the test cumbersome, annoying, and even intrusive. This is likely to lead to a negative candidate experience and even scare away some good candidates.

There is also an important difference between using the GMA as one of the prerequisites of success and using it as the main predictor. As Thomas Sowell describes in his book *Discrimination and Disparities*, a candidate typically needs to have a combination of qualities to be successful. He writes, "Even extraordinary capacities in one or some of the prerequisites can mean nothing in the ultimate outcome in some endeavors." Just as one strong leg will not prevent a three-legged stool from breaking down under pressure if the other legs are feeble, candidates cannot do the intended job if they excel in one dimension but lack significant capabilities in other areas.

A good example of this idea is Billy Beane, the hero of Michael Lewis's book *Moneyball*. Lewis writes: "When he was a young man, Billy Beane could beat anyone at anything. He was so naturally superior to whomever he happened to be playing against, in whatever sport they happened to be playing, that he appeared to be in a different, easier game."

Beane played baseball, basketball, and football in high school. He gave up football before getting to college. Despite this, Stanford University tried to recruit him on a joint baseball-football scholarship.

Unfortunately, the fact that Beane was incredibly athletic did not mean he had all the prerequisites to perform well as a professional athlete. As good as he'd been as a high school baseball player, he failed when he had to compete against major league competition. He did not take it well. "If there was one thing Billy was not equipped for, it was failure," writes Lewis. "The moment Billy failed, he went looking for something to break."

He was eventually reassigned to the minors, a demotion that made him seek a career as a scout instead, and he eventually achieved tremendous success as a general manager.

The limitations of certain predictors of success can also be seen in Lewis Terman's longitudinal study at Stanford University.[5] Terman followed over 1,400 gifted children into adulthood, collecting data on life outcomes of these talented kids. In some respects, many of them did quite well in life. Well over half finished college, compared with 8 percent of the general population. Terman also helped a number of them by, for instance, pulling strings to get them into college. (His study has therefore been rightfully criticized for not being scientific.) Despite his efforts to help some of these geniuses, Terman concluded, "We have seen that intellect and achievement are far from perfectly correlated," and many of the participants had selected professions "as humble as those of policeman, seaman, typist and filing clerk."

Another potential problem with job interviews and testing is that no matter how good a candidate's performance is in the evaluation stage, he or she may not perform well on the job. In the NFL, this phenomenon has given rise to the term "workout warriors," players who perform very well during drills and tests but fail to play effectively in actual games.

But Don't Throw the Baby out with the Bathwater

The point of highlighting the limits of scientific consensus and hiring assessments is not that you should completely dismiss these and revert to homemade methodology. Rather, it is to highlight that you need to apply some scientific findings and hiring methods with a healthy degree of skepticism. A friend who leads a company and read an early draft of this book kept struggling with the fact that there is also a downside to following many scientific recommendations. After a few discussions he caught himself searching for the One Big Idea discussed in the last chapter. He then jokingly paraphrased Churchill: "Atta, don't worry. You can count on me to do the right thing. I just need to try everything else first."

R^2 Versus R

I personally like to use R^2 instead of R when looking at correlation studies. While R (correlation) shows the degree to which two variables followed the same pattern, R^2 shows how much of the variation in B can be explained by the variation in A.

A GMA with an R of 0.65 has an R^2 of 0.42, which means that it can explain 42 percent of the variation in a hire's performance.

This does not mean that these results are causal, but for practical purposes, a high R^2 is a pretty good indicator of which variables matter most.

So why do I display the figures in my charts in *R*? Because several readers of the early draft of the book told me they were already used to consuming data in *R* and it was more helpful to them to compare the data in my book with other data points they had received if they were displayed in the same units.

USE JOB KNOWLEDGE TESTS WHEN RELEVANT

As I noted above, Google believes in hiring strong all-around athletes, i.e., candidates who are generally smart and capable, people who can be slotted into a variety of roles. However, when interviewing experienced engineers, it also asks them to demonstrate their skills.

Google provides pointers to candidates on how to prepare for their interview. (Go to YouTube and type "coding interview Google" and click on the first video for an example.) The company expects experienced engineers who will code on the job to discuss code during the interview. At our firm, ECA, we have found this practice to be helpful for some of our internal roles, as well. A candidate for director of finance performed very well in our initial verbal interviews. Later in the process, we presented him with a standardized quality control test. While most candidates catch more than 90 percent of the errors in the spreadsheet, this candidate discovered only 60 percent. Needless to say, we were eager to avoid a finance hire who was not good at catching QC mistakes.

One of our private equity clients was struggling to find a CFO who could act as a strategic thought partner to various department heads throughout the company. We worked with the PE firm to develop specific job knowledge tests for topics that fell outside the previous CFO's responsibilities where the client wanted the new CFO to excel in. For instance, we had the CFO candidates analyze a synopsis of the company's marketing spend data. The candidates then provided a list of questions they would ask the CMO that would help them understand if the spend could be optimized. After a full day of interviewing the three finalists, most of the board members were leaning toward candidate A. That is, until they saw the results from the job knowledge tests. Candidate B demonstrated superior skills in most tests, especially in how insightful his questions were for the CMO. Our client decided to go with Candidate B and has been so thrilled with this hire that the client now has candidates for other roles follow similar protocols.

The downside of job knowledge tests is that they are difficult and time-consuming to develop. A poorly designed test is more likely to destroy value by distracting you from variables that are more predictive of success. It's also not surprising that knowledge tests tailored to a specific job have proved to be more predictive of job performance than generic ones. This makes it particularly difficult and time consuming to create a feedback loop to measure the predictive quality of each individual test. These measures may take tens of hours to execute correctly. However, the alternative is to spend *hundreds* of hours coaching an employee.

FACTORS THAT EXPLAIN A CANDIDATE'S SUCCESS

Many hiring managers ignore the fact that two variables can overlap considerably, which requires them to use a variety of other ways to measure the same thing (see Figure 4.3). This, by itself, is not a major issue as long as

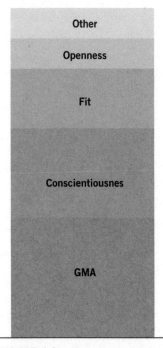

Other

Openness

Fit

Conscientiousnes

GMA

FIGURE 4.3 Factors that explain a candidate's success.

you are aware of it. The problem is that you cannot improve your predictive power beyond the limit of the main variable if all the tests highly correlate with it. If candidates must have five separate traits to make them successful, and most of your screening techniques are testing mainly for GMA, the other four traits are being ignored.

Once you have established which candidate evaluation technique works best in predicting job performance, the most desirable other variables are typically the ones that correlate *the least* with your strongest variable. These other variables will enable you to improve your predictive power by helping you measure candidate traits that your strongest variable fails to capture.

Let's walk through how a combination of variables improves predictive power in hiring.

Variables That Add Most Value When Combined with GMA

Since we already know that GMA is the variable that correlates most with predicting job success, the question is not whether you should use GMA in screening candidates. The question becomes, which variables add most value *in addition* to using a GMA? See Figure 4.4.

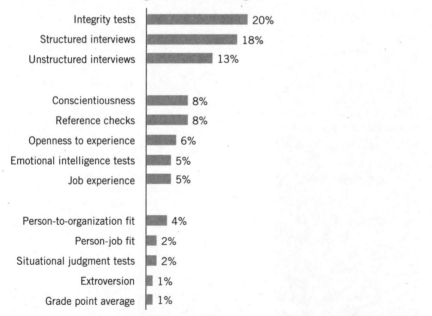

FIGURE 4.4 Percentage gain in predictive validity of job performance when using a second measure in addition to GMA.
Based on data from Schmidt, Oh, and Shaffer, 2016.

"You hire for skills and fire for personality" is an old saying among recruiters. So what are the personality traits that matter the most in making accurate hiring predictions? Integrity and conscientiousness.

Integrity tests add the most value, in part because their correlation with GMA scores is low. Integrity and GMA tests together correlate 78 percent with predicting job success for the average candidate. In my experience, that is quite a bit better than what most organizations achieve with their current methods.

After GMA and integrity, the structured interview (see Chapter 5) is the tool that adds the next-greatest value. While unstructured interviews do improve results, they are still 5 percentage points less effective than structured ones. Yet according to the Society for Human Resource Management, only one-third of companies conduct structured interviews for executive-level hires.

When the consulting firm, Deloitte, was hired to help a client determine how to select sales professionals, it found that the combination of a typo-free résumé and prior sales experience was contrary to traditional belief which is much more predictive of performance than where the candidate went to school or the candidate's GPA.

Similarly, Google has discovered that its prior emphasis on top-tier universities was not particularly useful. The company found that candidates from Tier 2 universities do just as well on average as candidates from Tier 1 schools. As a result, it has relaxed its requirement of a tier diploma. Google has also discovered that a candidate's GPA does not predict performance beyond the first few years after college, so the company no longer takes a candidate's GPA into account unless he or she is a recent graduate.

The Dilution Effect

One fundamental problem with job interviews is that access to more data, beyond a certain point of diminishing returns, can hurt predictive accuracy.

In a behavioral experiment performed by Jason Dana, associate professor at Yale University School of Management, a group of students was asked to predict the GPAs of other students based only on those students' past GPAs and course schedules. Given this information, 65 percent of the group's predictions were correct. When the predicting students added interviews with the other students to the information they already had, the accuracy of their predictions fell to 31 percent (see Figure 4.5).

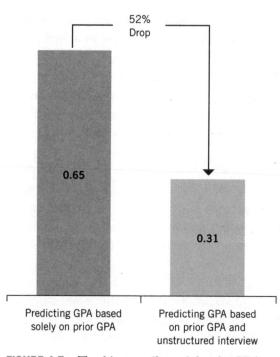

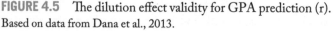

FIGURE 4.5 The dilution effect validity for GPA prediction (r). Based on data from Dana et al., 2013.

In his book *The Signal and the Noise*, Nate Silver summarizes best practices in making predictions. Silver's premise is that part of the difficulty of making predictions is distinguishing signals (factors with predictive power) from noise (factors with little or no predictive power). As much as most of us believe we will not be fooled and distracted by noise, that's easier said than done.

Most people struggle to assign the appropriate weight to the variable(s) with the highest predictive power. Instead, either we weigh all variables equally, or if we do assign different weights to them, we don't adjust sufficiently for the variables with the highest predictive power. This results in diluting the predictive power of the most predictive variables. Most interviewers are therefore better off understanding which one or few variables have the highest predictive power instead of trying to understand a large number of them.

One legitimate counterargument to having interviewers focus on just a few key variables is that they might then miss less common qualities that can prevent poor or even disastrous hiring decisions. My suggestion here is to check to see whether any of your interviewers have been effective in discovering such candidate attributes in the past. For instance, if some of your interviewers have displayed good people instincts and been able to predict candidate qualities related to job performance, have those same interviewers check for unusual qualities that may lead to poor hiring decisions. Other interviewers can then focus on probing the most predictive signals without getting distracted by noise. The key here is to have all interviewers write down their thoughts on a candidate *before* this person is hired. Otherwise you'll just end up with a bunch of past interviewers bragging that they were right all along with no way to know who is actually right and who is experiencing the well-known phenomenon of hindsight bias.

AVOID GROUPTHINK

In many organizations, the initial interviewer performs a detailed debrief with subsequent interviewers. Or if the two interviewers happen to meet in person, the first might make a thumbs-up or thumbs-down gesture.

In an article explaining Google's recruiting philosophy, one of its former recruiters, Kevin Grice, writes, "If you discuss your thoughts before someone else has had the time to process their own, the hive mind quickly becomes groupthink, and your biases (positive or negative) risk influencing theirs."[6]

In 1951, psychologist Solomon Asch used a simple experiment to demonstrate that most people can recognize the correct solution to a simple problem on their own.[7] However, these same people would point to an incorrect answer if influenced by other participants toward the incorrect solution. Participants in an experiment were presented with a figure (see Figure 4.6.) and asked, "Which line on the right most resembles the line on the left?" When answering by themselves, participants almost never erred (1 percent). But if they had to declare their opinions publicly, in a context in which all prior participants (who were covertly in cahoots with the experimenter) unanimously gave incorrect responses, 75 percent of participants made at least one error, starkly demonstrating the intense pressure to conform to group opinion.

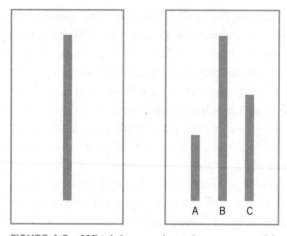

FIGURE 4.6   Which line on the right most resembles the line on the left?
From Asch, 1951.

Decision by Committee Is Not a Group Decision

In a *Harvard Business Review* piece titled "How to Avoid Groupthink When Hiring" I discuss how groupthink impacts hiring decisions and how savvy organizations avoid it.[8] Most organizations claim they are already making group decisions when hiring candidates. What they often mean is that they rely on a consensus-driven approach in their hiring committee. In reality, the person with the loudest voice typically overinfluences the committee's decision. This is usually the highest-ranking member, but it can also be someone who has been established as a "good interviewer."

Isn't this a good thing? Shouldn't the highest-ranking person or the best interviewer on the team make the decision since this person has the best judgment? No. Why not? Because no one gets it right all the time. More importantly, no individual will consistently get it right more often than a genuine group decision. Consensus-driven discussions in most organizations can provide a false sense of having reached a group decision. This is very different from a true group decision, one in which the insights of every member are duly considered.

Use Calibrated Independent Estimates

In order to reach equitable group decisions, follow what I call the calibrated independent estimates (CIE) process to ensure your interviewers maintain a healthy level of independence:

- Make it clear to interviewers that they should not share their interview experiences with each other before the final group huddle. It's OK for one interviewer to tell the others that she didn't have time to cover a certain topic or that she would like them to dive deeper into a particular area, but the individual members of the team should make a strong effort to not disclose their impression of the candidate by the tone of voice or the content of a request.

- Before the group huddle, have the interviewers individually:

  - Distill their interview rating to a single numerical score.

  - Write down their main arguments for and against hiring a candidate and what their final conclusion is. This will help them stick to their own impressions once the discussion begins and thus will lead to less biased predictions.

- If interviewers are e-mailing in their numerical scores and thoughts on a candidate, don't include the entire group in the e-mail. Have one person, ideally someone who did not participate in the interview, compile all the notes but keep them anonymous before distributing them to the group.

- Review the scores and interview notes; then have the group huddle for a live discussion. At this point, it is OK to be influenced by others and have interviewers change their scores if they wish, but interviewers should also know it's OK not to conform with the group.

I recently conducted a CEO search for a private equity–owned company. The chairman of the board kept reminding the other board members not to discuss their opinions on candidates with each other prior to going through a process similar to the CIE. Most boards I have worked with did not feel they needed such a disciplined approach. They thought they were mature enough to listen to everyone and not be negatively influenced by each other, so I was surprised to see how effective this process was in preventing the most charismatic person from taking over the discussion and overly influencing the other members while they were selecting a CEO.

WAS PEOPLE ANALYTICS A
SHORT-LIVED SPORTS AND TECH FAD?

Ben Lindbergh and Rob Arthur, contributors at the sports analytics site FiveThirtyEight, wrote, "In 2009, the first season of our sample—which was several years after *Moneyball* became a best-seller—a total of 44 [Major League Baseball] team employees fit our 'quant' definition, and at least a third of teams had yet to assign a single full-time employee primarily to statistical work. By 2012, the number had climbed to 75, and only four teams had no quants. Four years after that, the analyst count has more than doubled again, to 156." The Yankees, Dodgers and Rays were no exception in this regard (see Figure 4.7).

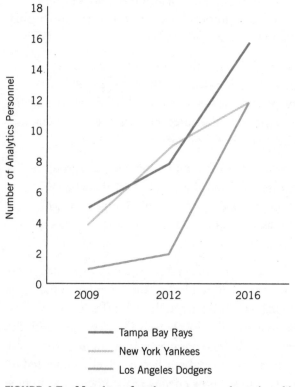

FIGURE 4.7 Number of analytics personnel employed by team.
Courtesy of FiveThirtyEight.

If your company is large enough, investing in an analytics team can give you a first mover's advantage. Most executives agree that the lessons from *Moneyball* are important. Why not invest in a team that analyzes your own data and instills discipline as you collect better data over time?

As Lindbergh and Arthur put it: "It paid to invest in analytics early. Teams with at least one analyst in 2009 outperformed their expected winning percentage by 44 points over the 2012–14 period, relative to teams who didn't."

Many executives I have spoken with dismiss the idea of investing in people analytics as something that "makes sense for sports teams, but not for other businesses." However, a look at the data shows that it's not only sports teams that are investing in people analytics. When our firm, ECA, pulled the data in March 2019, we identified 490 organizations that have started building out a people analytics team.

A number of executives I have spoken to refute the notion that they compete for the same talent as companies with talent analytics teams. They typically base their argument on two claims:

1. The type of candidate who would apply to a tech firm would not apply for a job in the more traditional industries that these executives see their own firms being part of.

2. The main players with people analytics teams are tech firms.

Even if their first claim is accurate, which I highly doubt, is it true that the main players with people analytics teams are tech firms? No, it is not. Our analysis indicates that 12 out of 17 companies that employ 10 or more talent analytics professionals are *not* tech firms (see Figure 4.8).

In an interview I conducted with Whirlpool's Marc Bitzer, he highlighted why the rapidly changing environment has increased the importance of building the right team: "Michael Porter's model for how to create a sustained competitive advantage is no longer fully sustainable. If you don't have a competitive edge in terms of talent, your market position will be difficult to defend."

A number of leaders have come to a similar realization as Bitzer. For example, hundreds of companies build up their talent acquisition analytics teams to improve the accuracy of their hiring predictions. These companies are slowly but surely tilting the odds of gaining a competitive edge in their

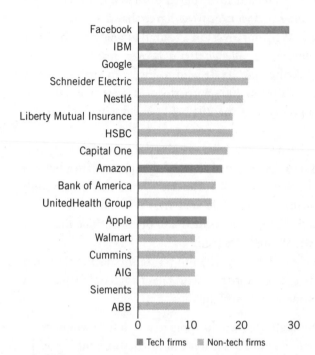

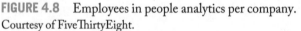

FIGURE 4.8   Employees in people analytics per company.
Courtesy of FiveThirtyEight.

favor by achieving better hiring results. It may not be the best strategy for a poker player who has recently learned how to calculate the odds of drawing to straights and flushes to openly advertise this new skill. Likewise, you should not expect these companies to tell you how much of an advantage they are gaining by tilting the odds in their favor.

And whether you know it or not, you are sitting at the same poker table as Google and all the other companies focusing on talent acquisition. While, of course, you should worry about companies trying to compete for your customers, remember that other companies are competing with you for the talent that will find ever better ways to get these customers.

It's also not true that only very large companies are making investments in this field. Yes, large organizations like Facebook, Google, IBM, and Schneider Electric, each with over 10,000 employees, have each built teams of over 20 people analytics professionals. But a number of midsized organizations, including Zillow Group, Etsy, Wayfair, and Evolent Health, have also invested in this field. The correct question is therefore no longer, "Will *Moneyball* make the leap from sports to the business world?" Rather the correct question is, "How rapid will this transition be?" Unlike in baseball, other companies will not have access to the performance of each of the players. It may therefore take a while before businesses that do not invest in talent analytics notice the impact of this shift. By then, however, they will face an even steeper uphill battle to recruit the few stars still out there. Steve Jobs allegedly often said that A players attract A players, while B players attract C players. Companies late to the game will therefore enter the talent arena with the deck stacked against them. Late entrants will not only have years' worth of knowledge gaps to close, but they will also have fewer A players with the star appeal to attract other A players.

One private equity firm that we worked with analyzed the success of its current and past deal makers. Success in this area was fairly easy for the firm to define. These deal makers were individuals who closed deals that needed to be approved by an investment committee, making the process equally unfair for everyone. Executives in the company compiled data on what they knew about 91 employees before the company had hired them. The results made the executives' jaws drop. Out of the 81 traits they analyzed, only 1 of the traits really stood out. What was somewhat surprising to the executives was that this trait was not difficult to identify. It was hiding in plain sight. Employees projecting strong signs of this particular trait were twice as productive in closing deals than employees displaying weak signs of it during the hiring process. Those displaying no signs of this trait during the interviews were nearly four times less productive than the top performers. To this firm's surprise, this trait had nothing to do with past deal experience. "Wait, so you are saying that instead of hiring *four* candidates who do not display this sign in the interview process, we can hire *one* who does and still close as many deals?" one of the executives asked. Unfortunately, the data had not been collected thoroughly enough to provide a definitive scientific answer to this question. However, this indicative finding certainly left the executives with a strong hypothesis and made them realize the value of better data collection processes going forward.

When analyzing the data further, the executives noticed that the top performers were not only closing more deals; they were also closing higher-quality deals with a higher return. "Four times more valuable" may therefore be an understatement.

IS THE FUTURE OF RECRUITING
WRITTEN IN THE HISTORY OF POKER?

> If I know something about the game that you don't,
> or you refuse to adapt to, I'll win your money.
> —David Sklansky, bestselling poker author and three-time
> World Series of Poker bracelet winner

In the movie *Maverick*, Mel Gibson plays a con artist and poker player. Trying to get a seat at the table in a new salon, Gibson promises to lose for at least an hour. He's as good as his word, but when the second hour begins, he starts winning hand after hand. When things are about to get rough because the other players suspect he is cheating, Gibson reveals his secret: "What do you think I was doing during that first hour? I was learning your tells." Gibson goes on to inform the men how the lack of their poker face gave away the strength of their hands.

I've long been fascinated by the commonalities between poker and recruiting. Like recruiting, poker is a game of both luck and skill. Poker players and hiring managers alike rely on picking up small hints that reveal "the other person's hand." I therefore sought out poker historian James McManus, who is famous for his books *Positively Fifth Street* and *Cowboys Full: The Story of Poker*. According to McManus, "poker evolved from European bluffing games, such as English brag, German *Poch*, and French *poque*, as well as Persian *As Nas*. In the nineteenth century," he continued, "and a few decades into the twentieth, poker was accurately called 'the cheating game.'"

The highest-stakes games tended to be dominated by cardsharps, who often worked in teams, using mirrors, cold decks, marked cards, and devices to slip cards hidden up their sleeves into their hand at key moments. Old road gamblers operated by depending on their gut instinct, by intimidating other players, and by trying to read the behavior of other players, as well as by cheating. In the late 1950s all the way until the 1970s, a number of poker authors changed the game, with David Sklansky, Doyle Brunson, and Herbert Yardley being the most notable ones. These authors taught players how to win by playing strategically and applying probability theory. This first mathematical revolution in poker gave rise to new stars including poker legends Brunson and Sklansky themselves, but also Amarillo Slim and Crandell Addington.

"The second and maybe the bigger mathematical breakthrough in poker came in 2000 when Chris Ferguson won the World Series of Poker main event," McManus explained. "Ferguson gives off a tough impression, having long hair and often wearing cowboy hats and leather jackets. Looks can be deceiving though. Ferguson holds a PhD and has a solid understanding of game theory." This newer approach in poker involved applying game theory on top of the probabilistic approach. Imagine you have a pair of fives. The probabilistic approach will tell you that this is a pretty good starting hand and you should open the pot with a raise. In game theory, you also need to take into consideration the game your opponents are playing. If one of your opponents only calls if she has a pair of sixes or above, you should play less aggressively if she calls. McManus concluded: "The game theorists have completely dominated the game since 2015. You can still get lucky and win against them, but it's getting increasingly difficult."

Curious to find out more, I got in touch with David Sklansky, author of what many consider the most influential book on poker, *The Theory of Poker*. Sklansky has written 15 other books on the subject, but he doesn't consider himself as purely a theorist. He has put his knowledge to use, winning three World Series of Poker bracelets and dozens of other tournaments, as well as long money in cash games.

"Instinct does matter," Sklansky told me, pausing to make sure I understood his point. "A math geek who has no instinct will still lose to a player who understands just a bit about probabilities but has a good instinct," he continued. "However, the mistake most players do is to think that their instinct matters more than understanding the math." These players get fooled by receiving sporadic positive reinforcement from winning once in a while. What they refuse to do, however, is keep track of the players with technical skills playing a disciplined game and admit that these players win far more often.

I asked Sklansky to explain how his probabilistic methods changed poker. "I didn't invent the idea that probabilities mattered in poker. Most players knew a thing or two about probabilities and if pressed would admit that probabilities mattered," he explained. "They just thought that probabilities mattered less than following their instincts, bluffing, or reading the other person's bodily clues. There is more skill and less instinct to the game of poker than even old-time pros and newer good amateurs realize."

Maybe the best example that can illustrate this is the Big One for One Drop series of tournaments. With $1 million buy-ins, they are among the most lucrative tournaments in history. The series' guiding force, Cirque du Soleil founder Guy Laliberté, ensures that a significant amount of the buy-in money is donated to charities supporting clean water initiatives around the world.

The seven-figure buy-ins attracted both business leaders and poker professionals. And make no mistake: the business leaders included hedge fund managers, loan sharks, and casino owners who knew a thing or two about probabilities, poker, and reading people, as well as having highly-tuned instincts. So how did the business leaders fare? In the opening 2012 a pro player, Antonio Esfandiari, took home the record-setting prize of $18 million. A pro won the 2013 One Drop event as well. And the next one. And the one after that. Laliberté worried that this might deter the business leaders, and so in 2016 he turned the tournament into an invitation-only event, practically banning pro players from at least the bigger $1 million buy-in events. Laliberté finally decided to allow some pros to participate, maybe because he was falling short of his goal for how many players would participate. He had earlier in the year announced 35 players being confirmed, but the final count, even after opening it up to the pros, was only 24. So who won the 2016 event? A pro. The same goes for the 2017 event. How about the year after that? You get the point.

In hindsight it can seem obvious that the businesspeople were doomed before the first card was dealt. Sure, they may have built billion-dollar businesses, but wasn't it obvious that they couldn't beat the pros at their own game? Since poker involves so much more than math skill, there were plenty of people who didn't have this obvious insight *before* the tournament.

The more important question for our purposes is whether CEOs and hiring managers realize that, when it comes to recruiting, they are sitting in a tournament in which 490 organizations and counting have already quietly started playing the odds and following a disciplined game. The biggest question becomes, do you have the foresight to realize that you can't beat this new type of recruiting pros at their own game?

Chapter Summary and Conclusion

Context:

- Complex jobs require leaders who can learn and adapt.
- A century's worth of hiring research indicates that GMA is the best predictor of hiring success, followed by tests of job knowledge.
- The question is therefore not whether you should use GMA in screening candidates; the question is, which variables add the most value in addition to using GMA? And the answer is that integrity tests add the most value when used as a second variable in addition to GMA, followed by structured interviews.
- Less is more when predicting on-the-job-success. Remember Jason Dana's dilution effect experiment.
- Avoid groupthink when making hiring decisions.
- People analytics is not just isolated to sports or to tech or to large companies.
- Poker and recruiting have a number of qualities in common. In both:
  - Outcomes rely on skills, tactics, and chance.
  - Participants are tempted to rely more on their instincts than math.
  - Executives are tempted to think they can beat the pros at their own game.

What you can do about it:

- Integrate an evidence-based approach into your hiring process.
- Most medium-sized and large companies would benefit from an investment in people analytics.
- Assign the appropriate weight to each hiring criterion.
- GMA, skills-based assessments, and integrity tests can help improve hiring decisions in most companies.
- Use calibrated independent estimates to reduce the chance of groupthink in hiring decisions.

CHAPTER 5

"Non-FDA-Approved" Methods

WHAT ELSE IS HIGHLY LIKELY TO WORK?

The last chapter covered candidate evaluation techniques that have robust evidence for and against their use. This chapter covers techniques that do not (yet) have a strong evidence base for their efficacy. This could be due to the fact that not enough research has been conducted on them or that research has been conducted but accurately designing a study and/or collecting bias-free data is difficult. The recommendations in this chapter are therefore based on my own subjective experiences and should be investigated further.

To borrow a line from our CFO and COO Brett Baker, you can view the methods in this chapter as the "non-FDA-approved methods." That is, they have not all been rigorously tested, or the evidence for them is still inconclusive, but you should still consider giving them a shot if they are right for your circumstances. The FDA analogy is good, but joking aside, one difference between medicine and the recruiting world is that rigorous methods that can prove a causal relationship (meaning if you use method A, outcome B will happen) have not yet been applied to a number of recruiting-related topics.

USE STRUCTURED INTERVIEWS

In the previous chapter, we learned that structured interviews produce 5 percent more predictive power than unstructured ones when both are combined with GMA tests. I personally believe that the value added by structured interviews would be significantly more for most jobs. However, the evidence base for structured versus unstructured interviews remains somewhat inconclusive. Schmidt and Hunter in their 1998 study argue that predictive power can be improved by 34 percent when structured interviews are used instead of unstructured ones (see Figure 5.1).[1] This finding, however, was not replicated in the 2016 follow-up study.[2]

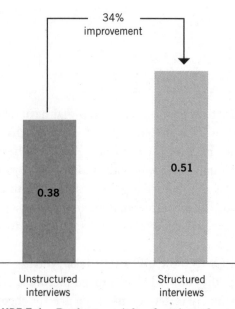

FIGURE 5.1   Predictive validity for job performance by interview method (r). Based on data from Schmidt and Hunter, 1998.

Further and more robust studies are needed before a definitive conclusion can be reached. However, having conducted thousands of interviews and observed hiring managers do the same, I highly recommend the structured variety.

Arguments Supporting Unstructured Interviews

One of the main arguments supporting unstructured interviews is that the interview questions and techniques need to be adjusted based on the perceived qualifications of each candidate. I am completely in favor of probing deeper where needed, of course. But if you're winging every interview, are you really measuring each candidate with the same standard ruler or with arbitrary rulers that change for every candidate?

Another argument I hear is that likability matters in a number of roles, and if a candidate is more likable in an interview, he or she will also be likable on the job and therefore better able to convince key stakeholders to make decisions favorable to the employer. Parts of this argument make sense. However, there is little evidence supporting this entire hypothesis. Proponents of it often point out that managers with higher extroversion have higher salaries. This does not show, however, that the most well-paid managers are in fact more productive; it shows only that they command higher salaries. As Tomas Chamorro-Premuzic points out in *The Talent Delusion*, "What is clear is that, in a world where most talent decisions are made by people who follow their intuition, likeability pays off." In a 2004 study on successful entrepreneurs, whose job interview skills matter less, Ciavarella et al. were not able to link the success of entrepreneurs to extroversion in the "big five" personality attributes, while conscientiousness did have a positive correlation.[3]

Why Many Thought Leaders Prefer Structured Interviews

Structured interviews are highly recommended by Google's former chief people officer, Laszlo Bock. In an article for *Wired*, Bock writes, "Structured interviews are predictive even for jobs that are themselves unstructured."[4] The only question in his mind is why more companies don't use them. To answer the question, he continues, "Well, they are hard to develop: You have to write them, test them, and make sure interviewers stick to them. And then you have to continuously refresh them, so candidates don't compare notes and come prepared with all the answers. It's a lot of work, but the alternative is to waste everyone's time with a typical interview that is either highly subjective, or discriminatory, or both."

Daniel Kahneman came to a similar conclusion when he evaluated interview techniques for the military. He found that interviewers who went through a structured set of criteria, rated each trait separately, and then assigned an overall score to the candidate significantly improved their predictive power.

Best Practices for Structured Interviews

Best practices for structured job interviews include the following:

- Write out in advance the questions you want to ask the candidates.

- Write out good and bad answers. If you can't articulate this clearly, chances are that you will ask questions to see if you like a person, not to determine whether the person will be good at the job.

- Use a numerical rating system, such as 1 through 5, for responses.

- Don't overcomplicate it. If you have many questions, sort them into four or five broad categories, to encourage interviewers to sort their ratings into a few categories.

- During the interview, actively try to be fair and consistent in how you rate similar responses from candidates you like and those who didn't make a great initial impression. If you really like a candidate but the person gave only a 2-caliber response on why he or she wants to work for your firm, rate the candidate at 2, not 3, 4, or 5.

- Assign scores to each category, and then combine these scores into a single candidate score at the end.

Many interviewers have a hard time separating how well candidates present during the interview from how well they will perform on the job. Interviewers are also affected by a variety of other biases. Most of us think it is unlikely that such biases will determine our impressions or decisions, but numerous studies show that even simple differences such as time of day or the applicant's name can affect interview results. Structured interviews help recruiters to mitigate and override their biases by sticking to predetermined questions and deciding ahead of time which answers are good or bad. These structures also help interviewers to avoid the dilution effect discussed in Chapter 4 and to focus on the most important interview questions.

NOT OVERSELLING THE POSITION WILL
HELP YOU HOLD CANDIDATES ACCOUNTABLE

> Show candidates your warts.
>
> —Ray Dalio

Unfortunately, I see too many hiring managers avoid telling candidates the truth about a job. Their logic is that if candidates find out how hard they will actually have to work or how boring the role truly is, they will turn down the job.

I could not disagree more with this practice. Finding good employees starts with being brutally honest about what working at your firm is like and what it takes to be successful in the role.

Hiring managers should by all means motivate their employees and prospective candidates alike. Hiring managers can do that by helping employees and candidates understand the importance of their work, appreciate how this work helps their clients, value what they learn, foster team spirit, and more. The inability of hiring managers to motivate their teams is a separate issue, and it should be addressed.

The Downside of Overselling the Position

Misrepresenting or lying about a role is very different from motivating prospective candidates. If a candidate decides that your company or the role is not a good fit, the candidate is probably right. Having the person decline the position will save you substantial time and resources onboarding, training, and starting to rely on a mis-hire, who will probably leave prematurely anyway.

In the end, the interview process is about finding a genuine fit. You cannot achieve this without being honest about what it's like to work at your company and what the job entails.

So it's only fair to design a process and train your interviewers in how to let candidates interview them as well as vice versa. In his book *Principles: Life and Work*, Bridgewater Associates founder Ray Dalio writes, "Show your job prospects the real picture, *especially* the bad stuff. . . . That way you will stress-test their willingness to endure the real challenges."

In *Please Lie to Me*, Thompson Barton articulates how lies and half-truths have become the norm in most businesses. Hiring managers lie about how great it is to work at their firm and how much fun the position is, but they leave out the fact that it also takes extra-long weeks of hard work to be successful in the role—which may not be fun for some candidates. Candidates, for their part, exaggerate past accomplishments and present their biggest weakness as "working too hard." Both sides know that the other one is fibbing or worse and are trying their best to figure out what they should believe.

These lies result in a lack of accountability, as neither party fully believes what the other says during the interview process. In some companies, people don't think twice about the fact that their new colleague is reluctant to perform onerous tasks that they said they would enjoy doing during the interview process.

Wouldn't it be better to paint a realistic picture for candidates before asking them if this is something they would be excited about and willing to sign up for?

If, after joining your firm, a candidate proves unwilling to operate in the capacity he or she recently committed to, you can at least feel good about having been straight about the job during the hiring process. This will make your job coaching, managing, and potentially letting go of the candidate easier by referring to your open and honest conversations before the person was hired.

Why a Tightly Controlled Narrative About Your Company No Longer Works

Another perspective is that you want to present your company in the best light possible. When I was in college, this was the predominant strategy among investment banks and consulting firms hosting recruiting events at our college. Each company would show up on our campus for a few hours once a year with a well-orchestrated pitch. Questions from the students were met with the same canned responses. And before the students had been able to take too close a look under the hood, the company reps were long gone. Since finding out more about each firm would have required hours of outreach to company employees and alumni—if the students even had access to those people—most students were forced to accept the self-portrayed image of most companies as close enough to the truth.

Companies trying to apply such tactics today would be in for a rude awakening. Jeff Weiss, founder and managing director of CCI, a national

CEO network, and I addressed this question in a *Harvard Business Review* piece titled "Stop Lying to Job Candidates About the Role."[5] In the era of Glassdoor, we argued, savvy job candidates can easily research the good, bad, and ugly about your company before interviewing with you. So the only question would be, who's fooling whom? Is it the candidate who accepts the job offer knowing that the company is misrepresenting itself, or is it the company that distorted the truth about the job by trying to project a positive image?

Smart organizations, therefore, no longer try to control and distort the realities of the job. Instead, they try to understand why their happiest employees love working there, despite what some may perceive as downsides of the company. These companies paint a more honest picture of what's attractive about the job, what some candidates may find tough about it, and what elements of the company's culture may be a positive, or not right for everyone.

HELP CANDIDATES BE HONEST WITH YOU (AND THEMSELVES)

> The most common lie is that which one lies to himself; lying to others is relatively an exception.
>
> —Friedrich Nietzsche

Unfortunately, most of us have experienced candidates who seemed highly motivated during the interview process but were actually not very motivated at all once they landed the job.

As a result, many hiring managers doubt every candidate's honesty, which takes us back to the issues addressed in Barton's *Please Lie to Me*. Skeptical hiring managers instead try to read between the lines and come to their own conclusions about a candidate's motivations and preferences.

A useful example of this is a hiring manager we worked with who did not ask sales representative candidates if they were OK with the firm's high-volume calling approach. Instead, he would assume that if candidates had past experience with high-volume calling, they would be OK with it. When we proposed to him that he should ask candidates if they would be OK with their assigned call volumes, he nearly laughed at us before saying, "Of course they will say they are OK with those volumes. They want the job."

Are Most Candidates for Senior Roles Lying to You?

In our experience, most candidates for senior positions will *not* misrepresent what they enjoy doing just to get an offer. Do they sometimes embellish their accomplishments? Of course. Do they intentionally lie when they know they won't be happy and successful in the new role? Of course not.

As a general rule, I feel that the risk of being intentionally lied to by candidates for senior positions is overestimated by most organizations. On the other hand, the risk of candidates not understanding whether a role is a good fit for them is underestimated by most companies. To better understand this, it might be helpful to ask yourself, do about 40 percent of U.S. marriages end up in divorce because the bride and groom intentionally lied to each other? Or is it more often the case that, before tying the knot, they didn't ask and answer the tough questions to understand if they would be a good fit for each other?

Some candidates simply aren't self-aware or mature enough to respond accurately to interview questions. However, most of them, especially those applying for senior positions, are just as interested in finding out whether the job will be a good fit for them as you are in discovering if they will be a good fit for you. Very few candidates are willing to accept a job they know they'll be miserable performing, or they think they might not succeed in, or they believe they might even get fired from.

But the truth is that when it comes to securing truthful interviews, the onus is more on the company than the candidate. The cost to your firm for a mis-hire is that one out of many of your employees does not perform well. The cost to the candidate is that the person will likely be miserable for a long time and have to explain another career transition on his or her résumé. The cost of a bad match is therefore often much smaller to your firm than the financial, psychological, and emotional cost to a candidate.

Helping Candidates to Be Honest with You

You can help candidates be honest with you—and with themselves—by getting them to snap out of interview mode and start thinking about whether *they* would be happy in the role. Tell them that the interview process is just as much about them finding out whether your company is a good fit for them as the other way around, and be honest about it. Encourage them to be open, reminding them that the more open they are with you, the more of their questions you can answer. Promise them, and yourself, that you won't switch to selling mode but will remain committed to giving them the full picture.

Chief marketing officer of ArcLight Cinemas Vincent Szwajkowski, who is also a Boston Consulting Group alum, asks top candidates if they would like to conduct a reverse reference check on him. If they accept his proposal, he introduces them to two people who recently reported to him and encourages the candidates to ask either or both any questions they might have. One of the references is typically someone who didn't work out in a role reporting to Szwajkowski. In an interview with me, Szwajkowski insisted, "Don't get me wrong, I don't want to lose a great candidate any more than anyone else does, but I'd really hate to have to refill this position in six months because the candidate didn't like working for me."

In an *HBR* piece titled "How to Negotiate with a Liar," Leslie John, associate professor of business administration at Harvard Business School, provides an overview of the research on best practices on eliciting honest answers.[6] It turns out that the best way is by asking direct and blunt questions.

You can also use the techniques listed in Table 5.1. One of these is the TORC technique (threat of reference check). Industry veteran Bradford D. Smart is a strong advocate of this tactic because, as he writes in a LinkedIn article, it "scares away low performers and liars—those who lie on their résumé and those who would lie in interviews."[7]

One point of caution is that candidates could perceive these questions as intrusive or manipulative and then leave a negative review on Glassdoor.com. In the era of Glassdoor, many employers have become wary of this move. Matthew Kohut, coauthor of *Compelling People*, points out that "interviewers using a tactic like this will clearly signal to candidates that the organizational culture has no room for people who can't back their words with deeds. At the same time, it puts candidates on the defensive, which may raise questions about trust and psychological safety within the organization. It's a show of strength at the expense of warmth." This might be the right move if you want to show candidates they can't mess around if they work for you; however, the lack of warmth will lead some candidates to get their guard up and become less open, and it will also make it harder for you to connect with and influence candidates down the line, say if you want to convince them to accept your offer.

TABLE 5.1 Verbiage to Use to Get Candidates to Be Honest with You (and Themselves)

	#	Technique	Suggested Verbiage and Techniques
Low	1	Candidate's Self-interest	We have asked a number of questions to make sure you will be a good fit for us. I'd now like to make sure that we will be a good fit for you. I'm sure it is important for you to be happy in your next job, so the more open you are with me, the more helpful I can be to you.
	2		Now fast-forward six months. Would you be happy with . . . (insert a realistic aspect of role or your culture)?
	3		Let's talk about your past two or three jobs/positions. What were a few day-to-day aspects of the roles (etc.) you enjoyed or did not enjoy? Follow-up: You mentioned that you did not enjoy _____. That is required for this role. Are you sure you will be OK with it?
	4	Accountability	Multiple times during the same interview, or during subsequent interviews, ask the candidates if they are OK with critical aspects of the role. For example: You told my colleague that you are OK with traveling 80 percent of the time. Are you sure that will not become too much?
	5	Threat of reference check	Whom did you report to in your last (few) positions? If I were to call this person and ask if you would be happy with this aspect of the role, what would the person say?
	6	Threat of post-employment action	To be open with you, this is a critical component of the role. One of our current employees in this role is not willing to do this and has therefore not been able to be promoted/earn full bonus/receive the responsibilities she wants.
High	7		In all honesty, we had a candidate who realized that he was not OK with this aspect of the role after joining us and we had to let him go. (More blunt language can be used.)

Likelihood of negative candidate experience

The tone, wording, personal maturity, and natural charm of the interviewer asking the questions matters, of course. You can alleviate some of the concern around creating a negative experience by reserving these questions for interviewers on your team who are best suited for this strategy.

We suggest hiring managers spend a good deal of their time asking questions designed to help candidates lower their guard and truly understand if they will be happy in the role. The techniques in Table 5.1 typically appeal to the self-interest of candidates and try to establish their accountability by repeating important aspects of the job over multiple interactions. Candidates, of course, may still lie to you. However, most of our clients were pleasantly surprised by how open candidates were—and how often they would give the "wrong" answer if they really wanted the job—when the interview was about their self-interest. For highly critical roles, or when we are uncertain whether the candidate will be happy in the role, we also clarify postemployment consequences in the event the candidate does not display the desired behavior or results. We use respectful but clear language when communicating our expectations.

Finally, being truthful is not just about removing bad experiences. More employers are seeing the benefits of a transparent culture. The interview serves as a unique opportunity to set the tone for the relationship you want to build with future employees. If you want to have a transparent relationship with your employees, it all starts with modeling the behavior during the interview process.

PROBE MORE DEEPLY AND READ
LESS BETWEEN THE LINES

If you want to become a better interviewer, you can start with remembering this simple rule: whenever you find yourself reading between the lines to get to a candidate's answer, stop for a moment and ask yourself if you can do a better job at clarifying what the candidate means. I'm referring to situations where you might think, "The candidate said A, which means he will feel B, which means he will do C." Sure, it can be uncomfortable or take up a bit of extra time to revisit a topic that a candidate has already answered. However, I've found that I'm always happy I asked a candidate to clarify a topic *in his or her own words* rather than my trying to read the person's mind and motives.

As discussed in the last section, you always run the risk of candidates not being frank with you. However, in my experience much of what is perceived as dishonesty during interviews comes from a candidate's fear of saying the wrong thing. Candidates know that interviewers tend to read between the lines, and some candidates have told me they get nervous in interviews because they are focusing on wordsmithing their responses so they can't be misunderstood rather than focusing on the core of the question.

This might also spring from either a simple misunderstanding or candidates not being honest with themselves. In such situations, a brief and open discussion will be more effective in getting to the truth than either guessing yourself or trusting a "psychic psychologist" who assures you she has read the candidate's mind. This isn't to say lying never occurs. But the question is, even when it does, how will you know? Much of the research suggests that most people are poor at detecting lies.[8] So you're better off trying to have a frank discussion and assume the candidate is doing the same. You can augment this with the techniques described above, as well as with background checks.

In my experience, too many interviewers ask questions intending to read between the lines of the candidate's response. This tactic often backfires. The CEO of a billion-dollar company we worked with would ask candidates, "What is your long-term career goal?" If the candidate didn't have a specific goal in mind or could not clearly articulate it, the CEO would take this as a sign that the candidate was not ambitious enough and would probably be unwilling to work long hours. The CEO almost certainly would have received better outcomes by simply asking candidates if they were OK with the long hours.

An executive at a major chain of medical clinics asked candidates for a regional director position what they would do if one of their top-performing doctors was demeaning some of his fellow employees. The leader wanted candidates to clearly state that while they would address the issue, they would try their very best to ensure that the doctor didn't resign from the regional clinic. If candidates did not articulate this clearly on their own, the executive would assume that the candidates, in the role of regional director, might fire the doctor or cause a number of the company's other top-performing doctors to leave, resulting in a steep loss in revenues.

I eventually convinced the regional leader that this was a highly unlikely scenario. We agreed on a middle ground. If a candidate failed to articulate the points the executive wanted to hear, he would:

- Probe until the candidate explicitly stated that he or she would display behavior the hiring manager feared. Two probing questions we came up with were:

  - What if I were to tell you that this doctor's leaving that clinic would be detrimental to the clinic's revenues, and the company may even need to shut down that clinic? (To his surprise, some candidates said that they didn't care about the revenue impact and wanted to do what they felt was right. However, most candidates would adjust their approach at that point.)

  - At what point in this process would you consult me or your peers? (Again, to his surprise, some candidates stated that they didn't want the job unless they had autonomy and full decision-making authority, but most candidates said they would appreciate the opportunity to consult with him before taking any action.)

- Try to determine how coachable a candidate was. One probing question we used was, "How would you feel if I told you that I'd rather take a different approach?" (Again, to the hiring manager's surprise, candidates who were fairly rigid in their approach often articulated their disapproval of the suggested approach.)

Why and How to Probe During Interviews

By probing, you are collecting additional data points. Each additional point will turn weak evidence into stronger evidence, which will enable you to make better decisions. You will also be able to better support your decisions when coordinating with your colleagues. Finally, you will be able to learn more from your decisions, as well as determine how to collect better evidence.

Unfortunately, many hiring managers are uncomfortable with probing during interviews. When I asked hiring managers why they didn't probe further on certain topics, some admitted their fear that they themselves might become irritated during the probing and come across as annoyed. Some were concerned that the candidate might have a negative experience (e.g., feel interrogated or simply annoyed with having to answer the same question multiple times).

However, I found that the majority of hiring managers who did not probe for clarifying responses were unaware that they failed to do so. They were focused on getting through their set of questions and didn't want to linger on one topic too long, or they had some of the fears just mentioned but had not articulated those fears to themselves.

As with the case of phrases that encourage candidates to be more honest with you, the tone, wording, and so on in which these questions are asked matters. Softening statements can be used this way, which will help you maintain a more positive tone.

I have found that interviewers feel more confident about drilling deeper into responses when they have practiced asking a few different types of probing questions. You may get more revealing answers by asking the candidate to not only clarify what they mean by a statement, but also explain why it is they have that perspective. Absorbing the underlying reasons for a candidate's responses will help you get a deeper appreciation for their preferences and thought processes.

A number of examples of softening statements and probing questions are listed in Table 5.2.

Utilize Panel Interviews

Another way to make sure interviewers don't read too much into candidate statements that could be interpreted in different ways is to use panels of two or more interviewers. Greg Hewitt, the CEO of DHL, in an interview with me noted: "Using panel interviews reduces the 'detective'-type guessing by interviewers. When we initially started utilizing panel interviews, we were surprised to see how differently our interviewers on the panel interpreted the same response to a question by a candidate." If two interviewers on the same panel can't agree about what a candidate meant by a statement, it's a good sign that they should go back to the candidate and probe further into the response. One way you can determine whether panel interviews are worthwhile for your company is to utilize them and see if they increase the prediction accuracy of your interviewers. If they don't, you can always go back to traditional one-on-one interviews.

TABLE 5.2 Softening Statements and Probing Questions

#	Softening Statements	Probing Questions (Clarifying What)	Probing Questions (Clarifying Why)
1	I want to make sure I understood you correctly.	Do you mean that . . . ? (E.g., Do you mean that you would do X and not Y?)	What led you to that?
2	Sorry, I still don't think I understood what you meant.	Are you saying that . . . ? (E.g., Are you saying that you were evaluated based on criteria Q and Z?)	Why is that?
3	Let me clarify that one more time.	Can you explain the piece about . . . ?	Why do you feel strongly about that?
4	Can we take a step back for a moment?	Could you please elaborate on that point?	Can I ask why?
5	Just so I am not misrepresenting what you are saying . . .	Do you mind explaining what you mean by . . . ?	What brought you to those conclusions?
6	I want to be certain that we are aligned.	Are you sure that . . . ? (E.g., Are you sure that you would be OK with the commute?)	Help me understand why.
7	Let's go over that one more time.	Help me understand your thought process behind that.	Where does that feeling come from?
8	That makes sense.	Can you give me an example of . . . ?	Why is that important?
9	I'm glad you brought that up.	I get the feeling that . . . (e.g., you would not enjoy this aspect of the role), is that fair to say?	Why?

HIRE MISSIONARIES, NOT MERCENARIES

I often hear hiring managers say, "If we want better talent, we need to increase our compensation bands." This statement is true in rare cases, but most of the time, once I speak with the hiring managers, I find out that they haven't really focused enough on how to make the role more attractive beyond the compensation.

My view is that you will find better talent by improving the opportunity first, the money second. Start by clearly articulating the problem you are trying to solve in the world, followed by how you can provide a superior experience to the candidates. This will help you to recruit missionaries instead of mercenaries. That is, you'll be able to attract employees who get extra satisfaction from their job duties beyond their compensation and will not jump ship as soon as they are offered more money elsewhere.

You can only achieve this by not trying to be the right company for everyone. If you offer the same enthusiasm about the problem you are solving in the world, the same benefits, the same hours, and the same vanilla office culture as everyone else, why should candidates join you unless they don't have a higher offer, are desperate for a job, or both?

In his book *In the Plex*, Steven Levy describes how Google attracted world-renowned scientists. At that time, working at Google was far less glamorous than the stories we hear today about their offices and perks. Most of the people who joined Google at that time had to take a pay cut, worked with refurbished equipment, and were crammed into small conference rooms.

Instead of a glamorous office and a lucrative salary, Google offered these scientists the opportunity to solve complex issues related to search engines while working with other brilliant minds in their field.

Peter Thiel, the cofounder of PayPal, had a similar view on how to attract talent. In his book *Zero to One*, he writes:

> The only good answers [to how you can attract talent] are specific to your company. . . . There are two general kinds of good answers: answers about your mission and answers about your team. You'll attract the employees you need if you can explain why your mission is compelling: not why it's important in general, but why you're doing something important that no one else is going to get done. That's the only thing that can make its importance unique. At PayPal, if you were excited by the idea of creating a new digital currency to replace the U.S. dollar, we wanted to talk to you; if not, you weren't the right fit.

BE FLEXIBLE ON THE START DATE

Unfortunately, I see too many hiring managers fail to land top performers because they refuse to be flexible on the start date or on some other fairly minor issue.

Take, for example, the VP of strategy at a Fortune 500 company who, after a five-month interview process, refused to let his top choice start two months after the offer was made. The candidate, a principal at Bain & Company, needed the time to wrap up a critical client project and also wanted time to plan for the relocation with his family.

The VP of strategy argued that he needed the position filled "yesterday" and could not afford to wait any longer. The candidate ended up declining the offer because of the start date. When the VP ended up needing another four months to fill the role, he eventually admitted that his company would have been much better off waiting for his top pick to be ready.

As the leader of a company, you can prevent such mistakes by actively discouraging yourself or your team from being too rigid around such things as start dates.

You should also be aware that many top performers aren't actively looking for other jobs because they're thriving in their current positions. Their current employers are rewarding them with attractive career-growth opportunities, praise, and star status, and they know their superiors have their backs. As a result, many such stars have developed a sense of loyalty and personal affection for their peers and superiors. They are hesitant, and in many cases unwilling, to leave people whom they respect and care about in the middle of a critical period.

On the other hand, bottom performers either have been let go, have left their positions, or have mentally prepared themselves to leave their companies because they're dissatisfied in their current roles. Such performers will naturally be more than happy to move over to your company immediately.

Top performers tend not to have the same flexibility. Although you should not necessarily read flexibility on the start date as a sign that a candidate is a bottom performer, you should not be surprised if a candidate asks for a few months to transition to your company. After all, wouldn't you want to be treated the same way by your most trusted employees if they were leaving for a new position?

HIRE PEOPLE WHO DON'T FEAR
GETTING THEIR HANDS DIRTY

There are very few people in today's economy who can be effective in their job simply by delegating. Everyone needs to dive into the nitty-gritty details on their own from time to time or get their hands dirty at least occasionally. Watch out for candidates who position themselves as being so accomplished that they don't need to do any "dirty work." Such candidates often say things like, "I'm not sure it's the best use of my time to . . ."

HIRE RESULTS-ORIENTED CANDIDATES

The best candidates are motivated by the results they will achieve. Candidates who aren't results-oriented tend to be more motivated by the tasks they have to perform.

I have found the concept of "pain avoidance" helpful in this context. Will candidates try to avoid doing something they think is cumbersome and painful, or will their motivation to achieve success help them overcome whatever pain is necessary? Will candidates pick up the phone and cold-call if they need to? Will they fix the coffee machine if they don't have the budget for a new one? Will they do data cleaning, even if it's been ages since they had to? Will they deal with investors one day, customers the next, and employees the day after that?

Results-oriented candidates will often speak about specific and measurable results they achieved in their previous jobs. Other candidates will talk about how they "massively improved" things without mentioning a single quantitative or objective way of measuring that improvement.

HIRE CANDIDATES WHO DEMONSTRATE
OPENNESS TO LEARNING

A number of studies have found that openness to new experiences can predict success. My experience is that you want to screen for candidates who sincerely want to learn from your team and are open-minded about opinions that contradict their own.

It can be difficult to test for these points in an interview setting. Few candidates would say that they *don't* want to learn from your team. You can screen for such candidates by applying active listening techniques. Are they pushing back? Do they revert to stating how they think the role should be performed, or do they seem to be genuinely energized when you tell them about your vision or processes?

You can tell whether candidates are open-minded if they ask questions indicating sincere curiosity about your point of view instead of just asserting their own opinion. Please note that it takes a fair bit of practice to probe a candidate's openness. Many interviewers have a hard time telling the difference between candidates who disagree with them and those who are closed-minded. (See Chapter 11.)

HIRE SELF-AWARE CANDIDATES

Many interviewers are on the lookout for candidates who might actively mislead them, but a bigger challenge is spotting candidates who are "incompetent but unaware." It is not always that these candidates actively want to mislead about how much they will hate your company culture or the job duties involved; they just aren't self-aware enough to realize they're doing it.

Self-aware candidates understand what they're good at and what they're bad at (Figure 5.2). As with candidates open to learning, self-aware

FIGURE 5.2 Hire self-aware candidates.

candidates rarely become defensive when someone tries to help them understand something they can do better. Instead, they make the other person feel comfortable with providing constructive feedback, and they relish the feedback as an opportunity to learn something new about themselves.

Sometimes, a self-aware person says, "I know that role is not for me." You should, of course, not hire candidates who don't want to perform the responsibilities of the job that needs to get done. However, their ability to articulate what roles and responsibilities made them happy in past jobs—and what made them unhappy—is a good sign they'll also be able to do so in the future with you.

Use techniques listed earlier in this chapter—in the sections "Helping Candidates to Be Honest with You" and "Probe More Deeply and Read Less Between the Lines"—to get better answers from candidates. To determine whether a candidate is sufficiently self-aware, you can also offer prompts and questions such as the following: "Let's go through your jobs one by one. What were a few things you liked about job number 1 (2, 3, etc.)? A few things you didn't like?"

Many candidates tend to make overly general points about their organization's goals, such as "I loved their product." Encourage them to instead think about more specific aspects of the job by asking these follow-up questions:

- "What were some of the day-to-day aspects you enjoyed about the role, and which would you prefer to avoid in your next role?"

- "Whom did you report to? What did you like about that person's management style? What did you not like?"

As much as possible, mention their prior bosses by name, and have the candidate give feedback specific to that person rather than speaking in general terms. You might ask:

- "Who were some of the colleagues (peers, direct reports, other colleagues) you enjoyed working with? What made it enjoyable? Who were some folks you didn't enjoy working with? What made it less fun to work with them?"

- "What are a few things you're good at? A few things you are bad at?"

Look for genuine responses. "I work too hard" is a terrible answer to what candidates are bad at. If candidates say that, you can remind them that this is less about impressing you and more about helping them determine whether this position is the right fit for them.

Answers like "I avoid conflicts but would like to work on becoming better at this" are, of course, context-specific and depend on how important a particular trait is for success in the role. That said, I would rather work with people who are self-aware and willing to be open about their areas of weakness than people who are unaware or try to avoid that subject.

HIRE CANDIDATES WHO BLAME THEMSELVES, NOT OTHERS

Most CEOs I have worked with use some version of the hiring criterion that candidates must take responsibility and not blame others—to hire candidates who have a strong sense of ownership. While the term "ownership" can mean many things, I have found it most helpful to determine whether candidates are willing to take responsibility for their own and their team's failures. Although I have not seen any formal research on this topic, I have found this criterion to be well worth applying.

One candidate I interviewed described his reason for leaving a past job this way: "It was a privately held company. The CEO hired me to launch a new initiative. After I had been there for a year and had not received the budget to do so, I left. I eventually realized that the CEO's son was against the initiative, and the CEO would not approve the budget unless his son was on board."

While much of what he said might have been true, I would have felt better about this candidate if he had focused on his own failure to correctly assess the opportunity during his interview process, or his failure to recognize the CEO's son as a key stakeholder who would have to be convinced to support any new initiative.

AVOID DRAMA KINGS AND QUEENS

Numerous studies have focused on the link between life outcomes and positive affect, which can also be described as a person's ability to handle life's challenges in a positive way. Sonija Lyubomirsky, Laura King, and

Ed Diener argued in a 2005 paper that positive affect is linked to higher income and better work performance.[9] The authors went further by arguing that the happiness-success link exists not only because success makes people happy but also because positive affect leads to success.

In my experience, screening for negative affect during a job interview is crucial. If candidates tend to cling to negative emotions when dealing with challenges, that trait is likely to negatively impact their work performance.

While nearly all candidates avoid temper tantrums or negativity during an interview, such tendencies can be revealed if you know what to look for. A common sign of negative affect is when candidates speak poorly of their past bosses or jobs. Besides a lack of professionalism, these candidates are revealing that they might be more concerned with the negative experiences in their past roles than with the positive aspects. Star performers rarely do this.

PAST BEHAVIOR SPEAKS LOUDER THAN CURRENT WORDS

When you can reliably infer something about candidates through their past behavior, weigh it more heavily than what they might tell you. It's easy for candidates to say, "I'd like this to be my last job," but if they have lasted only a year or so at previous roles, even if they mean what they say, they're unlikely to stay with your firm for the rest of their career.

Apply this healthy skepticism with caution, however. I have seen a surprising number of hiring managers jump to conclusions based on a few data points on a candidate's résumé or profile, unfairly concluding things like, "This candidate has never lived in our region and will not stay here."

RECRUIT FOR SKILLS AND CAPABILITY MORE THAN EXPERIENCE

Many hiring managers start a job description with requisite years of experience.

In a 2019 study, the scientists Van Iddekinge, Arnold, Frieder, and Roth reviewed over 1,500 studies that had tried to determine whether pre-hire work experience could predict performance in a new role.[10] As performance could be defined pretty broadly, they focused on three indicators:

job performance, e.g., as rated by their supervisor; job performance during training; and turnover. In the end, Van Iddekinge et al. included a total of 97 studies in their meta-analysis to evaluate these three outcomes.

They summarized their findings in the *London School of Economics Business Review*[11] using the following words to describe the relationships they were measuring:

- Prior experience to job performance: "quite weak"

- Prior experience and training performance: "also was weak"

- Prior experience and turnover: "essentially zero"

They concluded, "Overall, our results suggested that pre-hire experience is a poor predictor of outcomes that concern many organizations."

At our firm, ECA, analysis of our employee performance over the last few years has repeatedly confirmed this takeaway. As expected, experienced recruiters joining us ramped up faster than new hires without prior recruiting experience. After a year on the job, however, the experienced recruiters demonstrated lower productivity and lower-quality scores and also rated lower on qualitative performance ratings compared with their peers without prior recruiting experience.

One private equity investor who read an early draft of this book encouraged me to expand this section. "We have made the best hiring decisions when focusing on the skills, capability, and excitement an individual brings to the table," he told me. "Our best CEOs and executives have certainly demonstrated an ability to understand the challenges our companies were facing but didn't necessarily have prior experience in the exact same industry or even role. On the contrary, we have often felt that we made a hiring mistake when we overly focused on a candidate's prior experience matching the current roles and responsibilities we were trying to fill."

HELP CANDIDATES SEE THE PATH

Most candidates value more opportunity and a stronger career path over higher compensation. While many hiring managers do a good job articulating the current opportunity, many don't paint much of a picture of future career paths.

Some of the clients we work with have taken this point to heart, making a practice of talking to candidates about the career path for the role and offering a few examples of people who did that job in the past and what they are doing now. They also disclosed some career options with associated responsibilities and compensation ranges as part of the offer letter. Of course, they state that these career advancement options depend on a number of factors that may change over time. Most candidates have reacted so positively to this practice that our own firm has adopted it.

DON'T JUST PLAY DEFENSE

In a quest to avoid mistakes, I have seen hiring managers who turn down candidates for anything that could be taken as a remotely negative sign. These managers are focusing on how likely it is that a candidate will fail, not on how likely this person is to succeed. Such defensive behavior reminds me of a satirical piece in *The Onion*, claiming that since so many people have displayed poor judgment of character on social media, there's now only one viable candidate left for the 2040 presidential election, a 20-year-old who lives with his mom in an RV and is completely offline.

Don't get me wrong. I too would love to hire picture-perfect superheroes soaring straight out of the pages of DC Comics, but so far I've only been able to hire smart humans.

Businesses trying to manage risk better should consider inviting poker theorist David Sklansky to train them in this topic. Sklansky has offered seminars for companies ranging from hedge funds to more traditional industrial manufacturers. "What is the main thing you try to teach these executives?" I asked him. Sklansky didn't hesitate:

> To think more about the size of the pot than the chances of winning individual hands or not. Risk and reward matter much more in poker than how many hands you win or lose. Most people are very risk averse. Many companies have not realized this. Most executives would rather take a bet with an 80 percent chance of yielding $100K in profit for their firm than a 40 percent chance of yielding $1M in profit. The latter has a five times higher expected value. The best poker players are not the ones who consistently take enormous risks. Nor do they consistently play a

conservative game. Instead they take large risks when the expected rewards are high.

There are three instances when you don't want to go with the decision with the highest expected value, Sklansky explained:

1. The scenario with the higher expected value has a fairly high probability of disaster.

2. You can easily change your decision in one direction, but not in the other. For example, if you want to improve the productivity of your manufacturing facility, you may have two main options: (i) trying a new shift schedule which will require a $20K investment and will take three months to fully evaluate, but has a lower expected value; (ii) ordering new machinery which will require a $2M investment and will take six months to fully evaluate, but has a higher expected value. You may want to start with option (i).

3. The scenario with the lower expected value may have the biggest possible upside.

If you find that a hiring manager is turning down a number of candidates with the potential to become superstars, it may be because the hiring manager is "just playing defense." This hiring manager is focusing too much on whether a candidate may fail while ignoring if the risk of failure may be worth the expected value a superstar candidate can create for you. You can coach this hiring manager to balance minimizing risk with assessing an expected value that this caliber of a candidate well might create for you.

PRIORITIZE

Unless your organization has a history of embracing large changes at once, you are better off prioritizing how you want to improve your candidate evaluation techniques.

Pick one or two of the techniques discussed above and focus on implementing them before moving on to another area. For instance, if you want to implement skills-based assessments and structured interviews, make sure at least one of them is implemented correctly before taking a stab at the next candidate evaluation tool. Most organizations are not going to be able to improve in all of the mentioned areas above at once.

Chapter Summary and Conclusion

Context:

- Many hiring managers prematurely jump to the conclusion that a candidate is lying.
- Companies can no longer tightly control the narrative about what it's like to work at their firm.
- While a number of methods lack scientific consensus, hiring managers can adopt a variety of hiring strategies to find better candidates.

What you can do about it:

- Don't oversell the role or your company. Instead, have an honest conversation about what the role entails.
- Practice using interview techniques that help candidates be honest with you in return.
- Don't assume candidates are lying. Instead, probe more and read less between the lines.
- Prioritize among various candidate attributes and candidate evaluation techniques, experimenting until you find a few that help you predict job success. These may include techniques such as:
  - Structured interviews.
  - Panel interviews.
  - Flexibility on the start date.
  - Past actions by candidates might tell you more than their current words.
  - Recruiting for skills and capabilities more than for experience.
  - Helping candidates see the path to growth in their role when you make them an offer.

- Not just playing defense. Take chances if someone has the potential to be a star.

Candidate attributes:

- Hire candidates who don't fear getting their hands dirty, especially for senior positions.
- Hire results-oriented candidates.
- Hire candidates who demonstrate openness to learning.
- Hire self-aware candidates.
- Hire candidates who blame themselves, not others, when projects don't succeed.
- Avoid drama kings and queens who easily absorb negative energy.

CHAPTER 6

Beyond "Post and Pray"

HOW ARE YOU EXECUTING AGAINST YOUR VISION?

Hardly, any company has a stated strategy to recruit subpar performers. True, not all strategies are created equal, and firms can achieve better hiring results by utilizing better hiring strategies. However, most often it is not a company's recruiting strategy that sets it apart. It's the company's ability and discipline to execute upon strategy that is the real differentiator.

While a good recruiting strategy can be useful in outlining *aspirational goals*, the execution of that strategy is what creates *real results*. This isn't much different from understanding who *wants* to work hard to get in good physical shape. Everyone checks that box. The more important question is, who has the willpower to consistently follow through with the necessary training and diet? Willpower is what sets apart those who actually achieve results from those who are merely "determined" to achieve them.

Spending Real Money to Get Theoretical Results

As noted earlier, there are several reasons why companies don't try to improve hiring results. Sometimes companies recognize the value of doing so in the abstract, but their previous attempts to improve yielded no results. For these companies, the benefits of improving hiring results remain theoretical, while the costs of trying continue to be very real. Things fail to improve partly because it is difficult to know in advance what will work.

Hiring managers can choose from thousands of recruiting methods, all of which promise superior results. The benefits associated with utilizing better hiring methods are therefore seen as theoretical, and it is difficult for executives to justify spending real money to achieve theoretical results.

Taking Pride in Ad Hoc Successes

Recruiters at Activision Blizzard are often asked to find a candidate as good as Eric Hirshberg, who works at the company. The problem is that Eric came to the company after he went to a party—a party that he might just as well have skipped—where he ran into the CEO. How often does that happen? Not very. Yet this is exactly what happened at Activision Blizzard, the video game publisher with $7 billion in revenues. Its CEO, Robert Kotick, ran into Eric at a party. They talked. Within weeks, Eric had taken over Activision's game publishing division. How did this happen? Eric was not an on-paper slam dunk by any stretch of the imagination. For one thing, he had never worked at a video game publisher. However, Kotick saw potential in him and decided to give him a shot, and Eric soon became one of the most valuable employees at the firm. Under his management, Call of Duty: Black Ops II generated $1 billion in sales in 15 days. The inside joke at Activision Blizzard was that its recruiting strategy should be to send its CEO to more parties so that the company could land more stars like Eric.

Are Your Best Hires Coming from Systematic, Repeatable, and Scalable Hiring Processes?

The question all CEOs should ask themselves is, "Are our best hires sourced through a systematic, repeatable, and scalable process, or did they come to us through a series of random events?" If the answer is the latter, and you truly want to improve the quality of your hires, you have to focus on changing that.

Unfortunately, in most companies, sourcing good candidates involves posting their job on a job board followed by e-mailing the posting to a few friends and colleagues to see if anyone knows someone who should apply. A small prayer doesn't hurt, either.

The same executives advocating these practices often talk about how they take their recruiting very seriously. If everyone is following the same post-and-pray strategy, how does doing the same thing demonstrate that you are trying to gain an edge in today's fierce competition for talent?

Doesn't it show instead that you are, at best, expecting average results and average-quality candidates?

If your talent acquisition playbook is the same as most other companies', you're in trouble. Chances are that another firm is going to run the same plays with more resources and superior talent—and win.

In *Work Rules!*, Google's Laszlo Bock stresses the importance of employee referrals in Google's recruiting success. Bock's advice holds true for our firm, as well. A fifth of our candidates who make it to a first-round interview for a recruiter role with us come from employee referrals. Roughly half come to us through active outreach (see Figure 6.1). As a result, over two-thirds of recruiter candidates come from systematic and repeatable processes outside of job boards.

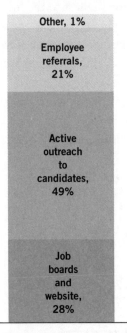

FIGURE 6.1   Share of recruiter candidates who made it to the first-level interview with ECA.

Why Repeatable Hiring Processes Are More Important Than Ever

If your firm does not have a systematic and repeatable sourcing strategy beyond posting on job boards, chances are you are not truly competing for top-tier talent in the market.

Unemployment rates are near historic lows, so one could argue that catering to candidates in this environment is particularly important. However, I believe that competition for star candidates will remain fierce even when unemployment rates inevitably move higher. The battle for talent is and will remain much more about quality than quantity. Companies that expect high-quality talent to come to them instead of actively looking to engage such talent will be making a serious mistake.

As you can see in Figure 6.2, the unemployment rate for college-educated individuals has remained relatively low during the past 20-plus years, even during the last two economic downturns. If there were official statistics on star performers, their numbers would be even lower. My former employer, L.E.K. Consulting, was disciplined about stack-ranking the performance of every consultant from the highest to the lowest performer in each hiring batch. Of the consultants who reported to me and were rated at the top of their class, I can't recall any that was unemployed during the 2008 downturn. I can, however, think of several lower performers who were

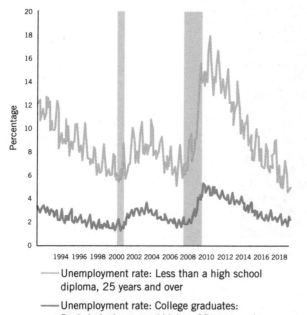

Unemployment rate: Less than a high school diploma, 25 years and over

Unemployment rate: College graduates: Bachelor's degree and higher, 25 years and over

*Shaded areas indication U.S. recessions

FIGURE 6.2 Unemployment rate percentage over the last 25 years.
U.S. Bureau of Labor Statistics.

unemployed. I realize this represents only a small anecdotal sample, but I'd be curious to see a larger study on this topic. Stars rarely search job boards for new opportunities. Recruiters have to creatively find ways to reach out to engage them, regardless of how the rest of the economy is doing.

Where to Start

What if you just don't know how to create a repeatable sourcing strategy beyond job boards? My best advice here is to try new tactics until you see what works for your company. The best solutions, after all, are the ones that make the most sense in both theory and practice. And what works for your industry, company size, geographic region, and even company culture and the capabilities of your existing team can be very different from what has worked for other companies in the past. Finding out what works for you requires some time investment, of course, but the alternative is to keep relying on a recruiting strategy that yields fewer and fewer attractive candidates while your competition is finding new ways to tempt them.

Helping your recruiters and hiring managers demonstrate success will turn them into believers in the fact that the time and resources invested pay off.

At our firm, we have found, through trial and error, when actively sourcing candidates, the following tendencies:

- For some roles, e-mails that do *not* include a job description are 27 percent more efficient than those that do. This could be because candidates have more trust in e-mails without a link or attachment, or it could be that e-mails including job descriptions are simply longer.

- Personalized e-mails are about 75 percent more effective than generic ones.

- LinkedIn messages are about six times (!) more effective than e-mails.

Don't Stop Testing

Demonstrating a few early wins is critical to getting your recruiters on board with a more systematic approach. But don't stop there. Make A/B testing, e.g., by testing if subject line A or B in an e-mail engages more relevant candidates, a continual part of your process. Without taking this critical step, you might be applying yesterday's methods while trying to attract today's candidates.

Our own testing underscores the importance of ongoing A/B testing. Methods that were highly effective two years ago no longer work. Simply putting a candidate's first name in the e-mail subject line used to generate up to twice as many candidates to engage in our searches. Now, perhaps because this tactic has been overused, we have abandoned this approach as it no longer increases candidate engagement.

Overcoming the Objection to A/B Testing

If you have data that prove A/B testing has been effective, it's easy to convince skeptical colleagues. You can simply point to the fact that your LinkedIn campaign was six times more effective than their e-mails. At the start of the workweek on Monday, you could send off your LinkedIn messages and take the rest of the week and the following Monday off, while your colleagues are still sending out their e-mail messages. Next Tuesday, you both will have been equally productive in attracting qualified candidates.

But what if you don't have the data to prove it? How can you convince your colleagues about the value of A/B testing? Individuals objecting to A/B testing initiatives often say it's a waste of time and that anyone with good intuition will spot the better method. If you belong to the vast majority who feel it's a waste of time to A/B-test two different e-mail templates going out to candidates, take me up on a challenge. Go through the headlines in Table 6.1 and write down which version you think received the most clicks. Don't just say the answers to yourself; write them down. (The answer key is provided at the end of this book on page 232).

You can use the same test on individuals who feel that A/B testing is a waste of time. One of these headlines was 10 times more effective than the other one. Would you rather send out 10 times as many messages or spend an hour in the beginning of a search and set up an A/B test?

TABLE 6.1 How Good Is Your Gut Instinct? Guess Which Headline Performed Better

	Headline A	Headline B
1	Can the Snotbot drone save the whales?	Can the drone help save the whales?
2	Of course "deflated balls" is a top search term in Massachusetts	This top Mass. Google search term is pretty embarrassing
3	Hookup contest at the heart of St. Paul rape trial	No charges in prep school sex scandal
4	Woman makes bank off rare baseball card	Woman makes $179,000 off rare baseball card
5	MBTA projects annual operating deficit will double by 2020	Get ready: MBTA's deficit is about to double
6	How Massachusetts helped win you the right to birth control access	How Boston University helped end "crimes against chastity"
7	When the first subway opened in Boston	Cartoons from when the first subway opened in Boston
8	Victim and family in prep-school rape trial blame toxic culture	Victim and family in prep-school rape trial releases statement
9	Guy in "Free Brady" hat is only one able to foil Miley Cyrus prank	Pats fan gets an eyeful for recognizing an undercover Miley Cyrus

Source: Seth Stephens-Davidowitz, *Everybody Lies: Big Data, New Data, and What the Internet Can Tell Us About Who We Really Are* (HarperCollins, New York, 2017). Used with permission.

Chapter Summary and Conclusion

Context:

- It's not a company's recruiting strategy that sets it apart. It's the company's ability and discipline to execute that strategy that is the real differentiator.
- Don't take comfort from the fact that you have landed a star performer or two through a series of random events.
- The battle for talent is much more about quality than quantity, and companies that expect quality talent to fall in their lap are not being realistic.

- Many hiring managers are overconfident about their ability to predict messaging and engagement techniques that will attract high-end candidates.

What you can do about it:

- Create a systematic, repeatable, and scalable process; then track to see if your best hires emerge from this process.
- Continually test and improve the efficiency of your hiring tools.
- Don't wait two years until you can prove the value of better hiring techniques. Helping your recruiters and hiring managers demonstrate success will make them believe that applying more creative hiring solutions pays off.
- Have hiring managers test their ability to predict which messaging and engagement techniques will be most efficient. If their predictions are correct, then you can stop wasting time and money on A/B testing. If not, you have demonstrated the value of A/B testing.

CHAPTER 7

The Importance of Goal Setting

CLEARLY DEFINE WHAT YOU ARE LOOKING FOR

Predicting on-the-job success is difficult. After all, we are dealing with humans, who are complex, multidimensional creatures. Some may reasonably wonder, is accurately predicting on-the-job success even possible?

In his book *The Signal and the Noise*, Nate Silver sheds much needed light on predictions for a similarly complex topic by using an example about meteorologists. This profession is often mistrusted, and there is a notion that meteorologists can't truly predict the weather. After all, how can they? Weather events are dynamic and multifaceted and are impacted by numerous variables. Just 25 years ago, the average 3-day prediction for where a hurricane would make landfall was off by 350 miles. That was hardly useful for evacuation plans when you consider that the radius drawn out from, say, New Orleans covered an area from Houston, Texas, to the Florida Panhandle (Figure 7.1). Today, the average forecast is off by only 100 miles. While this is still a large area, the 70 percent improvement has made evacuation planning much more manageable. Vulnerable areas can now be evacuated 72 hours in advance. In 1985, the same accuracy was available only 24 hours before a hurricane struck.

Much in the same way that meteorology has seen vast improvement, I believe it is possible to better predict on-the-job success, but only if we

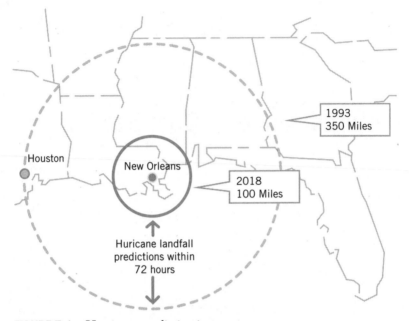

FIGURE 7.1 Hurricane prediction improvement.
Based on data from Nate Silver, *The Signal and the Noise*.

keep in mind that it is a complex topic and we can't achieve greater accuracy using simplistic models.

So how do we do it? As I explained in a joint article with Scott Thomas, the former global head of performance management at Google, *it all starts with carefully defining what it is that you want to become better at predicting.*[1]

I have executives ask, "How do I attract the best talent?" on a weekly basis. When I ask them how they define the "best" talent, I often receive lengthy answers including every imaginable personal attribute. I hear a lot of buzzwords, such as "team player" and "entrepreneurial," words that mean little when trying to evaluate candidates. Few executives define the *results* they are looking for. Even fewer mention quantitative, measurable results.

Be Specific

> Strategy is choosing what not to do.
>
> —Michael Porter

Weather forecasts have improved dramatically in part because meteorologists know *what* they are trying to improve (see Figure 7.2). They focus on

the most important criteria while deprioritizing thousands of less important ones. Similarly, if you clearly define the most important criteria for
your organization, you will help your recruiting team improve its results.

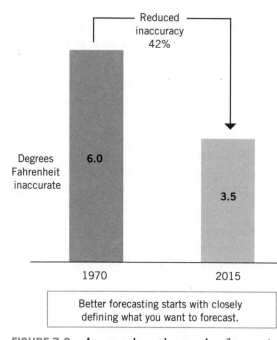

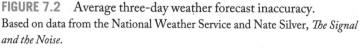

Better forecasting starts with closely
defining what you want to forecast.

FIGURE 7.2   Average three-day weather forecast inaccuracy.
Based on data from the National Weather Service and Nate Silver, *The Signal
and the Noise*.

What does all this mean for recruiting? It means you should be as precise as possible when defining what you are looking for.

Imagine that your local high school approaches you and asks you to set
up a baseball team for the school. You have recently read *Moneyball* and feel
like you're up for the challenge—except that, in this case, that book won't
do you much good. You don't have years of performance data on the players.
All you can do is observe all the students during next week's physical education classes before drafting your team. What criteria will you use to evaluate them? Athleticism? In what sense? What if you have too many students
you think are athletic? How will you differentiate among them? Will you
pick the best general athlete or the one who is terrible at track and field but
makes one 3-pointer after the other?

Whenever people ask me how they can *Moneyball* great hires by testing for one general trait, I ask myself, "Isn't this where Billy Beane's true genius was revealed?" Beane understood that a combination of on-base percentage and slugging percentage is a better predictor of offensive success than old notions to recruit for general athleticism. By clearly defining the traits that led to the most wins, he could try to sign players who were undervalued by the rest of the teams.

In other words, to answer the question about how to *Moneyball* great hires, there isn't one general trait to test for. It all depends on what position you are looking to fill.

Star Hires Are Not Picture Perfect

This may be counterintuitive for hiring managers who believe that there is one single trait, such as being an Ivy League MBA, that all-star hires across all firms have in common. And if you look hard enough, you might well come up with a few traits that these star hires have in common. However, you will achieve better results through fundamentally understanding what the OPS, the on-base plus slugging percentage, is for this specific role in your specific company.

Back to your job as a high school baseball coach: with this information in mind, you might want to take a few extra minutes to define what you mean by "athleticism" before choosing your team members. You'll probably decide to focus on their ability to throw, catch, run, or do anything requiring hand-eye coordination.

When ESPN had a panel of experts answer which sport required the most athleticism, they graded 60 sports on 10 mostly physical qualities: endurance, strength, power, speed, agility, flexibility, nerve, durability, hand-eye coordination, and analytical aptitude. The panel included sports scientists on the Olympic Committee, researchers who study human muscles and movement, an athlete who competed successfully at both baseball and football, and sports journalists who spend their lives documenting the rise and fall of the best athletes.

As seen in Figure 7.3, the term "athletic" can mean very different things in different sports. Even when selecting for athleticism, being specific matters. More precise definitions led to a clearer understanding of the skills required. This will, in turn, enable your recruiting team to focus their efforts on finding you a superstar who spikes in the dimensions most important to you.

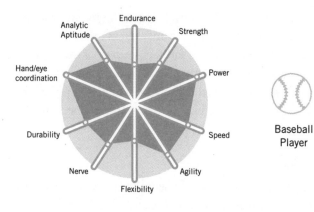

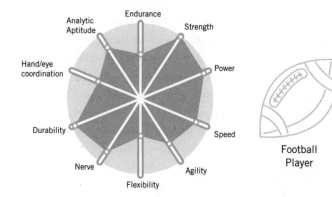

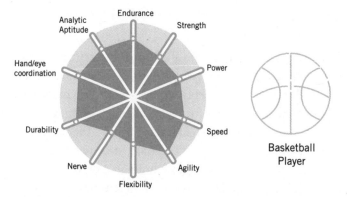

FIGURE 7.3 Which sport requires the most athleticism?
Based on data from the ESPN website.

You also want to consider whether you prefer team members who are strong in all the same skill sets and traits or who are each talented in unique areas. Imagine that each player you pick is superb in one-half of the circle in Figure 7.3, but well below average in the other half. Would you rather have all your players excel in the same half of the circle, or would you rather tilt toward the more important half, but also include a few at the other end? I'd personally go for the latter.

Look for Fit

The examples above highlight the need for searching for a precise fit rather than applying the same formula as everyone else. In a 2018 *Harvard Business Review* article, Patty McCord, the former chief talent officer at Netflix, describes how she "really dislike[s] the term 'A player.'"[2] She argues that we need to get over the notion that certain candidates are A players and others are B players. That is, there is *not* a set of people who are good at everything and a set of people who are bad at everything. It's all about fit. "One company's A player may be a B player for another firm," McCord continues. "Making great hires is about recognizing great matches—and often they're not what you'd expect." She could not be more right.

RESIST THE TEMPTATION TO REPLACE *MONEYBALL* WITH *FRANKENSTEIN*

Moneyball Is About *Reducing* the Number of Variables Where You Expect Perfection

I truly enjoy it when hiring managers obsess about hiring great employees. Many of them want to emulate Beane's success with the Oakland A's, which I believe is the correct talent strategy. I deeply respect such hiring managers, not least because they often raise the bar for the rest of their organizations. I have, however, observed that some managers trying to find the perfect fit share one common mistake: they want the candidate to be nearly perfect across the board. They list dozens of traits they admire in a number of past hires and insist that their ideal candidate possess *all* these traits.

In my experience, managers trying to assemble the perfect Build-A-Bear candidate from scratch more often end up with a Frankenstein. They insist on a candidate who checks too many boxes, instead of a strong performer who can get the job done. The genius of *Moneyball* recruitment is Billy Beane's obsession about reducing the number of variables to focus on while building the best team the A's could afford. He never looked for players who were great at every aspect of the game.

HELP HIRING MANAGERS BECOME SPECIFIC BY ASKING THE RIGHT QUESTIONS

As previously discussed, recruiters can help hiring managers define what they mean by a "great" candidate. Two key questions recruiters can ask hiring managers are (1) "What is the mandate for the role?" and (2) "How can I objectively measure success in this role?"

Make the latter question quantitative. Our economy is becoming increasingly complex, and many hiring managers find it difficult to define success by a few quantitative measures. A typical answer can be, "It's too hard to say. Success is qualitative." Don't give up too easily in such discussions. Sample probing questions can include:

- "Who are some of your current top performers in a similar role/level?"

- "What output did these individuals produce?"

- "What activities did they undertake to achieve that output?"

- "What other behavior did you observe in them?"

- "Are you intending to reward the new hire for similar output, activities, and behavior?"

If success is qualitative, understand how decisions around a person's performance reviews, promotions, firm recognitions, and bonuses are made. What skills does an ideal candidate bring to the table to execute against that mandate? Distinguish between hard skills and soft skills and between must-haves and nice-to-haves. What is the most likely profile for this job?

You want to carefully decide what types of background to target. Avoid the trap of making the profile too broad. The goal here is to narrow down the pool from a few million candidates to a manageable list you can reach out to. Challenge hiring managers who say something like, "The person's background doesn't matter; it's really about the person's mindset." Ask the hiring manager, and yourself, "What is the prioritized list of profiles that are likely to have this mindset?"

Ideally, these are attributes you can look for in résumés, LinkedIn, or other databases. If a candidate's background actually fails to increase his or her chance of being successful in the role, try to uncover traits that can be inquired about in referrals and/or can be screened for early in the process. For example, describing the candidate as a "good manager" is not very helpful in yielding referrals from your network. How can you screen for an excellent candidate? In other words, how can you tell whether a candidate just has a great résumé or will actually be a great performer?

I have listed a number of screening methods throughout this book, all of which can help you improve your interviewing process. Use these techniques to design a set of screening tools that you and the hiring manager agree on. Make sure to answer these questions:

- How will the interview process be structured?

- Who is doing the first interview screen?

- Who is doing the second screen?

- When will the candidate meet the team?

- How many rounds does a candidate have to go through before receiving an offer?

- Whom does the candidate need to meet before receiving an offer?

- How long in advance do you need to book time on the interviewers' calendars to make sure they are available?

Many of the companies I have worked with typically do not clarify these basic questions up front, which at times causes significant delays in their process. There is one more point recruiters should keep in mind during conversations with the hiring manager. For most of these topics, recruiters will add the most value to the search by *asking the right questions*, not by lecturing the hiring manager.

Chapter Summary and Conclusion

Context:

- Hiring managers make a few common mistakes when trying to define their talent strategies:
  - They say they want to hire "good" candidates but are often not specific enough about what "good" means.
  - They might be setting an unrealistically high bar by creating a long list of attributes they want the candidate to excel in and insisting that they won't compromise on anything.

What you can do about it:

- Carefully define what it is that you want to become better at predicting.
- Be specific when defining your hiring strategy. Strategy is choosing what not to do.
- Resist the temptation to replace *Moneyball* with *Frankenstein*. If you try to find a perfect candidate who meets a long list of criteria, you may be compromising more on quality than you realize.
- Empower your people operations leaders to prevent hiring managers from trying to hire candidates who are perfect in too many aspects.
- Help hiring managers be more specific by asking the right questions.

CHAPTER 8

Setting Your Recruiters Up for Success

LOOK UNDER THE HOOD

A number of hiring managers have expressed their frustration to me over the fact that their internal recruiting process or their external recruiters have not yielded enough quality candidates. In trying to be helpful, I often ask them about such key search levers as:

- What types of profiles are your recruiters targeting?

- What job boards have you tried posting this role to?

- How many candidates have your recruiters actively reached out to on their own?

- How much of your recruiters' time is dedicated to this search versus other searches on their plate?

To these questions, I typically receive a wide range of answers:

- "I don't know."

- "I don't know."

- "I don't know."

- "Je ne sais pas."

- "Atta, I just have no freakin' idea."

The standard position tends to be "I don't care how the results are produced, just as long as I receive the right candidates." Some of these hiring managers go on to tell me that they feel it's just the recruiter they worked with, who didn't care or wasn't competent. They just need to hire a new recruiter and their problems will be solved. In most cases, I need to take those recruiters under my wing, even if they don't belong to my organization, and help the hiring manager take a step back by asking the hiring manager, "Has that approach worked for you in the past?" It's rare that it has, so my next question is, "For what other part of your business would you consider creating success in the same way?"

If your manufacturing line stops working, would you simply think, "I don't know why they're not producing more gadgets, but I'll just keep telling them that I want better results, then hope and pray they will get there. If that doesn't work, I'll keep firing the plant manager and hire a new one until one of them figures it out." What if the problem persisted for a couple of days? Or for weeks, or months, or years? How would you treat a similar issue with your accounting processes or with your marketing results or your sales team drivers? So why would you treat recruiting any differently?

The vast majority of recruiters I've worked with *do* care and *are* competent. They just face unrealistic expectations from hiring managers: that they should be able to split their time on 30 or more openings, work without the tools or the budget they need to add more stars to their team, and still produce stellar results. I understand that some of these managers don't make budget decisions. However, they can still help the recruiters prioritize better by understanding the trade-offs that the recruiters must make, and they can then help the recruiters reprioritize their most productive activities.

Or as our managing director Peterson Loftin puts it, "They can always hope that the seventeenth time's the charm."

PRIORITIZE YOUR MOST PRODUCTIVE ACTIVITIES

Successful organizations "help their recruiters help them," to paraphrase Tom Cruise in *Jerry Maguire*. But how? It starts with a commitment to making talent acquisition a higher priority. Not just with words and motivational speeches, but also through budgets and action.

Talent acquisition needs to be part of the senior team's agenda. As described in the beginning of this book, Google's top 50 or so executives, including the CEO, gather every week for three to five hours to discuss recruiting results.

It's not just companies with an abundance of resources that focus this intensely on recruiting. When in 2013 I met Inanc Balci in the Philippines, he was one year into cofounding Lazada, now often described as the Amazon of the Philippines. Balci told me about the struggles of getting a business off the ground: "It's a grind! Last week we had listed a wrong version of a product on our website and someone bought it. I had to track down a friend in Singapore and ask him to send it to me, so I could fulfill the order."

When I asked him how he spent most of his time, Balci had a clear response: "I spend four hours every day interviewing candidates. In addition to that I also have to meet with the recruiting team and other company leaders to make sure we are on the same page regarding our recruiting goals." Four hours a day on recruiting? As the cofounder? Yes. And he had a clear reason for why he needed to dedicate so much time to recruiting: "It's a lot of time, and it may sound like a cliché, but I can't afford not to do it."

Balci led a sale of his firm to the Alibaba Group, which between 2016 and 2017 paid $1.5 billion for a majority stake in Lazada. By 2018, Lazada was the largest e-commerce retailer, not only in the Philippines, but by some estimates also in Malaysia, Vietnam, and Thailand.

Balci is not the only high-growth start-up CEO spending so much time on recruiting. DoorDash CEO Tony Xu in an interview disclosed, "I spend 50 percent-plus of my time in recruiting, as I find it has the highest output to input ratio."

You, as the leader of your company, need to think long and hard about where you are getting the most value from your talent strategies. If it's from managing your staff, spend most of your time managing. If it's from selecting the best talent, spend most of your time recruiting.

ASSIGN ONE OF YOUR FIVE BEST PEOPLE
TO TALENT ACQUISITION

Having one of your best employees in charge of talent acquisition is critical if you want to significantly improve your results. As always, "the team with the best players wins." This is especially true in areas of the business that can't rely on already-established processes to succeed.

A friend who read an early draft of this book told me that this recommendation seemed a bit obvious. I asked him, "So how does it work in your organization? Is one of your best five people leading talent acquisition?" He cut himself off halfway into saying, "Well, no. But . . ." We both smiled and nodded, as the point had been made. If you were to ask yourself the same question, what would you respond?

SET ATTAINABLE GOALS FOR YOUR RECRUITERS

After going through the process described in Chapter 7, how many great hires should you expect? Can you tell your recruiters that *all* your hires must be star performers? Aim for the stars, so that if you fail, you'll land on the moon, right?

The short answer to that question is no. As a CEO, you are in a position to empower your team to achieve ambitious goals. However, your team will stop trying if these goals are completely out of reach or unanchored to business reality.

If you're the CEO of a leisure and hospitality firm, for example, your employee turnover may be 9 percent per annum. If you're running an IT firm, your employee turnover may be over 4 percent per annum (see Figure 8.1). In both cases, reduced employee turnover could be one of the goals you set for your recruiters. However, setting the goal at an arbitrary number, such as 2 percent, will not help anyone. Setting unreachable goals is likely to be counterproductive. You'll simply seem irrational, and your recruiters will become demotivated. A much better approach is to "look under the hood," understand the drivers behind the attrition, and then in a collaborative way agree to which of those drivers can be improved and by how much.

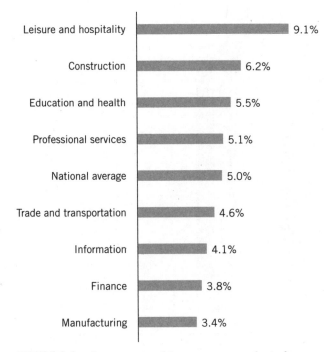

FIGURE 8.1 Average monthly turnover rates by industry. Based on data from the ADP website.

MEASURE SUCCESS AT AGREGGATE LEVELS, NOT THROUGH ANECDOTES

One of the reasons why setting quantitative and attainable goals is useful, is that you'll start measuring the performance of your recruiters across all their hires, not just through one-off anecdotes. A surprising number of companies form opinions about who their best and worst recruiters are based on a few anecdotes. "Julie is fantastic. She's the one who found us Sue!" or "Matt went to bat for Eric, who's turned out to be really awful."

In the social arenas we work in, this is an easy mistake to make, but it does very little to improve your recruiting results. Mike Trout, LeBron James, and Tom Brady are all athletes but are each held to different standards (see Figure 8.2). Your recruiting team should be, as well.

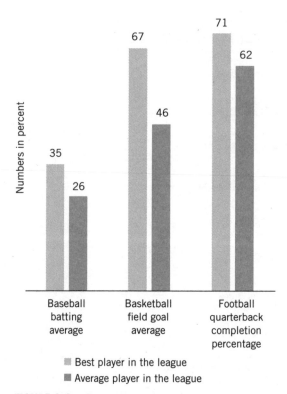

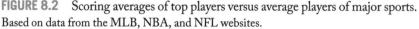

FIGURE 8.2 Scoring averages of top players versus average players of major sports. Based on data from the MLB, NBA, and NFL websites.

Unless you are clear and reasonable in setting your goals, you will not improve your results. Instead, you might end up rewarding self-promoters who claim they found the occasional star instead of those who increase your team's overall winning percentage. Most managers who have run sales organizations, for instance, have noticed that it's much easier to understand who is a good performer by reviewing sales numbers rather than listening to the salespeople brag about their performance or even trying to observe their behavior. So why wouldn't you define performance as clearly for other roles as well?

MAKE SURE HIRING MANAGERS ARE ENGAGED IN THEIR OWN SEARCH FOR NEW TALENT

Hiring managers who simply hand off searches to a recruiting partner show that they don't want to be involved in their own hiring process. Either they don't believe there is intense competition for the talent they're seeking, or if they do believe there is, then they are showing through their lack of involvement that finding the best talent is not a priority for them, regardless of what they say. In either case, you're unlikely to find strong talent if they stay unengaged with the search.

In an interview with Netflix's Patty McCord, she told me that she would reassign her recruiters to other parts of the business if they were not getting the partnership needed from hiring managers. "Many hiring managers would get upset at me, but I would tell them that I had many other hiring managers that would be delighted to provide the partnership we needed to help them be successful. I made it clear to hands-off or disengaged hiring managers that I couldn't afford to spend twice as much of my recruiters' time to achieve half the results for them as for their peers who were engaged in their own searches."

Hiring managers who ask for stellar candidates but neglect to partner up with their talent acquisition team remind me of one of Sacha Baron Cohen's Ali G episodes. Ali G pitches his brilliant idea to produce hoverboards modeled on those in *Back to the Future* to a venture capital investor. When the investor asks how this product will technically work, Ali G behaves like the classic "idea guy," telling the VC investor that his contribution to the partnership will be to solve these little technical details: "That's where you lot come in! You come up with the science."

GIVE YOUR HIRING MANAGERS MORE INTERVIEWING EXPERIENCE

A number of organizations focus on improving their hiring managers' interviewing skills with extra training and development. Whirlpool CEO Mark Bitzer stressed the importance of exposing hiring managers to a large number of interviews: "A number of hiring managers don't interview more than a handful of people a year. That's not enough. You need to interview hundreds of people a year until you get really good at this skill."

Data reported by former Google chief people officer Laszlo Bock in his book *Work Rules!* reveal a similar conclusion. Bock's data indicate that Google interviewers who had conducted fewer than 50 interviews typically achieved a prediction accuracy of more than 20 percent, while the equivalent number for interviewers who had conducted at least 50 interviews averaged more than 50 percent. Googlers who'd conducted more than 100 interviews were more than 60 percent accurate, and those who had conducted more than 150 interviews tended to be more than 70 percent accurate in their hiring predictions.

Amazon has come to a similar conclusion. Before candidates receive an offer, they need to be interviewed by a so-called bar raiser. Besides being a top performer, an Amazonian bar raiser needs to have conducted a minimum number of interviews (quantity) plus have a track record of hiring recommendations aligned with the outcome of the hire (quality).

TRAIN YOUR INTERVIEWERS
HOW TO ATTRACT STRONG CANDIDATES

Strong candidates are evaluating you and the opportunity as much as you are evaluating them. You, therefore, want to train your hiring managers and interviewers on how to attract strong candidates. In doing so, please keep the discussion from Chapter 5 in mind. Don't go so much into selling mode that you are bending the truth about the role. So, what are the tactics that are advisable?

Substance Attracts Better Candidates Than Kool-Aid

In trying to excite candidates, take a step back and think about what your best employees value most about being with your firm and what a strong performer would appreciate about this position. Make sure your interviewers are able to articulate how these key selling points manifest themselves in the job. Don't rely on interviewers coming up with these points on their own or being able to articulate the key selling points well. Debrief with the interviewers in advance of interviews, hold training sessions, role-play, use PowerPoint presentations that speak to these key selling points, etc. You, of course, want your interviewers to be truthful and to talk about what excites them about your company in their own words, but you also want to help them think about what will entice the right candidates and how to speak to those points. Also, please note that these key selling points must be real. Empty statements, trendy recruiting jargon, and lofty rhetoric seldom work. I can't tell you how many bureaucratic companies I've seen inaccurately describing themselves as entrepreneurial. Wouldn't you want strong candidates to see through that type of smokescreen? If not, are you going to respect their judgment once you hire them?

Instead of trying to be *good enough* for all candidates, focus on a smaller segment of candidates and being *a very good fit* for them. Emphasize how your company is different from others in your field. If all you can offer candidates is vague Kool-Aid, such as "In this role you'll have tons of exposure to senior management, and you'll get a lot of responsibility," you will be competing with all the companies that spout similar jargon. Instead, focus on tangible examples of how you are different. And better for the right person.

Ted Sarandos, head of content at Netflix, knew that he couldn't attract top-tier talent by just telling them that this would be an "amazing opportunity where they could be part of a game-changing model." Most senior executives I have met in Hollywood are good at that sort of pitch. Instead, Sarandos focused on identifying the best creative talent who could also execute their vision. He gave them enormous freedom unheard of among the larger Hollywood studios to execute their vision. While traditional studios would, for instance, require all shows to go through a painful pilot process, Netflix would greenlight producers to create full seasons of episodes. *Orange Is the New Black*, for example, was greenlit for production before it even had a script. Patty McCord, in her book *Powerful,* writes of Sarandos's bold new approach: "That has been the greatest differentiator between Netflix and the Hollywood studios."

Why People Change Jobs

Data from LinkedIn's survey "Why & How People Change Jobs" indicate that the primary reason that candidates switch jobs is that they care most about the opportunity to forge an exciting career path. Compensation is important to them, but it comes second to new opportunity. These and other important factors are listed in Figure 8.3. Even if these other factors are, on average, less important than compensation, they are all still important, and most candidates make a holistic decision based on all the criteria that are important to them.

Companies that compete for talent mainly through base compensation will soon find that their competitors have followed suit and, in effect, will merely have raised the compensation bar for their industry.

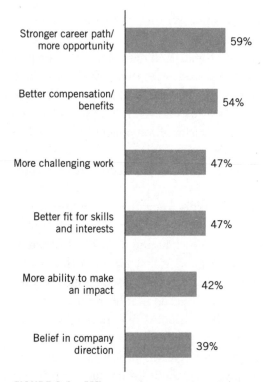

FIGURE 8.3 Why people accept a new job.
Based on data from the LinkedIn survey "Why & How People Change Jobs."

What You Can Learn from the Battlegrounds of the War for Talent

One area in which the importance of not competing exclusively via salary has been clearly demonstrated is in the competition for graduates from the top 10 MBA programs. Leading organizations have fought over these graduates for years, and this is where the war for talent is fiercest. The hiring strategies of employers who have gained ground over the past few years can therefore be seen as indicative of winning strategies.

As shown in Figure 8.4, the share of graduates from the top 10 MBA programs going into tech has increased significantly since 2012. This has come mainly at the expense of financial services and consulting firms. As tech firms gain ground in the war for talent, it is crucial to better understand their hiring practices.

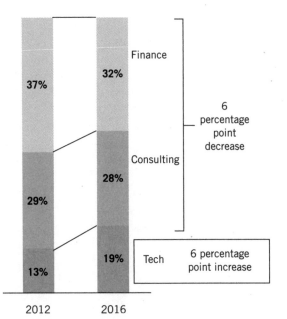

FIGURE 8.4 Percentage of top 10 MBA program graduates entering selected careers (by year).
Based on data from MBA alumni websites and ECA analysis.

In 2012, financial services and consulting firms not only had higher base salaries than tech; they had also increased these salaries at a faster rate (see Figure 8.5). But despite lower salaries, tech has been able to attract more talent from these elite programs.

Tech companies are winning talent by challenging conventional wisdom and offering "softer" attributes, such as a more compelling career path and superior perks, instead of hard attributes such as base compensation.

In 2017, Maria Renz, an Amazon VP, wrote in Vox's *Recode*: "At Amazon, opportunities to move, grow and take on new challenges are abundant. Our dynamic environment—where there is no shortage of interesting problems to solve or opportunities to build—is what has kept me here for so long. Amazon encourages employees to create their own career paths, and we have great flexibility to move between departments and roles."[1]

Companies like Amazon focus on creating more interesting career paths and learning curves, which for many amount to a "post-MBA MBA." Business students see this as a training ground for starting their own

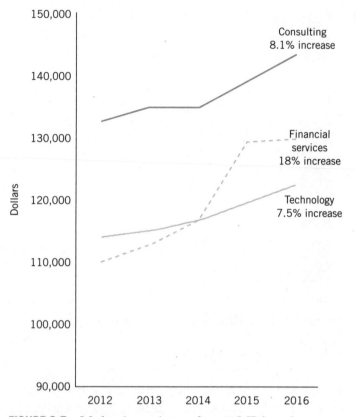

FIGURE 8.5   Median base salaries of top 10 MBA graduates entering selected career (by year).
Based on data from MBA websites and ECA analysis.

companies one day, or they see it as way to acquire a more complete set of tools to grow professionally and make an impact.

Companies like Google are also famous for competing less on base salaries and more on perks and a larger upside in other forms of equity.

This doesn't mean you have to offer Google-caliber perks to attract talent. Successful companies can emphasize how their employees can customize the softer attributes to the culture *they* intend to create and thereby attract talent that is a better fit for *them* (see Table 8.1).

TABLE 8.1   Hard Versus Soft Attributes

Hard Attributes	Soft Attributes
High compensation • Base salary • Sign-on bonuses • Year-end bonuses	Larger upside • "Equity" (options, RSUs, etc.) that could be worth millions, or if the employee does very well, billions in the future • Fast-track promotions into high senior roles
Known linear career progression and salary development	The "post-MBA MBA" • Fast learning curve • Great responsibilities Perks • Fun and creative offices • At-work perks such as free food Mission • Stronger focus on clearly articulating the problem they are addressing in the world

UNDERSTAND WHAT IS IMPORTANT TO STRONG CANDIDATES, AND TAILOR YOUR OFFERING FOR THEM

Each candidate's needs are unique. While you can't tailor your entire benefits and perks program to every single candidate, you may be able to customize aspects of the role, responsibilities, career path, opportunities, mentorship, and other factors such as flexibility with the start date or working hours for the strongest candidates. But how do you understand what is important to the individual candidates? You simply ask them.

During the interview, you can ask such questions as, "If you could design this role by yourself, what would you change about it?" In a second- or third-round interview, you can ask, "Based on what you have heard so far about our company and the role, what would give you pause about accepting a potential offer from us?"

Encourage candidates to speak their minds, and help them lower their guards. Make it clear you're not trying to trap them. The more you can do that, the more open and honest the discussions will be. With that openness comes the information that can provide you with a competitive advantage over a huge multinational with more rigid career paths or policies.

While you want to avoid favoritism, you have to balance that by tailoring (within reason) your value proposition for strong candidates. These candidates are highly sought by other companies, so your sharpest competitive edge will be your ability to cater to the specific needs top candidates care about, not from using a checklist that mainly applies to the needs of an average candidate—that is, to the needs of the masses.

It's important to listen carefully to the individual candidates and understand what *they* think is important. If you believe you can satisfy those needs, talk about how you and your colleagues can help them attain those very things. Don't give them a canned spiel about your firm. Candidates like those about as much as you like canned interview answers from them.

What if a candidate doesn't mention any perks or opportunities available at your company? Then it is not a good fit. Accept that, thank the candidate for his or her time, and move on.

Chapter Summary and Conclusion

Context:

- Recruiters often face a number of challenges:
  - The hiring managers' level of involvement may not match their ambitions for achieving their hiring goals.
  - Hiring managers may ask recruiters to produce ambitious results, but not help them understand how to accomplish them.
  - An organization may set unrealistically high goals for its recruiters, hoping this will inspire them to at least achieve some of these goals.
  - One unfortunate irony is that the talent acquisition department might not receive its fair share of star talent within the organization.
  - They partner with hiring managers with little interviewing experience.
- The most common reason cited for switching jobs is a stronger career path or more opportunity, not higher compensation.
- Tech companies are gaining traction in the war for talent.

What you can do about it:

- Successful organizations address these topics by:
  - Asking hiring managers to be involved in their own searches and encouraging them to "look under the hood"
  - Having hiring managers partner with their recruiters in understanding *how* they best can execute the desired hiring strategies, after determining whether these strategies are viable
  - Setting achievable goals for their recruiters
  - Assigning one of their best five people to talent acquisition
  - Ensuring that at least one experienced interviewer is involved in each search
  - Understanding what is important to strong candidates, and tailoring job offers to these candidates
  - Keeping in mind that substance attracts better candidates than Kool-Aid

CHAPTER 9

Strong Versus Weak Evidence

THE THREE CURRENT EXTREMES

"He didn't take the time to chat with the secretary. He's therefore not a warm person and will not succeed in this role. So we're not going to move forward with him."

Statements like this are common in the hiring process. Managers regularly have to make decisions about candidates based on limited or somewhat irrelevant data. I have observed three extreme viewpoints on how to make hiring decisions given the limited data.

First Extreme: Abolish Interviews

The first extreme view is that job interviews are completely useless. Proponents of this position typically favor evaluating candidates in purely quantitative terms and/or based on past experiences or results. Many proponents of this view favor a purely data-driven approach.

Tomas Chamorro-Premuzic, an organizational psychologist and the author of *The Talent Delusion*, asks, "What would happen if we all agreed to scrap job interviews tomorrow, and focused instead on other indicators of career potential? Unthinkable as it may sound . . . replacing interviews with other, more predictive measures is the way to go."

While I agree that most interviewers would benefit from integrating more objective and number-driven methods into their evaluation process, I believe that interviews can still play an important role in the selection of talent. The sabermetrics guru Nate Silver seems to agree when he argues that human scouts still add value in baseball and that meteorologists can make precipitation forecasts 25 percent more accurate and temperature forecasts 10 percent more accurate than computer-generated forecasts alone.

Ben Lindbergh and Rob Arthur, contributors to Silver's stat-obsessed sports analytics site FiveThirtyEight, write, "Stats haven't killed the scouting star." Their analysis shows that all but five MLB teams increased their number of scouts between 2009 and 2016 (see Table 9.1). The number of full-time scouts throughout the league increased from 1,246 to 1,539 in the same time period, an average increase of almost 10 scouts per team.

Why would MLB teams, which in many ways pioneered the data-driven approach to recruiting, increase their budgets for human recruiters if they were not adding value? Perhaps for the same reason that it is rare for organizations to refrain from using job interviews: because there is information value to be gained that is not easily captured by data alone.

Second Extreme: Ignore All the Data

The second and most common extreme viewpoint is seldom explicitly stated but often still implicitly held. Hiring managers who ignore all the data might do so for much the same reason they ignore the latest fad diet. Since no recruiting tool can successfully predict *all* hiring outcomes, they dismiss anything inconvenient that scientists tell them, choosing to stick with their own method.

Third Extreme: Any Negative Signal Should Result in Candidates Being Rejected

The third extreme holds that any indication, however minor, that candidates might not be a perfect fit will be used to not hire them.

This raises the question of how confidently we can establish certain facts. It is true that being certain that a candidate will be a star—or a mishire—based on a few limited interviews is almost impossible. In reality, we can't know with absolute certainty whether a candidate will perform well or not. In the interview process, we are just collecting evidence for and against our hypothesis that a particular candidate will be a good hire.

TABLE 9.1 Number of Scouts at MLB Teams, 2009 Versus 2016

Team	2009	2016	% Change	
WAS	28	47	67.9	
NYY	45	74	64.4	
SDN	36	55	52.8	
TOR	38	58	52.6	
TBA	43	65	51.2	
ARI	41	61	48.8	
ATL	32	46	43.8	
CHW	32	46	43.8	
LAD	43	61	41.9	
CIN	46	65	41.3	
ANA	34	48	41.2	Teams increasing scouts
MIN	35	46	31.4	
KCA	36	47	30.6	
TEX	38	49	28.9	
MIL	38	48	26.3	
PIT	39	48	23.1	
COL	36	44	22.2	
BOS	59	71	20.3	
CHC	51	60	17.6	
CLE	41	48	17.1	
MIA	38	43	13.2	
STL	39	44	12.8	
DET	40	44	10.0	
OAK	38	40	5.3	
PHI	33	33	0	
SFN	59	56	−5.1	
HOU	55	52	−5.5	Teams decreasing scouts
BAL	34	32	−5.9	
SEA	67	62	−7.5	
NYM	52	46	−11.5	

Source: FiveThirtyEight analysis. Used with permission.

HOW STRONG IS YOUR EVIDENCE?

Evidence That Is Easy to Verify

What is good evidence as opposed to poor evidence? For recruitment purposes, good evidence is information that you know is true with high certainty and that you can use to predict the future performance of a candidate.

The best evidence is objective and can be easily verified. It is often referred to as "hard facts." For instance, it should be easy for the *Wall Street Journal* to find out whether Kevin Durant really is six foot nine, as his official NBA profile claims he is, or six foot eleven, as the *Wall Street Journal* claims he is (see Figure 9.1). As long as Durant agrees to it, the *Journal* can settle the issue once and for all by measuring him.

FIGURE 9.1   How tall is Kevin Durant?
The Wall Street Journal. Used with permission.

Why would Durant want to be perceived as shorter than he is? Durant himself admitted in an interview with the paper that he's more effective as a small forward. Even though he's almost seven feet tall, he doesn't want people to think he plays small for his size, so he claims to be only six-foot-nine. "Really, that's the prototypical size for a small forward. Anything taller than that, and they'll start saying, 'Ah, he's a power forward.'"

Maybe for this reason, the Air Force does not ask hopeful cadets about their height. They simply measure the aspiring pilots to ensure they are between 64 and 77 inches tall and can fit in a fighter jet cockpit.

Evidence That Is Somewhat Difficult to Verify

Job applicants are not usually so naïve as to mislead employers about hard facts. The challenge arises when trying to assess whether candidates are being honest about statements or résumé items that are less easy to confirm.

Take, for instance, Christian Eberhard, who was employed as a medical doctor by the University Clinic of Erlangen in Germany. He took part in 190 procedures and surgeries, including amputations. What the clinic didn't know was that Eberhard had faked his medical degree. The clinic could have found out before hiring him if it had called Oxford University, where he claimed to have earned his degree. Today we could also use social media to look up people who attended the same university and reach out to his alleged cohort to see if anyone could verify that he had at least studied there—even if there was still a question of whether he earned a degree or not.

Even though the evidence presented by Eberhard (a fake but convincing doctor's diploma) was possible to verify, it was somewhat difficult for the German university to do so. No one there was familiar with the British system or wanted to invest the time to verify the information. The evidence Eberhard presented that he was a doctor should have been treated as "medium strong," because it was cumbersome to verify.

Evidence That Is Very Difficult to Verify

Then we have "Jennifer," a very likable talent acquisition executive who interviewed with one of the billion-dollar companies we serve. She thoroughly charmed the CEO and the COO. She also interviewed with, and equally charmed, all six talent acquisition professionals who would report to her in her new position.

The company had repeatedly told her during the interview process that its style of management could best be described as "servant leadership." To them this meant a friendly, collaborative, and nurturing leadership style. Jennifer seemed excited and energized by this description, describing in depth how this closely matched with her preferred style.

Within a week of Jennifer starting, the COO had received multiple e-mails from the talent acquisition team members saying that they would most likely leave the company if Jennifer did not change her style. The e-mails described how she had yelled at them, spoken to them in a demeaning tone, and humiliated individual members in front of the team. She was brought in for an open conversation with the COO and given a clear warning. On the first day of her third week, Jennifer was let go.

It's easy for some people to be quite charming during a job interview. They might have better acting skills, and of course they're highly motivated to leave a positive impression. Being charming day after day, even when their job requires it, can be a lot harder. Interviewers should therefore understand that a candidate's charm during an interview must be considered soft evidence of how charming the candidate will be on the job. They should instead be focusing more on hard evidence, such as a candidate's oral or written language skills, which can be verified more readily.

Unfortunately, evidence from interviews tends to be soft, so how do you know which information you should rely on most heavily when making your hiring decisions?

What Evidence Can You Rely On?

Both Christian's and Jennifer's cases involved "asymmetric information." That is, in both cases, the candidates knew more about themselves than their potential employers did, and they withheld the information they knew would keep them from being hired. Asymmetric information poses a problem not just for employers but also for job candidates.

Imagine a candidate who would genuinely enjoy applying a friendly management style, but the company he or she applied to was so tainted by its experience with Jennifer that it no longer wanted to risk hiring someone it did not know personally for at least a few years. In this case, one candidate bears the cost for another's asymmetric information. The interests of strong performers are therefore aligned with those of the hiring firm; that is, both would benefit from their counterpart's ability to verify the information displayed by the candidate.

The economist and Nobel Laureate Michael Spence coined the term "signaling" as a way for candidates to overcome this issue. He argued that "good" candidates can credibly convey information about themselves to employers by sending signals that are too costly for "bad" candidates.

"Costly" refers not only to monetary cost but also to effort, ability, and preference. There are always exceptions to the rule, but most companies will benefit from looking at what works best on average in these scenarios. One point of caution, however, is that companies can miss out on great talent and unconsciously discriminate against certain groups if relying too heavily on preestablished signals that favor certain groups. This point was discussed more in depth in the section "Limitations of GMA and Other Hiring Assessments" in Chapter 4.

THE SIGNALING ARMS RACE

What types of signals should you look for in a job interview? Signals that clearly indicate values that are difficult or undesirable to fake. Strong candidates will eagerly display these signals, in part because they are the hardest for weak performers to fake.

A growing number of employers favor candidates who have acquired an additional language or two. Such language skills are not always directly useful in many jobs, but employers still read the ability to speak another language as a signal that someone is curious, smart, and capable, with the long-term discipline required to learn something as complex and rewarding as a new language. Students who lack any talent for picking up new languages can live with the fact that they won't project this signal, or they can fake the signal and, by working even harder than students who are gifted in learning new languages, go through the painstaking exercise of learning a new language. They can also embellish their résumé and hope they don't get caught. A candidate did just that, claiming on his résumé to be "fluent" in German, but he froze when I began speaking that language to him during the interview.

The Case of Google

A major problem with signals is that once it becomes known that a variable is being widely used as a signal, that signal loses most of its value.

It could be argued that if it had not been for this problem, Google might not exist. Before Google, the major search engines looked for relevant keywords in a website. The more often a relevant keyword was displayed, the higher the rating it would get in Yahoo, AltaVista, and the other early search engines. This practice led to websites repeating popular search terms on their pages to receive a higher rank. All those extra keywords, though, were poor indicators of how helpful these websites would be to the user. Pornography websites typed in thousands of unrelated but popular keywords, hidden in ways that kept users from seeing them, cynically boosting the number of searches by people looking for those unrelated terms.

Larry Page and Sergey Brin, the founders of Google, noticed that looking for keywords in a website was not a reliable signal for how useful the site was to a person looking for specific information. They favored a system already in use in the academic community. Academic papers were ranked by how often they were cited by other academic publications, not by how often a keyword was used in the paper. Page and Brin reasoned that looking at the number of these "backlinks" to a website was therefore a better indicator, or signal, of how useful other people found the site. They could not have been more right.

Ironically, Google's success demonstrated an important point about the difficulty of finding good signals. In order for a signal to be useful, it must be costly to fake for those who don't actually possess the trait someone is looking for. This was not the case with the backlinks. Search engine optimization companies started offering services to set up thousands of fake websites to backlink to a company's website. If Google had failed to counteract this behavior, it would have displayed less useful search results for its users and become less helpful as a tool.

Google fights these tricks by constantly tweaking its algorithm. It is an ongoing cat-and-mouse game between Google trying to find more credible signals of actual quality and websites trying to fake those signals to get better rankings.

Signaling Among Candidates

Employers and candidates engage in a similar cat-and-mouse game. Once applicants understand that employers are looking for particular signals, the applicants do their best to project them. This misleading behavior has become so ubiquitous that most people don't even realize they're doing it.

A sloppy and unmotivated teenager is encouraged by his parents to study hard throughout high school and apply to prestigious colleges. If his grades are below those of his peers, he or his parents complain to his teachers. Once he is ready for the job market, his mother writes his résumé and has a few friends QC it to ensure it is error-free. His career counselor puts him through rigorous interview training so he'll be able to respond to any question without shooting himself in the foot. Finally, his father makes sure he shaves and wears proper attire to the actual interview.

"What's wrong with that?" you may ask. "Isn't that just common sense?" It has become common sense, but before it did, most companies used high school grades, college admission and performance, the quality of the candidates' résumés, their attire, and their responses to interview questions as ways to screen candidates. And in some fields and parts of the world, these signals are still effective. Stephane Vedie, the CEO of the billion-dollar-plus automotive parts supplier Varroc Lighting Systems, told me how he has experienced this phenomenon: "Candidates are very prepared in the U.S. compared to Europe. They seem to have a good answer for the most common interview questions. There is nothing wrong with being prepared, but I have had to adjust my interviewing style to make sure I'm receiving genuine responses."

Part of the problem is that in the signaling arms race, positive signals often lose their value sooner than negative signals. That is, far more job applicants are bragging about high GPAs, college degrees, and other credentials on their résumés than ever before. With this type of signal inflation, each positive signal is worth less. This makes it challenging for employers to spot extraordinary talent among the sea of ordinary candidates projecting the same signals. Any serious negative signal, however, will still retain its value. A candidate throwing a temper tantrum during an interview would have been rejected 50 years ago and will still be rejected. The danger is that, amid all these comprehensively groomed candidates, employers out of desperation to rely on *any* signals give too much weight to the tiniest negative signal, even if this signal no longer is predictive of negative outcomes. Such hiring managers may find themselves reasoning: "This candidate had a small typo in an e-mail three months ago. He is clearly unprofessional, so we should not hire him."

A university such as Harvard aims to attract the very brightest students not only from each class but also from each school district. Needless to say, Harvard will no longer be able to use a 4.0 GPA as a credible signal for selecting that caliber of student. Neither will the 67 percent of companies that, according to the National Association of Colleges and Employers, screen candidates by their GPA. (See Figure 9.2.)

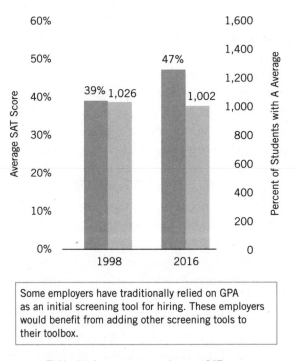

Some employers have traditionally relied on GPA as an initial screening tool for hiring. These employers would benefit from adding other screening tools to their toolbox.

■ % with A average   ■ Average SAT score

FIGURE 9.2 Grade compression among high school students. Based on data in article in *USA Today*.[1]

What Signals Can Be Trusted in a Job Interview?

In addition to looking for signals that are difficult or undesirable to fake, you can look for signals that have not yet become "common sense" for candidates to project. That is, until lots of employers start looking for these signals, most candidates won't think they'll get much value from projecting them (see Table 9.2).

Many interviewers intuitively sense this and adjust their style, no longer directly asking candidates what they actually want to know. I want to emphasize that there are typically more downsides than benefits with this approach. It's not that this approach can't be helpful; it can. In my experience, however, most interviewers take it too far. They fail to follow a systematic process, read too much between the lines, and often don't try to verify information by probing further while checking for signals that are difficult to fake.

TABLE 9.2   Signal Reliability

Difficulty to Fake	Signals			
Candidate Attributes	Low	Medium	High	Very High
Team Player	Likability during interveiw	Reference checks	Brief work trial	Long work trial period
GMA	Brain teaser	High school GPA	College GPA	SAT
Quality of Work	Interview questions	Work samples	Work tests	Long work trial period

Paul Ericksen of *Industry Week* argues that the point when some companies started favoring MBAs in their recruiting strategy marked the decline of MBAs: "They went from being used by individuals to try to increase their business savvy to being used by HR to represent a simple differentiator in evaluating candidates. . . . This approach changed the whole reason for someone getting an MBA. In my experience the primary driver of many MBA students today is not the knowledge and background they provide. It is just to check off another 'credential box' needed to succeed in applying for a job." Eriksen goes on to describe how this once-useful signal for identifying good candidates became much less useful when candidates started gaming the system.

Pitfalls of Relying on Signals

There are a number of pitfalls with trying to discover signals displayed by candidates. Hiring managers can get so caught up in unearthing what they believe are signals, that they don't take the time to check if those candidate traits are predictive of job performance.

The Novel Information Bind

Let's start with what I call the "novel information bind." That is, hiring managers who unearth a novel piece of information about a candidate often feel a painstaking urge to use that information regardless of how helpful it might be.

Being able to accurately evaluate an intrinsic quality in a candidate does not have a value in itself and should not be confused with a signal. We also, of course, want to understand intrinsic qualities that are strong predictors of job performance.

Candidates with a tan (a signal) in Southern California may very well like to surf (an intrinsic quality). However, since there is no known link between surfing and having what it takes to be a good employee for most jobs, this is a useless piece of information. This point is ignored or misunderstood by many hiring managers, who can't avoid feeling a detective's pride when having uncovered a novel piece of information about a candidate. Since it requires work and even skills to discover underlying information about a candidate, many hiring managers take that information and commit to fitting it into a story about why it is predictive of job performance. Unfortunately, out of the thousands of pieces of information about each candidate, only a few are predictive. So regardless of the effort and skill it took to unearth a choice nugget of background information, hiring managers should avoid overvaluing things they could see were not predictive if they looked at them more objectively.

The Illusion of Validity

I have seen interviewers spend hours debating whether candidates are extroverts or introverts without the slightest proof that either of those traits predicts performance for the position they're trying to fill.

In an interview, you are trying to predict future outcomes based on several criteria. In this context, it doesn't matter whether you are right that a candidate is an introvert—or have a correct understanding of a candidate's other traits—unless those criteria actually predict anything relevant to the job.

This can be particularly hard to accept when a screening test produces criteria that seem to make logical sense. Nobel Laureate Daniel Kahneman named this phenomenon the "illusion of validity."

In *Thinking, Fast and Slow*, Kahneman describes how he experienced the illusion of validity when he was in the military. He had been assigned to predict which candidates were better suited for office positions. His role was to administer a leaderless group challenge with eight military candidates who didn't know each other. The candidates were instructed to carry a long log over a six-foot wall without touching the wall. If any of the participants or the log touched the wall, the group had to start over again. At the time, Kahneman thought that "the task [of predicting their job performance] was not difficult, because we had already seen each of these soldiers' leadership skills." However, he had to confess later on that "our forecasts were largely useless. The evidence was overwhelming. Every few months we had a feedback session in which we could compare our evaluations of future cadets with the judgments of their commanders at the officer training school. The story was always the same: our ability to predict performance at the school was negligible."

What was also surprising to Kahneman was his own reaction to the data. "The dismal truth about the quality of our predictions had no effect whatsoever on how we evaluated new candidates and very little effect on the confidence we had in our judgments and predictions."

I have observed this phenomenon most often when sophisticated screening tools are being deployed. One of my clients was trying to convince me that he and his staff had discovered a great signal. They had come across a personality test that they felt was highly accurate in predicting certain personality traits. I took the test and agreed that some of the results would be accurate if candidates responded honestly. However, finding personality tests that can accurately assess a job applicant's personality is only half the battle. Once you have such a test, you should stay critical of your initial hypothesis, take a step back, and determine whether those personality traits actually predict better performance, which, in this case, I did not believe they did. As a result, I disagreed that the described personality traits were good predictors of performance for the role our client was hiring for.

In my experience, the illusion of validity is so strong that it is often difficult to notice once you are already impacted by it. One effective way to prevent this from happening is to be disciplined in testing your hypothesis. Be explicit about the results you expect to see from using a prediction method. Make them quantitative and be clear about when you expect these results to become apparent. And then believe the numbers even if they go against a strong hunch. You can also research how to find and test variables with high validity.

MAKING DECISIONS WITH LIMITED DATA

Hiring managers often have to make decisions on candidates based on very limited data. There are few other areas in which companies have such limited time and opportunity to gather data points before making such an important and costly investment.

Several kinds of professions have to quickly make crucial decisions based on limited data. Police officers on a DUI stop typically spend less than a minute with a driver before deciding whether the person might be under the influence, and if so, whether the person needs to be investigated further.

Hiring managers seldom have to deal with drunks, but they often have to solve multidimensional problems based on limited data. What do I mean by that? A good candidate can't be evaluated on a one-dimensional scale such as "good or bad" or "sober or drunk." Hiring managers can't rely on a two-dimensional scale, either. As Jim Williams, a TPG executive who has filled over 200 CEO roles, explained to me: "Selecting the 'best athlete' is a common recruiting strategy, but it often leads to poor outcomes if not done right. Being smart and a good leader is not enough. You also need someone with a deep passion for the product of the company and also someone with the right skills for the challenges that the company is facing. Business context truly matters."

The Long List of Traits

Some hiring managers create a long list of traits they want candidates to possess and (often as important) qualities they want to avoid. The larger the number of interviewers who are part of the process, the longer these "wish lists" tend to become.

One company we worked with had come up with a list of more than 30 specific traits it wanted each candidate to excel at. The main challenge with these extra-long wish lists is that unless hiring managers spend significant time with each candidate, they end up spending *less time per criterion* they are assessing. This inevitable imbalance often forces them to make decisions based on lower-quality information.

Some firms try to divide up the traits they are assessing among multiple interviewers, hoping this will allow each interviewer to drill deeper into each topic. My experience has been that this practice leads to a number of challenges. Sometimes the interviewers fail to coordinate effectively. Even when they do coordinate, there tends to be overlap on some basic topics, such as "What attracts you to this job?" Let's say there are five interviewers and each interviewer covers five to ten topics. After allotting time for introductions, candidate questions, and other things, the interviewers probably have somewhere from two to ten minutes per trait they need to evaluate.

The *One* Difficult Test

Many hiring managers try to resolve such time constraints by evaluating candidates through *one* very difficult question or test, one they believe will reveal the presence or absence of a quintessential quality.

Depending on only *one*, albeit very difficult, test can be a great method if that test is reasonably predictive of what you are trying to measure. And interviewers aren't the only ones trying to determine whether one well-chosen data point is predictive of something important. Sports bettors and fans often think that the "wrong" team won. Well, did it? Let's take the World Cup in soccer as an example. Did the "best" team win the 2018 World Cup? The answer goes back to our definition of "best." Before you roll your eyes, let's think about this for a moment. What does winning the World Cup mean? To most of us, it simply means that the winning team was skilled, was able to rise to the occasion, and had the right amount of luck at key turning points.

Another reasonable statement is that the winning team is the best team in the world. If this interpretation is correct, it would mean that if the World Cup were to be played again this month, the recent trophy holder would win it again. Winning the cup, in other words, should provide valuable information that can be used to predict future performance. I would, however, argue that this would rarely happen.

In this regard, therefore, the FIFA World Cup trophy is a less convincing indicator of the best team than a World Series trophy is. The World Series has a best-of-seven format. How often does the team that loses game one go on to win the World Series? The answer to that is 36 percent of the time (see Figure 9.3 and the sidebar). That's fairly often. And because of the more rigorous best-of-seven format, I often feel that the team winning the World Series *was* the better team—and if a subsequent game were to be played, I would put my money on the same team winning again.

> For all the sports fans that have started drafting me an e-mail explaining that the nature of baseball creates much higher variance and its skill-to-luck ratio is lower than that of basketball, I can only say that the Dodger Dogs are just too tasty for me to pass up an opportunity to pay tribute to them. Hang in there for a second, and you'll see my point as it relates to recruiting.

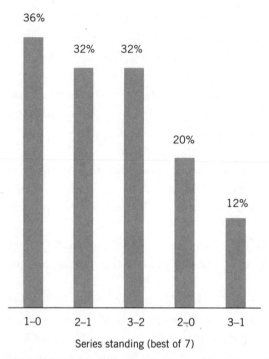

Series standing (best of 7)

FIGURE 9.3 Historical probability of the losing team winning baseball's World Series given standings in seven games.
Based on data from Douglas Jordan, "World Series Game Situation Winning Probabilities: How Often Do Teams Come Back from Behind?, *The Baseball Research Journal*, 2014.

The 1992 European Championship provides an interesting insight into the *one*-difficult-test method used in soccer. Denmark was given just a few weeks' notice to get a team to the tournament. This was after a last-minute decision to not allow Yugoslavia to participate due to its ongoing civil war. Denmark, a team that had not even qualified for the tournament and was ill prepared to play, went on to win the championship.

Twelve years later, in 2004, it was Greece's turn to shock the world. ESPN sports reporter Roy Smith remarked that "they had never won a game in a major tournament. They had never even scored a goal." Yet Greece went on to win the European Championship that year.

If you were to place a $500,000 bet on which team would win the next European Championship in soccer, which one would you pick? Denmark? Greece? After all, they have both proven that they can rise to the occasion by passing one very difficult test in the recent past. Or would you rather go with a safe bet and place it on Germany or France, which have since then each won multiple championships and World Cups?

This analogy obviously has its limits. For one thing, soccer rosters are constantly changing, as older champions move toward retirement. But the point is that since baseball rechecks the same data point a few times, i.e. by having teams meet multiple times to answer the question "Is team A really better than team B?," winning a championship in baseball is more predictive than in soccer, which relies more on the one-difficult-test method.

How does all this information translate to hiring? How can hiring managers balance the constraints of decision making under uncertainty with what little helpful data they've been able to acquire? A number of investment banks and consulting firms still rely on arbitrarily chosen brain teasers to assess a candidate's GMA. These firms would get much better results simply by checking a candidate's SAT scores.

Other employers may not use brain teasers but still collect only one data point on each candidate dimension to predict which ones will succeed. The fact is that most of their interviewers aren't measuring much at all. There are few if any one-question tests whose answer can reliably predict who will succeed in one position or another.

The Death of the One-Question Psychological Tests

In 1969 a woman showed up at the admission's office of a psychiatric hospital with a sole complaint. She heard voices. The psychiatrist on duty believed that he had heard everything he needed to hear. Or had he? The woman was part of an experiment run by psychology professor David Rosenhan.[2] Rosenhan had convinced seven friends and students to show up at mental hospitals with similar claims. Recruiting the participants required some convincing. Rosenhan reported that they were worried they'd "be immediately exposed as frauds and greatly embarrassed."

It turned out that the participants had worried about the wrong things. Rosenhan, who himself also participated in the experiment, and his seven participants were all admitted to the hospitals they approached. All but one were diagnosed with schizophrenia and placed in a psychiatric ward; the "lucky" one was diagnosed with "manic-depressive psychosis" and also placed in a ward. The pseudo patients showed no other symptoms linked to schizophrenia, reported that the voices had gone away soon after being admitted, and didn't fabricate any details about their lives aside from their real names and professions. Yet over the course of their "treatment," they were forced to take a total of 2,100 antipsychotic pills.

Not only did the hospital staffs fail to notice that the study participants were faking, but some staff members even described normal behavior as symptoms of the patients' conditions. Meanwhile, 35 out of 118 actual patients called out the study participants for faking, with some even confronting the participants with statements like "You're not crazy. You're a journalist or a professor." Rosenhan's landmark 1973 paper "On Being Sane in Insane Places," published in *Science*, highlighted the need for more accurate methods in diagnosing mental illness.

Two other psychologists contributing to the field around the same time, Amos Tversky and Daniel Kahneman, had noted that many psychologists would diagnose and design treatment plans based on very limited data. Imagine a patient who often does not seem to listen when spoken to directly. Should this person be treated for ADHD based on this observation alone?

The clear takeaway from Rosenhan's as well as Kahneman and Tversky's work was that a data-driven approach, using checklists, would yield better diagnostic outcomes for patients. The work of these three researchers has profoundly helped to promote evidence-based practices in clinical psychology.

Very few psychologists still base a diagnosis entirely on one strong factor. Instead, they examine patients for a range of criteria from a subset of possible symptoms. Table 9.3 lists the diagnostic criteria used for ADHD. Patients must display at least five of these symptoms before being diagnosed with the condition.

However, over time, even this approach to diagnosing patients continued to evolve. If one patient has most of the symptoms for a condition and another patient exhibits only the minimum required, should they both receive the same treatment plan? Of course not. Patients' symptoms are now typically placed on a continuum instead of the prior practice of yes-or-no binaries. That is, instead of stating that a patient does or does not have a condition, psychologists refer to patients as being somewhere on a spectrum for the condition. This continuum takes into account the number of symptoms displayed and also how severely these symptoms impact the patient's day-to-day life. For instance imagine two patients who both

TABLE 9.3   DSM-5TM Diagnostic Criteria for ADHD Describing Symptoms of Inattention, Hyperactivity, and Impulsivity

Symptoms of Inattention	Symptoms of Hyperactivity and Impulsivity
Often fails to give close attention to detail or makes mistakes	Often fidgets with or taps hands and feet, or squirms in seat
Often has difficulty sustaining attention when doing tasks or activities	Often leaves seat in situations when remaining seated is expected
Often does not seem to listen when spoken to directly	Often runs and climbs in situations where it is inappropriate (in adolescents or adults, may be limited to feeling restless)
Often does not follow through on instructions and fails to finish schoolwork or workplace duties	Often unable to play or engage in leisure activities quietly
Often has difficulty organizing tasks and activities	Is often "on the go," acting as if "driven by a motor"
Often avoids, dislikes, or is reluctant to engage in tasks that require sustained mental effort	Often talks excessively
Often loses things necessary for tasks or activities	Often blurts out answers before a question has been completed
Is easily distracted by extraneous stimuli	Often has difficulty waiting their turn
Is often forgetful in daily activities	Often interrupts or intrudes on others

display the same number of symptoms, one of which is "Is often forgetful in daily activities." However, Patient A as a result keeps getting let go from his job, whereas Patient B has no trouble holding on to her job. So despite both patients displaying the same number of symptoms, Patient A most likely places higher on the spectrum since these symptoms are having a bigger impact on his life. Hiring managers can achieve better outcomes when interviewing candidates by adopting similar methods as those used by psychologists. Instead of focusing on if a candidate displays a specific trait or not, hiring managers should ask themselves, "How certain am I about the candidate having this trait, and if so, how severely will it impact the person's performance?"

Implications for Hiring Managers

In a study published in 2018, Maria Ramos-Olazagasti and her colleagues showed life and career outcomes of ADHD patients who had been tracked for 33 years, beginning when they were 8 years old.[3] What if the authors had selected their ADHD study participants based on only a single question instead of following the list in Table 9.3? What if they had conducted the study about a psychological construct that was less precisely defined than ADHD, such as how "fierce" the study participants were? Would you take their study results seriously? Probably not. Yet this is exactly what many hiring managers do. They "measure" and predict ill-defined psychological constructs about candidates using what I call "one-question psychological tests."

What about the alternative? How about trying to more closely define what you are measuring and asking a set of questions to measure that trait? Isn't that time consuming? Unfortunately it is. Depending on the condition, it can take a trained psychologist anywhere from two to ten or more hours to diagnose a patient. And that is just for one condition, not thirty. Spending ten-plus hours per trait to interview candidates you are evaluating is obviously impractical. What is a better solution?

Most organizations would benefit from reducing the number of traits they try to evaluate in each candidate and spending more time confirming that their evaluations are accurately predictive. After all, the organizers of the SAT ask 154 questions to estimate a single candidate attribute: general mental ability. The only plausible explanation for the test designers going through the mind-bending process of formulating 154 novel questions is that their research has told them that precisely 154 questions are needed to accurately measure the range of GMAs among test takers. In other words, even for well-tested constructs such as GMA, a large number of questions are needed in order to get reliable and valid results. Using one singular question will not be helpful in most fields.

When interviewing candidates, collecting multiple data points on each trait you believe is a strong predictor of job performance will give you more reliable data. You can also use tips outlined in Chapter 5 in the section on probing questions ("Probe More Deeply and Read Less Between the Lines") and in Table 5.2 to drill further into each topic.

You can further check how accurate your interview questions are against those of other interviewers by comparing responses, even on the same questions. As strange as it sounds, one of the topics that test designers struggle with is that when candidates take the same test more than once, their performance may fluctuate dramatically. If you and your colleague frequently draw opposite conclusions about a candidate after asking the same interview questions, you may want to consider using other questions. You can also research how to design interview questions with higher reliability.

THE FOUR MAIN METHODS USED TO ASSESS CANDIDATES

Imagine that you can pick any three sales professionals currently working at your company to support an important territory that you want to grow. How do you go about determining who the best three salespeople are? Most people find this question easy to answer if they assume that none of the salespeople have preferences that make them more suitable for the role or give them an advantage, such as stronger technical knowledge about the product or an existing book of business. You would probably look at how much in sales each rep has delivered over the past few years and then reach out to the top performers to understand how motivated they are to get the new position. You would probably put aside other hiring tools, such as personality tests. Not surprisingly, past results tend to be considered the most reliable predictor of future results for candidates you know.

There are four main ways of determining a candidate's skills and attributes:

1. **Observational.** Looking at past behavior and outcomes. This can also include work sample tests.

2. **Self-reporting.** Asking candidates or using questionnaires.

3. **Other reporting.** Asking others who know the candidate or who are qualified to assess the candidate.

4. **Ability testing.** Having the candidate perform a task or take an exam to measure skills.

The main pros and cons of these methods are listed in Table 9.4.

TABLE 9.4 Pros and Cons of Methods to Determine a Candidate's Skills and Attributes

Method	Pros	Cons
Observational: Looking at past behavior and outcomes	+ Typically more reliable	– Difficult to get data in most cases – Difficult to know if work sample done by candidate or somone else
Self-reporting: Asking candidate or using questionnaires	+ Easy and convenient + Not intrusive + Perceived as fair by candidates	– Candidate may not be honest – Candidate may not be self-aware
Other reporting: Asking others who know the candidate or who are qualified to assess the candidate	+ Easy and fairly convenient + Reasonably accurate when done well	Requires raters to: – Know candidate well – Be good at assessing skills and traits – Respond honestly
Ability testing: Having the candidate perform a task or exam to measure their skills	+ After observation, typically most reliable in measuring a number of skills + Difficult to "fake" good	– Time consuming and difficult to develop – Burdensome for candidate – Even small errors are perceived as more unfair than other methods – Rigid in what it tests – Candidate can cheat

Self-Report Tests

In reality, interviewers mostly rely on the self-report tests and try to augment these with a few ability tests by asking situational ("What would you do if . . .?") and behavioral ("Tell me about a time when . . .") questions. While these types of questions can be helpful, they are limited in their capacity to correctly estimate a candidate's ability.

Most interviewers know that candidates are motivated to get a job and may therefore not always respond to questions honestly. Another issue is that candidates may be incompetent but unaware that they are. That is, even if candidates are honest, they must have both skill in the relevant area and enough self-awareness to accurately assess how skilled they actually are.

Side Note: Subjective Versus Objective

Many human resources professional object to the claim that their qualitative performance reviews are subjective with a statement like, "We are extremely professional in our company, and all levels are required to be objective when writing a performance review." In today's business world, while the word "objective" has the connotation that someone *tries* to be unbiased, one should note that for information to be truly objective, it needs to be able to be easily verified by any external person reviewing it.

Some forms of feedback are more efficiently captured through subjective experiences. This is not to say that subjective feedback can't be quantified or that personal biases can't be reduced. The call center industry has addressed this issue through brief surveys after customer calls. Call center agents no longer must rely on their manager's subjective impression of how happy customers are with their service; they can simply look at the survey data.

Netflix tries to find someone within its organization who has a common connection to a candidate and asks that person to conduct a blind reference check. Netflix CEO Reed Hastings once said in a workshop, "People can buffalo [trick] you in four or six hours. Don't pay too much attention to the interview: you really go deep on the blind references." He continued, "You have to work [your] network to get" those blind references.

Observational Studies and Reports from Others

Observational studies (looking at past results) can produce highly accurate data. The problem is that you can't easily determine past results for most roles you hire for, in part because you lack an objective definition of results. While in most sales roles results are measured against quantitative and objective metrics such as revenues or profits, results are not as easily quantified in most other roles.

Some companies do performance reviews with quantitative ratings for roles with nonquantitative goals. The first issue with using quantitative ratings for hiring purposes is that they are not as objective as such factors as a candidate's height, number of baskets scored, or revenues delivered. Another issue with such performance ratings is that while you can ask for these ratings in an interview, it is difficult to know how to assess the information. Did the candidate embellish when she provided you with her last performance rating score? If so, can you verify the number? Assuming the candidate was truthful about the score, a 4 out of 5 rating may be phenomenal at one company and just all right at another. Even within the same company, rating standards between offices or supervisors can vary significantly. Unless you or someone you trust is familiar with the proper context for a candidate's ratings, the numbers won't always be helpful.

Given these difficulties in assessing a candidate's performance in his past job, most hiring managers rely on alternative data points, including:

- Any indicators of past results, even if they are not what a candidate was formally evaluated on.

- Behavior that leads to results.

- Personality traits or belief systems that lead to behavior, which in turn produces strong results.

- Experience that is assumed to lead to an understanding of problems, which in turn leads to behavior that produces strong results.

One theory says that personality is linked to performance. For instance, in sales roles, we can assume that extroverts are more likely than introverts to enjoy making social connections and will therefore take more meetings and sell more.

There is nothing wrong with this hypothesis. However, let's apply Occam's razor to this theory. This is the problem-solving principle that stipulates that, in general, the fewer assumptions you make, the higher your chances will be to get to the right answer. Another way of saying this is that the more assumptions needed to support a hypothesis, the weaker the evidence tends to be.

How many assumptions do you need to make to select the right candidate? Let's assume that when the relevant information is available and reliable, predicting a candidate's performance by using last year's results has a 70 percent chance of being accurate. Even so, trying to predict whether candidates will be good salespeople by determining whether they are extroverts still requires at least three assumptions:

1. You can correctly assess which candidates are extroverts.

2. Extroverts will take more meetings.

3. Those who take more meetings will sell more.

By applying a 70 percent chance that each of these assumptions is correct, you have a 34 percent chance (70 percent × 70 percent × 70 percent) of hiring a good candidate.

This exercise isn't meant to merely criticize personality tests; most current hiring methods face a similar issue. The more links required to get you to your prediction, the higher the chance that one of the links is weak and the entire chain will break.

Table 9.5 provides an example of the minimum number of steps required for a useful sampling of hiring techniques. Given the drawbacks of the "other report" method, ability tests should constitute an important part of the hiring process.

TABLE 9.5 Probability of Making Good Hiring Predictions When Using a Multistep Logic

Predictive Variable	Explanation	Probability of Individual Prediction	Probability of Predicting a Great Hire
Last year's results	Last year's top performers are 70% likely to be top performers again this year	70%	70%
Smart and driven	There is a 70% chance to correctly determine if a candidate is smart and an equal probability if the candidate is driven. When these two variables are determined correctly, they predict good hires 70% of the time	70%	34% = 70% × 70% × 70%

Ability Tests

As previously discussed in the section "Use Job Knowledge Tests When Relevant" in Chapter 4, ability tests have a number of advantages. For one thing, while many candidates might be good at talking a big game about how good they are, it's difficult to fake the ability to perform a task live (see Figure 9.4).

FIGURE 9.4 The IKEA job interview?
Canary Pete Art. Used with permission.

I personally have had a very good experience with them and highly recommend them for most senior level roles. So, what are the downsides of ability tests? Many hiring managers argue that while ability tests are good for determining hard skills, they don't work as well for softer candidate traits such as emotional intelligence. I addressed this topic in a joint white paper with Yale psychologist David Caruso, whose research focuses on emotional intelligence. We argued that ability tests, although difficult to design, can lead to more accurate predictions, even of traits such as emotional intelligence. These tests should, of course, be combined with other recruiting methods.

HOW TO CONVINCE CANDIDATES TO SHARE MORE INFORMATION IN INTERVIEWS

I have worked with hiring managers who have made unreasonably high demands on a candidate's time during the interview process, asking the person to spend days on a take-home assessment. I've already established in Chapter 2 that this process needs to be a positive experience for both sides. Other managers make the opposite kind of mistake, not spending enough time to explore questions whose answers would be crucial to any hiring decision. In my experience, this happens most often with interviews for senior-level roles, when companies want to be maximally respectful to candidates.

So how do you convince candidates to share more information about their past experience or go through interview and vetting steps without making it painful for them? To answer this question, it's helpful to know that it's the better candidates who will pay the highest price for any lack of credible signals that would allow you, as the employer, to distinguish them from weaker candidates. Informing candidates about this phenomenon will help them appreciate the complexity and depth of your interview process. Strong candidates tend to, within reason, be happy to spend a bit of extra time to allow you to assess their skills. One example of this is how two PhD candidates reacted very differently to our internal interview process for our project manager role. After a full day of interviews, we decided that candidate A should definitely receive an offer, while candidate B should not. Before we had a chance to reach out to them, candidate A dropped me an e-mail, saying how impressed he was with our thoughtful and involved interview and testing process. Candidate B, on the other hand, gave us the feedback that our process was excessive.

If you're still not fully convinced about the fact that star candidates have the most to gain from showcasing their skills, you may want to compare the range of salaries paid by NFL teams for their college draft picks with the range of salaries among undergraduates hired by top-tier consulting firms. Both the athletes and consulting firm hires are known to be at the top of the top of their class at the best colleges in their fields. In the 2018 NFL draft, Baker Mayfield, the first pick in Round 1, signed a four-year contract with the Cleveland Browns for approximately $33 million. Trey Quinn, the 256th pick, signed a four-year contract for approximately $2.5 million, less than a tenth of Mayfield's. Most consulting firms have standardized salaries for entry-level hires per region, adjusted in some regions to the cost of living. One reason among many that NFL teams pay so much for their top draft picks and why there is such a wide spread among the salaries offered is that they have access to years of data on the athletes, dating from their college and even back to their high school performances, which increases the accuracy of their predictions.

Some law firms have recognized the difficulty in obtaining credible signals from entry-level applicants and have reinvented their hiring strategy. The firm Greenberg Traurig, for example, has announced that it will hire law school graduates into one of two programs. Candidates credibly signaling high value are hired into a traditional associate program with a high salary (close to $190,000 in 2019, according to Glassdoor). Candidates signaling less value during the hiring process, but still deemed to have strong potential, are hired into a one-year "residency" program at less than half the associate's pay. After that first year, the residents move into an associate's role, are offered a different path, or are asked to leave the firm.

If some day more companies were able to more accurately predict the performance of their hires through improved methods and algorithms, pay discrepancies among their hires would increase.

HANDLING CONTRADICTING EVIDENCE

Hiring managers often face contradictory evidence about candidates. For example, imagine that a candidate was referred to you as "one of the smartest people I know" by your best friend, but the referral struggled to grasp a concept that most other candidates readily understood. Would you still trust your friend's judgment? Many hiring managers fail to systematically evaluate such evidence. Instead we hear such remarks as "You never know." Ironically, instead of using such comments to stress that we should not draw conclusions based on evidence we don't fully understand, these comments are often followed by an anecdote about a former hire who in one way or another resembled the current candidate and turned out to be great (or awful). The statement is then used to support a decision in favor of (or against) the candidate.

A better approach, of course, is to weigh stronger evidence more heavily. A disciplined hiring manager uses an evidence-based approach and prefers beliefs and conclusions that are reliable and valid to ones that are comforting or convenient. In doing so, it is important to be skeptical of claims (especially your own) and to be aware of the pitfalls of human reason, as well as the methods commonly used by those who present false or deceptive claims. I've found the best way to accomplish this is to take pride in the methods and process I use to reach conclusions, as opposed to coming up with the "right answer" to begin with.

Indicators of Evidence-Based Data

What evidence should you believe? In interview situations, you often have extremely limited data on which to base a decision. Should you trust one specific data point indicating that the candidate may be strong (or weak)? This is where you start evaluating the quality of your evidence.

In his open class "The Deceptive Mind," Yale professor Steven Novella provides in-depth descriptions of the kinds of evidence or knowledge you should believe in and the kinds you should not. He opens the course with an example of the water engine. There are many companies and people, he notes, who claim that they have developed or can develop an engine that can burn water as fuel. The incentive to develop such a piece of technology is obviously enormous.

Imagine if we could replace all fossil fuels, nuclear power, and other sources of fuel with something as simple as water. Unfortunately, that is not possible. The things that keep getting reinvented are new ways to electrolyze water. Water is separated into its hydrogen and oxygen components, resulting in a mixed gas of oxygen and hydrogen. The gas is burned, and the by-product of that process is . . . water.

What is the evidence that anyone can use water to fuel engines? It is always very thin, though it doesn't keep fraudulent companies from claiming to be "one step away" from being able to do it—they just need a bit more money from investors in order to make the next breakthrough. But their demonstrations are always highly flawed. Or they cheat, often running a separate engine behind the curtain to make their "water engine" run. They never deliver what they promise, which is certainly grounds for questioning the validity of their claims. A large-scale example of this is Theranos, a company that claimed to have revolutionized blood testing by only requiring very small samples. In the beginning of 2015, the company founder Elizabeth Holmes was named the youngest and wealthiest self-made female billionaire. Theranos had by then raised over $400 million in venture capital and reached a valuation of $9 billion. By the end of the year, the house of cards designed by Holmes collapsed following an article in the *Wall Street Journal* reporting that Theranos had fabricated the results.

Novella goes on to ask his students: "What is knowledge?" "How can we know anything?" "What does it mean to know something?" The scientific method is based on methodological naturalism, which simply means that natural effects have natural causes. When we try to model and understand the world, we shouldn't invoke magic or supernatural causes because they're not testable.

It also means that all conclusions in science are provisional and all discoveries are subject to revision. There is no truth with a capital T in science. We must be continuously open to revising our understanding of the world whenever new and credible evidence is presented to us.

Novella articulates a number of methods used by those who present evidence-based and not evidence-based data. A number of these points are summarized in Table 9.6.

TABLE 9.6   Indicators of Evidence-Based and Not Evidence-Based Data

Evidence-Based	Description	Not Evidence-Based	Description
Transparent	Method, arguments, logic are clear and open for review	Black box	"Secret sauce" only revealed to or understood by those advocating for the method
Falsifiable/ specific/ objective	Specific hypothesis that is possible to be proved incorrect by objective measures (if the evidence points that way)	Vague/ subjective	
Replicable		Not replicable	Invokes special "skill" only known or "properly" understood by the person making the claim to perform correctly
Predictable	Assumes the world is predictable, at least to a certain extent. A hypothesis will most likely have a number of implications, even if not able to replicate in a lab, e.g., evolution	Specific power	

Humble/ conservative	• Admits limits of predictive power • Admits limits to knowledge • Cautious about making grand claims that go beyond limits of evidence	Confident/ bold	• Confidence does not go down even if evidence is limited • Explains unknown with unknowable (e.g. ghosts, which cannot be falsified) • Makes big, bold claims even with weak evidence
Flexible and self-correcting	Will change ideas/ become critical of hypothesis in light of new evidence that contradicts the prediction of how it should work	Rigid	Will not change mind about original hypothesis even if new contradicting evidence is presented
Accountable	Willing to commit to changing mind in light of specific proof	Non-committal	Moves the goalpost in light of new evidence
Skeptical of own ideas	Uses evidence to understand what is actually true	Skeptical only of ideas of others	Uses evidence to promote ideas they wish were true
Presents proof for hypothesis		Asks others to disprove their ideas	Puts burden of proof on others
Quantitative	Large enough sample size so that result and just noise are seen	Anecdotal	
Rigorous and thoughtful	Systematic, thorough, and quantitative; e.g., understands common problems that arise from sampling biases and tries to prevent them	Haphazard	Satisfied with any method that supports hypothesis
Supported by consensus of experts		Most experts in fields do not believe it	

Source: Based on a lecture series given by Professor Steven Novella.

Although none of these methods guarantee the quality of the information, the more indicators that the information is based on solid evidence, as shown on the left side of Table 9.6, the more reliable the information tends to be. Conversely, the more apparent the signs on the right side of Table 9.6 become, the more skeptical you should be about the information you have.

MANAGE THE TEMPTATION TO PREDICT THE UNKNOWN UNKNOWNS

Another good question to ask is, do you usually know what you don't know? If so, do you accept a higher margin of error for your predictions that rely on several unknowns?

Most hiring managers who deploy an evidence-based approach will soon become frustrated with the limits of our knowledge for predicting the quality of hires. Our current understanding allows us to measure traits that predict, if we are being generous, only 60 to 80 percent of the variation in performance among candidates. As we saw with the example of fad diets (see Table 2.3 in Chapter 2), we are often tempted to come up with alternative factors to try to explain the other 20 to 40 percent variation.

In his classic book *The Black Swan*, Nassim Taleb discusses our need to predict the unknown unknowns and our miserable track record in predicting them with even minimal accuracy. A specific variable might be crucial to getting a prediction right. However, there is a stark difference between our need to predict a variable and our ability to do so.

This is also the case in medicine. For centuries, we had a limited understanding of what is needed to sustain life. Everything about living organisms that we didn't understand was labeled "life energy."

Eventually we discovered more and more about what is necessary to sustain life, but the term "life energy" is still used today for a variety of reasons. Most people still don't know enough about biology to understand even basic medical issues. Others are skeptical of the scientific community and look for other, usually simpler, explanations. And then there are those who find it nice and comforting to believe in "life energy" and similarly vague notions.

It is completely understandable that some people prefer to be comforted. After all, such notions invoke pleasant feelings. However, if you want to understand what is actually true and even use this information to make predictions, then you need to embrace uncomforting truths. This means recognizing that the idea that your gut feeling is the best way to predict a candidate's job performance is as outdated of a myth as the idea that "life energy" is an acceptable explanation for why life exists.

However far it takes you from your comfort zone, you must resist the temptation to lazily interpret a lack of evidence for one theory with evidence for an alternative theory. Until alternative theories are supported by strong and independent evidence, you're better off acknowledging the limited accuracy of your predictions. This acceptance will help you make better contingency plans for events that are likely to go wrong. It will also clarify the limits of your knowledge and highlight the need for finding solutions that actually work instead of those convenient, easy, or comforting solutions you wished would work but now understand simply won't.

How Good Are You at Coming Up with a 90 Percent Accurate Range?

Prominent Swedish researchers David Cesarini, Örjan Sandewall, and Magnus Johannesson ran a simple experiment that illustrates some of the pitfalls that can arise if we interpret subjective evaluations too literally. They administered a test of confidence to a sample of students at an elite Swedish institution. The test, originally developed by Russo and Schoemaker,[4] worked like this: Subjects were asked 10 trivia-type questions, such as "What is the distance between the earth and the moon?" (The correct response is approximately 238,900 miles, which equates to flying 25 times between New York and Singapore, the longest flight in the world.) But rather than providing a single, numerical answer to each question, subjects were instructed to give low and high estimates they felt 90 percent confident the true distance fell somewhere between. Study participants who followed the instructions and understood the boundaries of their knowledge should have reported an average of nine confidence ranges that contained the true value.

In practice, the typical respondent gave only four to six correct answers, which Russo and Schoemaker interpreted as evidence that most people are overconfident. Cesarini et al.[5] added the following twist: after subjects had provided their first 10 ranges, they were asked, "How many of the ranges you provided do you think contain the true value?" Most study participants answered with a number far smaller than nine. But wait, you say, if the instructions specifically said to provide a 90 percent confidence range, why didn't subjects do that? Cesarini et al. suggest that most subjects did not interpret the instructions too literally.

How can you apply the insights of Cesarini et al. to hiring predictions? Next time a hiring manager says something like "I want you to be 90 percent sure on this hire!," take a step back and try to clarify what the manager really means by this. Cesarini et al.'s experiments show us that we should not always infer that 90 percent confidence intervals supplied by others, including experts, will necessarily contain the true value nine times out of ten. Resist the temptation to please this manager temporarily by giving her the answer she wants to hear. Better to make sure you both understand the true actual meaning of "90 percent sure." Explain how accurate your predictions have been in the past, and find a candid way to convey the reality that in many hiring decisions, the risks involved are often too large to guarantee anything even close to 90 percent certainty. The hiring manager may be disappointed to hear this, but in the long run, your candor will help you build trust with all your colleagues. After all, if someone you care about had cancer, would you rather have him go to a doctor that tells him the real chance of the treatment working or go to a person who tells him that there is a 100 percent chance that the "unique techniques" will heal your loved one?

Valid and Reliable Predictions

There are two psychometric concepts that can help you determine whether or not proposed solutions will actually help you make better predictions: test validity and test reliability.

Test validity shows the probability that a test or variable will accurately measure what it is supposed to measure, such as how successful a candidate will be in a job. If a specific skills-based test can predict 40 percent of the variation in performance between candidates, it is said to have a validity of 40 percent. If a personality test can predict only 5 percent of the variation in performance, its validity is 5 percent.

Test reliability shows how consistent a measure is. For instance, SAT tests are fairly consistent measures of IQ. We all know people who have received two very different outcomes on two different SAT exams, but these are simply the exceptions that prove the rule. For the vast majority of test takers, SAT scores stay within a narrow range. If a thousand people had SAT scores of around 600 and retook the test a year later, they'd be highly likely to produce test results well within the same range.

As Arthur Jensen points out in *The G Factor*, IQ scores are often more reliable than blood pressure scores. By contrast, judgments made about candidates in a job interview often have low reliability. Multiple interviewers might not agree among themselves about whether a candidate has a warm or cold personality. Moreover, the same interviewers may not agree with their own assessment of a candidate's warmth a month or two later. And a test can't be valid or useful if it's that unreliable.

You will achieve better recruiting results if you focus on factors you can reliably predict. After all, centuries of belief in concepts like life energy or the use of leeches to bleed patients did nothing to cure diseases, instead causing endless pain and injury and death, while an evidence-based approach to developing medicine has saved billions of lives, to say nothing of the pain and suffering modern patients have been spared.

Chapter Summary and Conclusion

Context:

- There are generally four ways to determine a candidate's skills and attributes. Each method has pros and cons:
  - **Observational.** Looking at past behavior and outcomes. This can also include work sample tests.
  - **Self-reporting.** Asking candidates in person or using questionnaires.
  - **Other reporting.** Asking people outside the search who know the candidate or who are qualified to assess the candidate.
  - **Ability testing.** Having the candidate perform a task or take an exam to measure their skills.
- Hiring managers make important decisions, often in the face of uncertainty, because the evidence they base their decisions on can be confusing or even contradictory. This leaves a lot of hiring managers wondering what evidence they can rely on.
- The difficulty of making accurate hiring predictions has been exacerbated by the signaling arms race, in which candidates try to first understand the signals that employers value and then teach themselves to project these signals, often falsely.

- The limits of interview data for making accurate hiring predictions has led to three extreme viewpoints on how to weigh interview data:
  - All interviews should be abolished.
  - Since no recruiting tool can successfully predict *all* hiring outcomes, everything behavioral scientists tell managers should be dismissed and instead managers should wing it with methods they're comfortable with.
  - Any negative signal should result in that candidate being rejected.
- Hiring managers use many different methods to address concerns around making decisions under uncertainty:
  - Some try to gain insights about a long list of each candidate's traits and attributes. But since interview time is limited, these long lists often yield lower-quality information about each trait examined.
  - Others try to ask candidates a *single* difficult question the answer to which they believe will be thoroughly predictive of performance. However, unless and until this putative silver bullet of a question has been proved to reliably predict performance, the odds are that no single question or answer can be all that predictive of success on the job.
- Psychologists facing similar uncertainty when making diagnoses have abandoned both of these overly generalized practices, focusing instead on ensuring that they diagnose each specific condition more accurately.

What you can do about it:

- Successful hiring managers adjust their style to make better predictions given the limits of the available evidence.
  - They understand indicators of evidence-based data and assign the appropriate weight to each data point, based on how strong the evidence is for that point.
  - These hiring managers also understand how to convince candidates to share more accurate information about themselves.

- Finally, they use two psychometric concepts—test validity and test reliability—to make better predictions.
- Successful hiring managers also stay away from the following common mistakes:
  - Trying to predict the unknown unknowns
  - Sticking to the novel information bind
  - Being deceived by the illusion of validity

10

Why Do So Many Hiring Predictions Fail?

It's tough to make predictions, especially about the future.
—Yogi Berra, baseball coach/manager/player

WHICH EXPERTS ARE GOOD AT MAKING PREDICTIONS?

Recruiters have a bad reputation in some circles. A lot of this is due to their inability to accurately predict which hires will perform well. Even worse, the same recruiter who hired your best employee also might have hired a person who is underperforming. These factors make it difficult to tell whether recruiters who are accurate in their predictions got them right because of luck or skill.

Recruiting resembles poker in several respects. I recently had a hard-earned lesson in this when I participated in a small hold'em tournament with about 40 players, one of whom was Matt Damon. A friend asked me if I thought Matt would be any good. I said he was probably there just for fun, even if he was excellent at acting the role of poker prodigy Mike McDermott in *Rounders*. A few hours later, Matt—not Mike—took home the first prize, and I had to eat my words while my friend laughed at me.

Much as in poker, hiring predictions are impacted by both chance and skill. The shifting ratios of chance and skill make recruitment decisions quite challenging, especially because we often can't know whether a hiring manager was just lucky when he landed a star performer or his hiring methods had made all the difference.

In both poker and recruiting, a surprising number of people believe they can just wing it. When they lose, they convince themselves that their opponents got lucky. They fail to realize that other players usually won because they played a more disciplined game, relying on the odds and game theory, understanding that since their opponents miss the flop about two-thirds of the time, they should almost automatically bet. It was for these and other reasons that a couple of my mentors discouraged me from getting into talent acquisition.

Recruiters and hiring managers aren't alone in struggling with the accuracy of their predictions. A survey conducted by the *Economist* provides a fascinating example.[1] The magazine asked 16 individuals to make 10-year forecasts on growth rates, inflation, and other economic indicators. Four of the selected forecasters were former finance ministers, four were chairpersons of multinational corporations, four were economics students at Oxford University, and four were garbage collectors.

A decade later, the *Economist* checked with all 16 to see how their forecasts turned out. The results were summarized under the headline, "Garbage in, Garbage out." In other words, the forecasts were awful.

Simply responding with "no change" across the board would have produced better results than any of the four groups accomplished. Still, some of the groups were further off target than others. The garbage collectors and the corporate chairpersons did the best (or least bad), while the finance ministers came in last. While the results from the *Economist* study were startling, the study was not scientific. For one thing, the sample size was too small.

A much more rigorous study was conducted by Wharton professor Philip Tetlock, the biggest multiyear study of this form to date.[2] He recruited 284 experts to make predictions about the future. All were guaranteed anonymity so they wouldn't have to worry about embarrassing themselves. Altogether, Tetlock gathered 26,450 predictions.

What were the results? The experts would have been better off making random guesses. In other words, hiring managers can take comfort in the fact that they are not alone in making imperfect predictions. This seems to be a universal problem.

THE CONFIDENCE PARADOX

As tempting as it might sound, Tetlock's study does not suggest that we should stop listening to experts altogether. Nor should we dismiss every expert prediction as "garbage."

There was a wide variation among the experts in Tetlock's study. In his book *Future Babble*, Dan Gardner comments on Tetlock's study, saying: "Some experts are so out of touch with reality, they're borderline delusional. Other experts are only slightly out of touch. And a few experts are surprisingly nuanced and well-calibrated." Gardner continues: "What distinguishes the impressive few from the borderline delusional is not . . . their political beliefs [or whether they were] optimists or pessimists. It also made no difference if they had a doctorate, extensive experience, or access to classified information. Nor did it make a difference if experts were political scientists, historians, journalists, or economists. What made a big difference is *how* they think."

Paradoxically, the experts who did the worst were the ones who were the most confident that their predictions would be accurate. The experts who were, on average, better at predicting were less confident, not only about anyone's ability to make accurate predictions but also about their own.

The biggest takeaway from this study, according to Gardner, is that when you hear from experts who sound very confident in their long-term predictions, they are almost certainly wrong. They're precisely the sorts of experts we see on TV and hear on the radio. They are also the folks who take up the most space in meetings and "group decisions."

But shouldn't these confident experts realize that their predictions have usually been wide of the mark and that they should therefore adjust their thinking? Unfortunately, this seldom happens. As Gardner points out, it is the rare expert who's able to admit his predictions were wrong. "They will often concede that they were off on details here and there," Gardner writes, "but flat-out wrong? No. Never. Unless pinned down by circumstances as firmly as a butterfly in a display case, they will resolutely deny being wrong."

Overconfident experts are much more likely to lecture you on how your suggestion that they are w-r-o-n-g is itself wrong, even when clear evidence of their blunder is staring them right in the face.

Remembering the Peaks

Most recruiters and managers treat the star hires they've brought on board as trophies to be displayed in well-lit cases, while quickly forgetting about their mis-hires. They're not unlike the 1980s sitcom character Al Bundy repeatedly telling the story of how he scored four touchdowns to clinch the Chicago City Championship for Polk High, even though, unfortunately, Al failed to have much success after high school.

If someone throws a dart just once and hits the bull's-eye, does it prove that this person is great at throwing darts? But what if the person throws half a dozen and three hit the bull's-eye? The evidence for this person's being skilled has significantly increased. How about if the next dozen darts miss the board altogether? This is what often happens in recruiting, and yet hiring managers only want to talk about their bull's-eyes.

Many individuals want to measure success by pointing out a few anecdotal peaks (achieved using the method they advocate) and valleys (reached using the methods they oppose) in the performance. "Do you remember the time I was right about that candidate?" a hiring manager may ask. In reality, these anecdotes are poor indicators of how well a recruiter has done *on average*. Encouraging a culture of talking about aggregate success or failure will help provide a better understanding of the accuracy of past predictions by your colleagues. As the leader, you can help create that culture by creating recurring meetings in which you calibrate ever more precisely your company's defined metrics on prediction accuracy. And every time you hear someone using an anecdote to make the case that a specific recruiter or method is better, bring the conversation back to the stats. Anecdotes can still be used as powerful examples that help explain certain stats, but they should only *support* telling a story about the stats, not *replace* them.

LEARNING FROM PAST MISTAKES
STARTS WITH ADMITTING THEM

Table 10.1 summarizes some of the classic self-serving arguments and tricks used by people who make bad predictions to avoid conceding they were wrong. What makes these arguments effective, though, is that sometimes they're right.

It may also be helpful to keep in mind that these excuse makers aren't always intentionally lying to you, because they've even refused to admit to *themselves* they were wrong. Why would someone do that? Because lying takes effort. It's much easier to be intellectually lazy and refuse to admit errors. And after all, it's not lying if you believe it. Being aware of the prevalence of these psychological defense mechanisms will allow you to spot in advance overly confident experts who can't admit when they're wrong. Recognizing these signs can help you avoid getting cowed by or tangled up in their arguments. You might also admit to yourself that trying to use logical arguments to convince someone who is more comfortable being illogical on this topic won't be the best use of your time and that it's best to avoid listening to their advice going forward.

TABLE 10.1 Arguments Hiring Managers Use to Avoid Conceding They Are Wrong

#	The Type	Arguments and Techniques Used by Hiring Managers Wanting to Avoid Admitting Their Predictions Were Wrong
1	Mr. Insulted	"I'm insulted you could even suggest that I could be wrong. End of discussion."
2	The Vague Unproven Alternative	"It's easy to hire someone who can hit the hard metrics, but what really matters is to find someone who doesn't burn out the team while hitting the targets. Do I have any proof that my vague unproven alternative does a better job at hitting our soft targets? Of course not. However, I'd rather put the burden of proof on you."
3	The *Almost* Right One	"I was almost right if it weren't for this small flaw in the candidate that blindsided me. But no one really expected *that*. So I was fundamentally right."
4	The Patient Buddha	"I was wrong on the timing, but my main point will still happen. He will perform. Eventually. Someday. Just wait and see."
5	Mr. You Are Welcome	"My prediction of him being a bad hire became a self-negating prophecy. He turned out to be a great hire, but if it weren't for my feedback, he would have been an awful hire. You are welcome."
6	The English Teacher	"I never said she *would* perform well. I said she *could* perform well. Do you need an English lesson?"
7	Mr. Play it Safe	"Yes, I did say that Jake is extremely smart. But I also said that I had some doubts about his energy level. And he failed because of his energy level." In other words: "I wasn't born yesterday. I hedge my bets."

(continued on next page)

#	The Type	Arguments and Techniques Used by Hiring Managers Wanting to Avoid Admitting Their Predictions Were Wrong
8	The Emperor's New Clothes	"My prediction did happen. You are just too blind to see it. I'll be here if you need more advice. Lucky you."
9	The Deflector	"OK, I may not have been completely right on John (recruiting lingo for the painful term w-r-o-n-g), but I was right on Jenny—look what a star she is. And if you bring up my stats, I'll keep throwing anecdotes at you."
10	Mr. Attack the Messenger	"Let's talk about your awful performance on an unrelated topic. That should take your mind off me for a minute or two."
11	Mr. I'll Blame You Back	"There was nothing wrong with my prediction. You just mismanaged the candidate after she was hired. If you give birth to a child and I raise her and she ends up in jail, which of us did a worse job?"
12	Mr. I Wasn't Really Trying	"Yes, most of my hires last year were awful. But you see, I wasn't really trying. No one can make as good a hire as I do when I put my mind to it. Do you want me to start trying now?'
13	The Never Discouraged One	"Who cares that most of my predictions have been off? I'll keep making predictions with great confidence until some of them come through. Even a broken clock is right twice a day."
14	The Unblinking Denier	"Of course, I'll deny I ever made those past predictions that failed. Don't let that stop you from asking me for help about future predictions though. OK?"

How Past Mistakes Can Help You Make Better Predictions

Philip Tetlock found that the better predictors were quick to admit when they were wrong and adjust their approach. Good experts take more pride in getting to the right answer—even if it disproves their initial theory—than when they have the right answer to begin with.

But forget for a moment about outside experts. What if you want to improve your own predictions? Tetlock's study revealed that better predictions are achieved by making them abundantly objective and quantifiable. Those making them should point out in advance whatever obstacles might derail their predictions. For instance, if candidates are highly motivated but don't have the right skills, you might decide to still give them a shot, though you should also note that you're worried they won't pick up the necessary skills fast enough. If a candidate fails and the reason is clearly because he or she didn't manage to master key skills in due time, you will at least have learned something useful.

Meanwhile, you should leave no room for interpretation about whether or not you were right. Because you now have to do what very few people like doing: going back to check whether your prediction hit the wall, the bull's-eye, or somewhere in between.

If your forecast was off, take responsibility for having been wrong. Make a good-faith effort to understand what caused your original assumptions, or the conclusions you drew from them, to be off the mark. Don't simply blame an unforeseen event, brush it off, and presume you won't have any random obstacles bedeviling your upcoming forecasts. If your forecast was wrong due to unforeseen events, that, if anything, should make you more worried about your ability to accurately predict on-the-job outcomes. Why? Because you could have factored in the chance of unforeseen events into your prediction. The more carefully you track your predictions, the better you'll get at foreseeing things. Bridgewater Associates founder Ray Dalio has taken this lesson to heart. When estimating the time and budget for a project, he'll make the best estimate he can and increase this by 50 percent. Because despite serious efforts to get past estimates right, he has underestimated the time and budget required by roughly half.

Are Ethical People Immune to Overconfidence?

The purpose of the points made above is not to mock certain professions or cast shade on expert predictors. Nor is it to question anyone's good intentions. It's also not to imply that some experts are ethical or noble while others are not.

Few people would question the noble intentions of medical doctors. Yet a 2013 study showed that physicians' diagnostic accuracy between easy cases and difficult cases dropped by about 90 percent, even as their *confidence* in their conclusions dipped only about 10 percent (see Figure 10.1).[3] Taking advantage of additional resources, such as asking a colleague, looking up reference materials, and ordering more tests, did not increase as their diagnostic accuracy dropped. All of this is in line with findings about other overly confident experts.

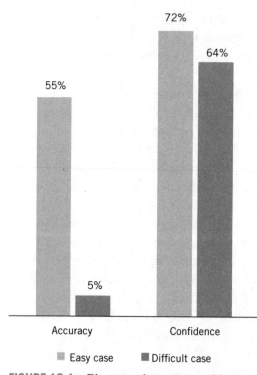

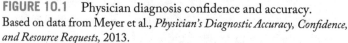

FIGURE 10.1 Physician diagnosis confidence and accuracy. Based on data from Meyer et al., *Physician's Diagnostic Accuracy, Confidence, and Resource Requests,* 2013.

My purpose in pointing out these mistakes is to show them to be natural human errors, not to make fun of any profession—even the most skilled and noble experts in a field are prone to making human mistakes.

In *Future Babble*, Dan Gardner reflects on reading a report from the Organization for Economic Co-operation and Development that projected "better than previously forecasted growth." He found that forecast reassuring until he realized that he had "just finished writing a book about how awful experts are at predicting the future and how psychology compels people to take predictions seriously anyway." Nevertheless, as he admits, "the mistakes and delusions I chronicle in this book are *human* follies. We are all susceptible to them, even authors who write about the mistakes and delusions of others."

ECA president Ken Kanara once told me that "the tough part about recruiting is that you don't know how people you said 'no' to would have performed if hired." In a refreshingly introspective LinkedIn post, former Netflix senior software engineer Robert Sweeney wrote:

> I turned down Daniel Buchmueller for a job at Netflix. After a 60 minute interview I was on the fence, so I concluded that he "wasn't senior enough." He went to Amazon instead where he co-founded Amazon Prime Air (their drone delivery service) and was #2 on Fast Company's "Most Creative People" list. At some point, we programmers are going to have to admit that we really can't judge another programmer's technical abilities in a 60 min interview. We end up hiring programmers that are good at interviewing, but not necessarily good at doing the job. And we miss out on engineers like Daniel.

It's the kind of intellectual humility displayed by Kanara and Sweeney that is necessary to improve our own recruiting results. Genuine expertise comes from recognizing the limits of our own minds, as well as our forecasting methods.

PREDICTING THE UNPREDICTABLE

> I can calculate the movement of stars, but not the madness of men.
>
> —Sir Isaac Newton

We know that experts in every field are often off on their predictions. Aside from overconfidence, why does this happen? And why do we even believe accurate predictions are possible?

One reason is that we can predict events like solar eclipses years, decades, and even centuries in advance. The discoveries of Sir Isaac Newton laid the groundwork for spectacularly accurate predictions that enable us to build skyscrapers rising more than 2,000 feet into the sky. We can send humans into space and build hundred-mile-long bridges and magnetic railroads that glide across the landscape. So why can't we predict something as simple as the performance of a potential hire?

Imagine a frictionless billiard table. Once a ball is set into motion, it can keep bouncing off the cushions of the table and other billiard balls indefinitely. How long in advance would you be able to predict the ultimate movements of each billiard ball? Indefinitely, at least in theory. However, if you'd made the tiniest error in calculating the gravitational force of a distant star, you would be off in your predictions not long after the cue ball hit a few other balls.

Now imagine that the other balls had eyes and ears and were able to see the cue ball coming at them. Or maybe their priorities shifted and they changed their minds about wanting to participate in the game altogether. What if their trajectory (performance) depended on their emotions or other complex psychological motivations? What if each of the balls knew that the others were also self-aware and feared that one of them was holding a grudge against them?

Now we're getting closer to the situation that hiring managers find themselves in every day. Shifting priorities, a different set of skills needed to do a job than when the person was hired, a new boss with a different management style, changing team members and interpersonal dynamics, and half the office are "hangry" since the delivery guy forgot to bring the Monday-morning bagels—could there be any more chaos? Described in different terms by Edward Lorenz, chaos theory outlines the difficulty of predicting the future, even when dealing with deterministic, relatively featureless components such as billiard balls.

"As grand as those motions and laws [of natural sciences] may be," explains Dan Gardner, "they are relatively simple. In a word, they are linear. A linear system is the sum of its parts. Gravity, for example, is linear in mass. Double the mass and you get twice the gravity. . . . Simply by doing the math we can know with great confidence precisely when a solar eclipse will next cast Rio de Janeiro into shadow at midday."

As late as the 1970s, researchers were confident that, as their understanding of the causes of earthquakes improved, so would their ability to predict them. Gardner notes, "If there's an equation, scientists once believed, there must be predictability." Most scientists have abandoned that view; today most of them agree that our ability to predict when an earthquake will erupt has not significantly improved. Some even doubt our ability to ever be able to do so with any useful accuracy. Meanwhile, people living along major tectonic faults wait and wonder.

Yale University historian Jon Lewis Gaddis observes the irony of this in his book *The Landscape of History*. "Social scientists during the twentieth century embraced a Newtonian vision of linear and therefore predictable phenomena," he points out, "even as the natural sciences were abandoning it."

As we've seen, understanding the limits of predictions is crucial to attempts to improve them. And instead of trying to predict the unpredictable, we can make better contingency plans for when events don't pan out as we thought they would or wish them to.

What Can You Do if You Can't Improve Your Predictions?

At our firm, we make every effort to recruit capable, experienced recruiters who are a good fit for us. We also closely track their performance and ramp. We know, based on data from past hires, how fast an average recruiter should ramp; and we also know, based on performance data from each new hire, when it is unlikely that a recruiter will ever meet our standards. If this is the case, we are open with the recruiter about it. Substandard recruiters often ask for a second chance, and we are happy to grant them that. We are also happy to invest extra resources to mentor them. In rare cases, a recruiter proves that our initial low assessment was wrong. However, most often our initial assessments prove correct. In these cases, we will talk with these recruiters about other roles in our organization that might be a better fit for them. Failing that, we try to help them find another job externally.

This proactive approach allows us to correct our decisions within a month or two of a mis-hire's start date. Before we adopted this approach, we wouldn't form an initial opinion about hires until their first performance review, about six months into the job, when we gave them a chance to course-correct. For most candidates, then, it would take us twelve to eighteen months to reach the same conclusion that we now reach in one or two months.

REWARD GOOD DECISIONS, NOT JUST GOOD OUTCOMES

A few years after my wife and I purchased our home in Los Angeles, experts redrew the fault lines that show where earthquakes are most likely to occur. Suddenly our home was within the danger zone. Thank you, seismologists.

These experts were telling us that there was a higher probability of an earthquake erupting in our neighborhood but were not predicting that an earthquake would destroy our home; nor were they predicting when one would strike.

Similarly, actuaries crunch vast amounts of data to inform me that there's a 73 percent probability that I will live to a certain age: 76. Life insurance companies use this information to sell me coverage for the unlikely event I don't make it that far. But only fortune-tellers would confidently tell me I will live to 78, or some other random number. The difference is that actuaries will tell me the odds of this event happening, 35 percent for an *average* 46-year-old male, while fortune-tellers would be 100 percent confident in their predictions for an *individual outcome*.

Actuaries rarely have to interact with people demanding to know the likelihood of the adverse effects happening to them on an individual level. Doctors, however, often face patients who demand exact predictions and answers. A cancer patient might demand to know how long he or she has left to live. A parent might demand to know why a child keeps waking up in the middle of the night with a stomachache. My wife is an MD, specialized in pediatrics where part of the patient population is highly acute. She therefore knows all about the agony of parents who are trying to help their children by demanding unreasonably precise answers from the doctors. At times, all that these parents want is for someone to hold their hands and say, "It'll all be OK. We have a solution." My wife does take her time to comfort patients and their loved ones, but not by bending the truth. When it comes to informing them about the patient's health, she sticks to the facts, which might include informing the parents that the doctors don't know what's causing the pain and are not even sure the other diagnostic tools will provide an answer. In their desperation to help their children, some parents may become frustrated and lash out. Other parents may lose trust in modern medicine and put their faith entirely in alternative medicine, which is not standardized or validated. A few go as far as threatening to ruin the doctor's career by going to the doctor's supervisor, giving the doctor poor online reviews, or filing a lawsuit. Regardless of these pressures, my wife and other doctors bring the conversation back to the limits of their knowledge and the probability that their estimates are accurate. "We have an ethical obligation to be truthful, including being honest about our limitations," my wife tells me. "That's our role, even if some patients may not appreciate that in the moment."

The demands made on recruiters and hiring managers more often resemble those of a client going to a fortune-teller than to a life insurance company. But smart company leaders can make more reasonable demands on recruiters and encourage a truthful dialogue. CEOs can empower recruiting teams to educate the entire organization on the benefits and limits of probabilistic decision making and how these apply to recruiting—and also let the recruiters know that the CEO has their back if a hiring manager is making unreasonable demands for accuracy.

How Poker Players Live with Good Decisions That Had Bad Outcomes

In a discussion with poker historian James McManus, he pointed out that what separates typical players from excellent ones is that the latter pride themselves on making good decisions while the former tend to focus on the outcomes. "If you make a tough but correct decision," he said, "and your opponent makes a terrible one but gets lucky and wins a huge pot, it's called a bad beat. And they're brutal. Amateurs smashed by these beats often berate their opponent or even go on tilt. That is, they allow their angry frustration about one hand to infect their future decisions. I've certainly done that. In fact, I've done it thousands and thousands of times." McManus laughed and went on: "The pros teach themselves to handle it better. Either that or they were born with a cooler temperament than I've got. But even some of the very best pros still go on tilt for a while after taking a particularly vicious beat."

Another problem is that no matter how confident you are about a decision, a small part of you often still thinks you should have made the opposite one. And when your decision turns out to be wrong, the part of you that advocated for the opposite one rubs it in with an "I told you so!" Poker players can objectively calculate the odds and know that they've made the right call, or at least the one with the highest expected value. Most recruiters don't have that luxury.

If even top poker pros go on tilt, it's easy to understand when hiring managers in LA go on tilt too. Then there's the fact that most companies fail to agree on the criteria for which hiring decisions were right or wrong. Even if they did, those criteria would be much more subjective than those in poker, where whoever outlasts all the other players wins the tournament, even if the winning player didn't necessarily make better decisions than every other player that week. Not only do hiring managers have to deal with bad luck, but they constantly receive conflicting signals from both their bosses and the various candidates. They also have to deal with work rivals fighting for more power within the organization.

Use Expected Value Wagers

Another thing that helps solid poker players avoid going on tilt is their commitment to making "expected value wagers." These are the expected value of each hand played. Pros who make a series of positive expected value (+EV) decisions can expect to win over time, while a series of negative expected value (−EV) decisions are likely to lead to going broke. So long as they are playing correctly, making as many +EV or GTO (game theory optimal) decisions as possible, pros can manage whatever temptation they might feel to trust their gut in big spots. Instead of getting elated or depressed by wild swings of good or bad luck, disciplined players rely on +EV wagers to keep them in the black in the long run.

How Google Prevents Hiring Managers from Going on Tilt

Many gamblers who lose a lot of money try to win it all back by making even larger, if less intelligent, bets. Similar behavior has been observed among fund managers after their investments underperform. They often begin to take higher risks, hoping to earn back the money as quickly as possible. While the riskier, higher-stakes decisions do give them a small chance of recouping their losses and saving face, such decisions also dramatically boost the likelihood that they will lose even more of their clients' money.

Google has instituted a practice that reduces the likelihood of hiring managers going on tilt. They do so by separating the people who make hiring decisions from those who conduct the interviews. A panel reviews the interview questions and the candidates' responses. If the review panel members don't agree with an interviewer's rating on a question, they will correct that rating or discard the question.

This practice can help prevent hiring managers from lowering their standards when in desperate need of help. It can also help prevent the opposite, hidden cost from loss aversion.

The Hidden Cost of Loss Aversion in Hiring Decisions

This is not to say that there are no costs associated with turning down great candidates. As discussed in the opening chapter, such costs are often enormous. It's just difficult to discern these costs clearly because they often are hypothetical.

There is a large and growing body of literature on loss aversion. Perhaps the most important thing we can learn from it is that most people get a greater disutility from a negative event (say, losing $100 on a bet) than they get utility from an equally positive event (winning $100).

The pressure can be intense to not hire potential stars who emit even the faintest negative signals. Some managers are filling a position on a very small team, so a particular hire would constitute a significant portion of that team. A new hire who performs extremely well for a team of any size can make the hiring manager a star, but hiring a person who underperforms can be disastrous for the manager.

How to Limit the "Losses" from Loss Aversion in Hiring Decisions

A former Google executive I interviewed explained how the management team was careful to not let great if slightly flawed candidates slip through the process. That's what makes a recruiting strategy *Moneyball*, remember? One of the interviewers, a former Boston Consulting Group partner, was so quick to turn down candidates that he had received the internal nickname of Dr. Death. Despite his seniority, Google went ahead and hired a number of candidates he had recommended should be turned down. As far as the executive I interviewed remembered, "These candidates did well at Google."

In a famous paper "Risk and Uncertainty," Paul Samuelson articulated with unusual clarity how loss aversion prevents individuals from making seemingly logical choices.[4] He also offered a solution to this challenge. Samuelson offered a colleague a heads-or-tails bet on a coin flip: a correct call meant the colleague would win $200; for an incorrect call, the colleague would only lose $100. The colleague said, "I won't bet because I would feel the $100 loss more than the $200 gain. But I'll take you on if you promise to let me make a hundred such bets." Enough said.

In his book *Misbehaving*, Nobel Laureate Richard Thaler shares an example of a wise CEO who recognized the negative impact of loss aversion on decisions made by his executives. Thaler sets the scene by explaining that he was teaching a group of executives along with their company's CEO. Thaler notes:

> I put to the executives this scenario: Suppose you were offered an investment opportunity for your division that will yield one of two payoffs. After the investment is made, there is a 50% chance it will make a profit of $2 million, and a 50% chance it will lose $1 million. (Notice that the expected payoff of this

investment is $500,000, since half the time they gain $2 million—an expected gain of $1 million—and half the time they lose a million—an expected loss of half a million. The company was large enough that a million-dollar loss, or even several of them, would not threaten its solvency.) I then asked by a show of hands who would take on this project. Of the twenty-three executives, only three said they would do it.

Then I asked the CEO a question. If these projects were "independent"—that is, the success of one was unrelated to the success of another—how many of the projects would you want to undertake? His answer: all of them! By taking on the twenty-three projects, the firm expects to make $11.5 million (since each one is worth an expected half million), and a bit of mathematics reveals that the chance of losing any money overall is less than 5%. He considered undertaking a collection of projects like this a no-brainer.

Making Money Not Enough to Motivate Executives to Go Against the Crowd

To an outsider, the executives in Thaler's example may seem wimpy in their unwillingness to take on a project with an expected return of half a million dollars. What kind of head honcho turns down a project expected to be that profitable? The issue is that it's risky to be a hero. Even responsible executives aren't robots always looking to maximize the expected profit for their firm, regardless of the personal cost to them. They also want to minimize the chances of failing.

Most executives in my experience, when given a choice, would rather fail conventionally than succeed unconventionally. If the unconventional plan fails, it could cost you your job. Until it succeeds, and maybe even after, you are likely to be branded as "somewhat crazy and unconventional." Failing conventionally, on the other hand, will get you sympathy from others who would have made the same choice.

In a study of professional money managers, David Scharfstein and Jeremy Stein show that most people would rather stay part of the herd, even when that reduces their chances of succeeding.[5] This may seem counterintuitive. Money managers must convince investors that they can outpace the herd that makes up the market. If they remain in the herd with other investors in most of their decisions, it will be difficult to keep their promise to their own investors—and justify their own hefty fees. James Surowiecki, in *The Wisdom of Crowds*, points out why: "mutual fund managers actually have to do two things: they have to invest wisely, and they have to convince people that they're investing wisely too." A friend who read an early draft of my book asked, "Are you surprised by this finding? In most firms, promotions are driven one-third by what you did and two-thirds by what others think you did."

Over shorter periods, even the best fund managers will underperform from time to time. Investors, of course, could wait patiently to see the long-term performance of each fund. Investors could also perform their own due diligence on the investment techniques and strategies of each fund manager. But most investors are neither patient nor willing to delve too deeply into why fund managers have underperformed in the short term and if their long-term investment hypothesis is solid. Investors would rather take shortcuts such as firing contrarian fund managers the minute they underperform, before waiting to see whether the dip turns out to be just a hiccup. Recruiters face similar dilemmas. They have to make good hiring decisions *and* convince their boss that they did, often before much evidence of this is available.

How to Encourage Better Hiring Predictions

Companies can encourage hiring managers to make better hiring predictions by following a few simple practices:

1. **Follow the law of large numbers.** When taking a risk, present it as a repeatable series of +EV wagers, not an all-or-nothing Hail Mary pass. Know that if you make the same bet enough times, you'll achieve results very close to the expected value, plus or minus a few percentage points. Just make sure that the bets are independent of each other and avoid systematic errors, such as relying too long on a single hiring manager with not so great judgment.

2. **Define success and failure up front, and be patient, especially when trying out new ideas.** Don't think, "We'll try and see how it goes." You may have some bad luck early on, but having defined success up front will help you stay patient long enough to see the experiment through.

3. **Share risks and benefits.** Instead of each manager hiring 1 direct report, if possible have 10 hiring managers hire 10 people and assign those individuals only after they have started at the firm. This will make it easier to see decisions as a "repeat game" as opposed to a single big bet. Some companies, like the video game company EA Sports, hire college graduates into a two-year rotational program before assigning them to a specific division.

4. **Make it safe for hiring managers to fail.** If you penalize them for every bad hire, they'll become overly risk averse. Instead, reward decisions that were correct at the time they were made (ex ante), not only decisions that turned out to be correct (ex post).

5. **Seek clarity.** Establish clear hiring criteria at the outset and make sure interviewers numerically evaluate each candidate. Less quantitative criteria provide too much opportunity for big egos to make a case that they were right all along.

6. **Remove the veto power of individual interviewers.** Studying the job performance of tens of thousands of hires, Amazon discovered that candidates who received an unfavorable rating by one interviewer performed better than candidates who received unanimously favorable ratings. It's difficult to know why this is the case, but my own hypothesis is that interviewers overvalue charm when making hiring decisions—and only charming candidates get a perfect rating. As a result, Amazon has adjusted its process. The direct hiring manager and most senior interviewer, called (as mentioned in an earlier chapter) a "bar raiser," still retain veto power, but other interviewers don't; and hiring decisions don't need to be unanimous.

HAVE A CONTINGENCY PLAN

Modern farmers must accept the fact that accurate long-term weather forecasts aren't possible. Since the farmers can't base planting decisions on forecasts or almanacs, they've learned to install irrigation systems and to delay or accelerate their harvests as weather patterns shift.

What can hiring managers learn from farmers? Farmers a long time ago stopped hoping for a perfect tool that could predict the weather for them. Instead they make contingency plans. Hiring managers too can stop searching for tools that help them make perfect hiring predictions. They can instead make contingency plans and learn to quickly adjust to new information. What would contingency plans in the hiring process look like? A number of methods can be learned from top-tier management consulting firms:

- **Grow your own talent.** While occasionally these firms hire externally for senior-level positions, the vast majority of their senior team members were internal employees who grew into those positions over time.

- **Build in enough time for the process to develop.** Growing your talent takes years of hard work. To sustain their growth, top-tier consulting firms have to be patient and learn to accurately estimate their needs for partners six or more years in advance. In an interview I conducted with Leon Schor, former senior partner at L.E.K. Consulting, he noted that "the alternative is to keep applying hiring methods that most often have failed in the past."

- **Allow for churn.** Management consulting firms are notorious for hiring large cohorts of new graduates after each school year while expecting most of these hires not to last more than one to three years. Operating this way allows them to be uncompromising while enforcing their standards, and to accept the fact that some hires, regardless of how smart and capable they might be, are not good fits.

How do these practices apply to other kinds of firms? "If you are not thinking about what your talent funnel looks like 10 years from now, you're underinvesting in the company's future," noted Ron Williams, former chairman and CEO of Aetna in an interview with me.

Several ECA clients are building a strong middle management team, expecting some team members to grow into more senior positions. "Some may argue that we could run our firm with a leaner middle management," noted Brian Kelly, the COO of a billion-dollar veterinary company and former Boston Consulting Group consultant. "However, we are also hiring for future leaders, not just current middle management."

Other companies deliberately build large internal strategy or consulting teams. The idea, again, is that some of these hires will take a leadership role in the business one day.

Google had a similar strategy of growing its own leadership talent through its Associate Product Manager program. When describing the program's rationale, Eric Schmidt, Google's CEO at the time, reasoned, "One of these people will probably be our CEO one day—we just don't know which one."

Larry Kutscher, who grew a private equity–owned hospitality tech company from a $900 million valuation to a $1.5 billion exit, has applied a similar strategy. Over the past few years, Kutscher has hired promising talent in individual contributor roles. These are people who reported directly to the CEO, who moved them into line roles when they demonstrated that they were ready. In an interview with me, Kutscher noted that "growing internal senior management talent has not only produced better results. It has also allowed us to save on expensive recruiting costs, which can get very high for senior positions."

Formal succession plans for senior roles have been put in place by large and small companies. Sometimes such plans work to perfection. When they don't, however, these are the most common reasons:

- Senior management assigning this task to someone else and not staying sufficiently involved themselves.

- Replacing quality with quantity. Companies eager to quickly build a succession plan often include too many hires of modest caliber in their line of succession.

- Not enough quantity. In a surprising number of cases, senior leaders have expressed to me a vision of a team built to be in position to take over for them if they and all their senior colleagues were to be suddenly "hit by a bus." In many cases, these leaders have had their eyes set on a particular individual to take over for them if they left. One issue with this approach is that they are not grooming enough future leaders for roles that might arise in the future. Another is that if their star hire suddenly leaves, either for another company or by growing into a different internal role, they won't have enough time to find and groom their next star executive.

The problem of insufficient quantity in the executive pipeline springs not only from unit leaders focusing all their efforts on grooming a star hire; it also occurs because the organization has failed to formulate an explicit strategy, with a big enough budget, to hire more stars at the appropriate levels. Company CEOs can address this issue by formulating an explicit strategy and assigning appropriate budgets to achieve those goals.

You know that your succession plan is failing if a sizable portion of your management team was recruited externally. Companies hiring most of their VPs and C-suite positions from the outside will also find that it demotivates current employees, who won't see themselves on a path to the C-suite or even into middle management. This isn't even to mention how expensive it is to hire outside mercenaries at the VP level and above.

Chapter Summary and Conclusion

Context:

- Recruiters have a bad reputation in some circles. A lot of this is due to their inability to always predict which hires will perform well.
- Recruiters are not alone in this. Experts in a wide variety of fields struggle to make accurate predictions.
- Finding experts who are good at making predictions is difficult because the most confident ones are often the least accurate.
- Loss aversion has a negative impact on hiring decisions.
- Executives, like most other people, don't like going against the crowd while making crucial decisions. Offering them extra money is often not enough to motivate them to buck common trends to make risky hiring decisions.
- Professional poker players, who face dilemmas similar to those faced by hiring managers, have learned to live with good decisions that sometimes have terrible outcomes.
- Many hiring managers do not measure their hiring success by metrics, but rather through remembering the peaks, i.e., a few anecdotal good and bad decisions.

What you can do about it:

- While these issues aren't easy to resolve, companies can make better hiring predictions by following a few simple practices:
  - Remember the confidence paradox. The level of people's confidence in their own predictions is often inversely indicative of the accuracy of their predictions. Less confident predictors display a healthy level of skepticism toward their *own* predictions, seek advice from others, use more external materials, reevaluate their frameworks, etc.
  - Recognize forecasters who don't learn from their mistakes, and stop taking their advice.
- Successful companies predict, measure, and reward aggregate success rather than rewarding or punishing individual outcomes.
- Successful organizations embrace the uncertainty that comes with all hiring decisions and develop contingency plans.
- Google prevents hiring managers from going on tilt and neutralizes biases in hiring decisions by deploying independent hiring panels.
- Smart companies reward good decisions, not just good outcomes.

CHAPTER 11

Using a Flawed Instrument to Make (Im)Perfect Predictions

THE ROOT CAUSE OF UNDESIRED HIRING BIASES

I'm assuming that most executives who have made it this far in my book have also read Daniel Kahneman's *Thinking, Fast and Slow* and Nassim Taleb's *The Black Swan*. Kahneman and Taleb are profoundly insightful in unpacking cognitive biases and other problems that arise when we use an imperfect instrument—our brains—to try to make perfect predictions. Any book on recruiting would be incomplete without addressing these biases, so I will highlight a few of them. However, I believe that most of my readers are already familiar with this part of the hiring story, and I am comfortable dedicating less space to this topic than it deserves.

In the frictionless billiard table example discussed in Chapter 10, I explained why it would be virtually impossible to make perfect predictions when such a vast number of forces impact the outcomes. This remains an important reason to recognize our limits of making precise predictions. An equally important reason is that our brains, as amazing as they are, place hard limits on our understanding of the world.

Research on this topic has only scratched the surface, and yet a number of studies already indicate how most of us are far more susceptible to systematic error than we would like to admit when we're trying to remember the past, make sense of current events, or use these data points to predict the future.

Accurately Understanding the Past

Most of us form opinions about the present based on remembered experiences. Some of these memories can be enormously helpful. "The last time I had too many tequila shots, I woke up in agony the next morning." But what if we couldn't rely on our memories? Or even worse, what if we unconsciously altered our memories when trying to make sense of particularly good or bad outcomes we're experiencing in the present?

Psychologists Ulric Neisser and Nicole Harsch ran an experiment whose results are particularly instructive for recruiters. Neisser and Harsch tested "flashbulb" memories, their term for recollections of major events. Flashbulb memories are assumed to be more resistant to change than other memories since they're usually more vivid and widely discussed after the event. Neisser and Harsch surveyed 106 students right after the space shuttle *Challenger* explosion that killed seven American astronauts in 1986. Then 2½ years later, 44 of the students were surveyed again. On a 0-to-7-point scale, with 7 being the most accurate recall, 25 percent scored 0, and half scored 2 or less. The same students self-rated their confidence in how accurate they were at an average of 4.17 out of 5.

Similar studies have been replicated with the deaths of loved ones, the death of Princess Diana, and the 9/11 attacks, with virtually the same results. These studies indicate that our memories, even when it comes to major events, are unreliable. Moreover, feeling confident in a memory being accurate is not of much help either and should serve more as a warning that you might be overconfident about recalling what actually happened.

Another example comes from Harvard researcher Edward Giovannucci.[1] He surveyed women about their eating habits over the last decade to see if high-fat diets impacted the chance of breast cancer. The answer was yes: women who at a younger age consumed a high-fat diet were more likely to have breast cancer. Or were they? These women had also completed a survey about their diets about a decade earlier, well before developing breast cancer. When Giovannucci compared the results of the two surveys, he discovered that while women without breast cancer recalled their dietary habits fairly accurately, those with breast cancer recalled having a fattier diet than they had reported in the past. In other words, these unfortunate women were harshly blaming themselves for something they had not done.

If we can't rely on our memories, how well can we rely on the models based on such memories to explain the world or predict what the future might hold?

Understanding the Present

Our perceptions of the present might be nearly as faulty, leaving us to wonder, how much can we rely on our brains to accurately convey information about current events?

At any given second, after all, our brains are receiving roughly 11 million pieces of information from our five senses, and yet we can process only 40 pieces of information per second. In order to function, we need to simplify this information to a manageable small number of conclusions. Making sense of more information than we already do would require our brains to operate at a higher capacity. Storing, or remembering, all that information is also costly, i.e., requiring a lot of energy and brain power. The more of that information we can turn into a pattern or story, the easier it will be to comprehend and store it.

Imagine a book about world history. If the book contained the names of all the world's rulers, the dates when they were in power, and a story about each ruler's personality traits, it would be extremely difficult to remember all these stories. Now imagine instead that the book had just one central theme, such as the rise and fall of rulers throughout times, and the book also often repeated that the rulers on the rise shared a few personality traits and the rulers on the decline shared a different set of traits. The central theme would not only help you to gather key takeaways; it would also let you remember more of the individual stories.

Fitting data into a pattern or story is critical to our brains' ability to understand and recollect the data. Without this ability, we could just as well try to remember thousands of randomly selected words.

As the brain struggles to understand and remember an endless series of events, it needs to sort them into narratives. If something that actually happened doesn't fit into that narrative, the brain prefers to alter the outlier fact to make it fit the story, rather than make up an entirely new one.

Once we've come up with a master narrative, we tend to look for more evidence to prove to ourselves that the narrative is true. Doing the opposite—that is, looking for evidence, as scientists do, that might disprove the narrative— would require more effort. And our brains, if they have a choice, will choose the activity that requires less effort and energy.

The same thing happens when there are holes in the narrative. We find ways of filling those holes, or papering them over. In brief, we start seeing patterns where there are none. The "cognitive shortcuts" require less effort from us than trying to make sense of each piece of information by itself.

The downside of these shortcuts is that they make us more susceptible to biases, even when we'd sincerely prefer to be free of them. Making clear sense of past or current events *requires* us to eliminate these biases. We want to evaluate individual candidates based on their own merits, not on ethnicity, gender, religious beliefs, attractiveness, or the pleasant sound of their name. The question is, can we do that?

My family and I personally experienced the downside of such biases when we moved from Iran to the countryside of Sweden in the mid-1980s. Swedes by many standards were, and are, some of the most tolerant and virtuous people in the world. Even so, a wave of neo-Nazi sentiment had infected a small portion of the population during this period. As an eight-year-old heading to school on my bicycle, I was sometimes chased by skinheads on mopeds, older kids trying to smash me with their helmets or chains. Meanwhile, my mother, trying to land a job to support her four children, was told, "We don't hire blackheads," a derogatory term for non-Swedes with black hair.

We're all incredibly lucky to live in a time and place where most hiring managers—indeed, most Americans—pride themselves on being free of such negative biases. Just a generation or two ago, this wasn't always the case.

Not only have most hiring managers today adopted more tolerant views, but they're proactively trying to counteract earlier biases. For the time being, however, the idea that any of us is entirely free of bias when making hiring decisions is also wrong.

Using Data Points to Make Predictions

As we've seen time and again, our memories and even our perception of current data points are often more biased or flawed than we realize.

A few of the flawed methods we use to make predictions are described in Table 11.1. Anecdotes can be more powerful than statistics, even for CEOs. And yes, even for authors who caution others against using anecdotes to make predictions. Likewise, the methods we favor when making predictions are often just as flawed. Some of these methods are listed in Table 11.2.

TABLE 11.1 Select Challenges with Making Predictions

Bias/Flaws	Description	Example
Small sample bias	Too few data points to make a conclusion	Flip a fair coin five times, and tails comes up four times. Does this mean that you should expect 80% of all future coin flips to come up as tails? Now try flipping the coin 100 times . . .
Large sample bias	The likelihood that *something* correlates if enough variables are tested	If enough people try it, it will work for someone. Mistaking correlation for causation.
Confirmation bias	The tendency to see information that confirms a hypothesis (and disregard information that indicates the opposite)	"I'm very good at determining when someone has a toupée." But how do you know when you don't notice someone wearing one? Or "psychic predictions."
Sharpshooter fallacy *or* data mining	Rationalizing a hypothesis after the fact to fit an outcome	Fire a gun into the side of a barn, draw a circle around the hole, and then claim that you hit the bulls-eye

TABLE 11.2 Additional Challenges with Making Predictions

Bias/Flaws	Description	Example
Survival bias	After the fact, it is difficult to find data on what didn't work	Interviewing surviving cancer patients on their diet habits. How different were these to those of nonsurviving patients?
Missing bullet holes	Another perspective on what the missing data are not telling you	If most WWII airplanes come back with bullet holes in their wings, is it the wings that need to be strengthened or the engines?
The illusion of validity	Believing so strongly in your ability to predict that even strong data proving you are wrong will not convince you	Daniel Kahneman admitted that during his military service, he maintained full confidence in his recruiting methods, even though they failed to make accurate predictions
Cognitive reflection	The tendency to gravitate to a simple answer even when, upon reflection, we realize the response was wrong	Brain teasers of simple math problems
Poor intuitive understanding of odds	Most people are intuitively bad at understanding odds	People who win the lottery believe it was an act of a higher power

This doesn't stop a CEO from making predictions based on some story he's heard. A CEO I recently worked with to hire a head of strategy told me he wanted the candidate to have experience at one of the top eight strategy consulting firms, but he preferred that the candidate not be from Bain. "All the folks we've hired from Bain have been arrogant," he said. We later found that he'd had one past employee from Bain and had also interviewed "a couple" of candidates from Bain in the past. To an outsider, it might seem obvious that no CEO should judge Bain's 8,000 employees by a few past interactions that didn't sit well with him. But as most of us can attest, we can't help feeling that way, at least momentarily, when we go through a similar experience.

For example, in a small town hit by a spate of cancer cases, suspicion may naturally fall on the electricity lines buzzing just outside of town—even after it has been noted that the number of cases in a town of that size is well within the range of a random statistical outcome. Even after learning that the vast majority of places with both the highest *and* the lowest cancer rates are small towns like this one, suspicion may linger.

Wanting to Believe

Our brains are profoundly limited in their ability to understand the business world, let alone the known universe. The sooner we accept this fact, the sooner we can make better hiring decisions. As Dan Gardner writes in *Future Babble*:

> We try to eliminate uncertainty however we can. We see patterns where there is none . . . and we treasure stories that replace the complexity and uncertainty of reality with simple narratives of what's happening and what will happen. . . . So we look to experts. They must know. They have Ph.D.s, prizes, and offices at major universities. And thanks to the news media's preference for the simple and dramatic, the sort of expert we are likely to hear from is confident and conclusive. They *know* what will happen; they are *certain* of it. We like that because that is how we want to feel. And so we convince ourselves that these wise men and women can do what wise men and women have never been able to do before. Fundamentally, we believe because we want to believe.

Why do we keep believing predictions that we know are flawed and are more likely to be wrong than right? Because we don't like uncertainty. We hate it. So much so that we find flawed predictions more comforting than the truth that our predictions are seldom worth the effort of making and tracking them.

Rob Paulsson, president of Strategic Healthcare Programs and author of the business novel *Hank's Office*, writes in his article "Beware the Lure of Confidence" how he has learned that "confidence is not competence" and that "some insecure people are very good at what they do." Paulsson concludes that "competent people are not afraid to acknowledge uncertainty and risk."[2]

All CEOs can improve their hiring outcomes by following Paulsson's example. They can help their teams embrace uncertainty rather than seek comforting predictions. Yet culture change can't begin until the CEO follows through. The CEO needs to make sure that the hiring managers, recruiting professionals, and other team members start to remind one another about the uncertainties that come with predictions. Finally, organizations can shift away from listening to overconfident execs by numerically tracking hiring predictions. It's easier to realize that no one gets all his or her predictions right when everyone is sharing the data that drives this point home.

"I Think, Therefore I Am"

We are influenced by our subconscious more than most of us realize. At the same time, we tend to identify with our conscious mind. "I think, therefore I am," the French philosopher René Descartes wrote around 1640. No one knows what Descartes would have thought of the unconscious, if he even suspected he had one. While most of us, living after Freud, understand that we have a subconscious, many believe that our conscious mind has the final say.

An alternative theory says that our conscious and subconscious minds might decide things together, making what might be called "panel-style" decisions. In a study by Chun Siong Soon and colleagues, MRI scans of brains indicated that decisions are made up to 10 seconds before they enter our awareness.[3] As much as we would like to think our wide-awake self is in charge, Soon's results indicate we are often unaware of our biases and other factors urging us to do things.

A study of 45,457 married couples conducted by psychologists Richard Kopelman and Dorothy Lang found that there is a 12 percent likelihood above chance that a couple will have names that resemble each other's.[4] Studies comparing the physical features of couples, such as height and nose size, have yielded similar results.

These studies indicate that even if we deliberately try to engage the deeper parts of the brain, we can't assume that we are free of biases in our subconscious.

HOW TO REDUCE BIASES IN YOUR HIRING PROCESS

If you agree with the fact that even the best-intentioned hiring managers aren't free of biases, the question becomes how to reduce the impact of such biases on your hiring decisions. You can do so by utilizing a number of the tools listed below. Some of them have already been discussed throughout the book, but I'm recapping them here as they relate to reducing biased hiring decisions.

Identify and Address Sources of Systematic Biases

As Timothy Wilson wrote in *Strangers to Ourselves*, we cannot address our biases if we don't know they exist. Relying only on your willpower to remain neutral is unlikely to remove every bias from your decisions. The more we're aware of such biases, the more likely we'll be to override or eliminate them.

In reminding yourself about how seemingly meaningless information and circumstances can impact your decisions, the following two examples can be helpful. In one study, researchers had participants rate a single writing sample.[5] The only difference between the papers was the number of initials, if any, in the name of the author. Authors with one or more middle initials received scores that averaged 20 percent higher (see Figure 11.1).

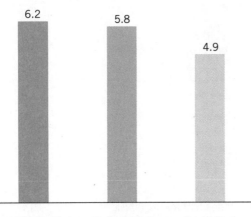

Average writing ability score by author name

When hypothetical authors had middle initials, the same writing sample was rated as significantly better.

FIGURE 11.1   Does having a middle name give one an advantage? Based on data from Van Tilburg and Igou, 2014.

Another study illuminated how biases can impact even life-altering decisions. Actual parole judges, unlike those depicted in daytime TV shows, often feel a deep sense of responsibility to their community when trying to decide whether or not to parole a prisoner. These judges also realize the gravity of their decisions for the prisoners themselves. Yet a study by marketing professor Shai Danziger and colleagues showed that prisoners who had their cases heard early in the day or right after a lunch break had significantly higher chances of being granted parole than prisoners who had their cases tried later in the day (see Figure 11.2).[6]

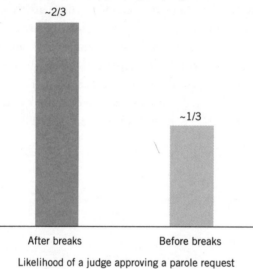

After meal breaks, parole judges are approximately twice as likely to approve a parole request.

FIGURE 11.2 Justice is what the judge had for breakfast.
Based on data from Danziger, Levav, and Avnaim-Pesso, 2011.

Amazon, for example, scrapped its résumé AI tool after noticing the tool was biased against female candidates. While some AI tools don't look at the names and official gender of applicants as part of their decision, Amazon assessed that the risk of the tool leading to biased decisions was still high as certain hobbies, educational tracks, etc., are more popular among female applicants, and the tool would be likely to indirectly discriminate against such applicants regardless.

Design Your Interview Processes to Reduce Biased Decisions

Shane Frederick, a professor at the Yale School of Management, has an assistant put tape over the names of his students before grading their exams. "I often have a sigh of relief after I take off the tape," Frederick said in an interview with me. "I find myself giving a low exam grade to students that I had a good impression of in the class, and vice versa. I'm glad to know that I wasn't influenced by that impression before grading the exam."

Private equity investor M-K O'Connell had a similar experience recently when we anonymized a job knowledge test taken by five finalist candidates for an investment role at the fund where O'Connell works. A McKinsey engagement manager, who was the front-runner after the verbal interviews, scored the lowest of all five candidates by both O'Connell and one of his colleagues, who rated the tests independently. The unbiased process didn't only help them avoid a hire who might have presented well but lacked depth. It also helped them prioritize a candidate whom they might have missed otherwise. One of the candidates had recently moved to the United States from abroad and had a few hiccups when trying to articulate his thoughts during the earlier verbal interviews. Communicating effectively to the investment committee was a critical part of the role. Arguing that written communication and depth of analysis for investment opportunities were more important than verbal communication, O'Connell decided to give this candidate a shot and allow him to take the written assessment, which required a fair bit of writing. How did this candidate do in the anonymized written assessments? He placed in a joint first place. The investors were clearly happy they had not turned down a top candidate. This is *Moneyball* at its finest. O'Connell relied on processes, not merely willpower, to limit his biases. He also prioritized the criteria most critical for success in the role, not a long list of criteria that would have narrowed down the list of available candidates to seemingly picture-perfect individuals, who in reality lacked the same level of depth.

In my experience, the best interviewers don't simply rely on self-restraint and a belief that they have pure moral (and unbiased) values. Willpower is seldom enough. They design the candidate vetting process in such a way that it reduces the chances of their interviewers being exposed to information that might bias them.

Recognizing this point, one CEO I talked to said that he always does the first-round interview over the phone because he had realized he otherwise might give too much weight to the candidate's appearance, as opposed to the quality of the person's skills.

Set the Table for an Interview

What if you can't change the design of the interview process? My recommendation is to admit that you're human and therefore likely to be impacted by biases. Remind yourself about how we all are affected by bits of information that often seem trivial. By doing so, you just might be able to "think slow," to use Daniel Kahneman's term, and thereby make wiser decisions.

You can do so by "setting the table." Whenever you notice something that could unfairly predispose you, simply take note of it. To make sure you are taking this seriously, write it down.

Depending on if you noticed this bias before or during the interview, you can then follow the advice below.

Opt Out Before an Interview

So, what types of clues are you looking for when you set the table? It can, for example, be that you have previously held negative beliefs about or had negative experiences with a certain group or minority. University of Chicago, for instance, assigns those professors who have a background in certain regions to conduct the initial screening of applications by international students to its PhD economics program. The logic is that these professors have better knowledge about the nuances in signals projected by candidates in regions where the professors themselves grew up. Is an "A minus" GPA excellent or awful for a student from a certain university in Sweden? One of the professors, wanting to give students from all backgrounds a fair chance, asked applicants from one country to be assigned to someone else. The professor has visited the said country multiple times and enjoyed his interactions with its people. However, in his younger days he did not hold a favorable view of the country as the rhetoric between that and his home country were intensifying. Not knowing if some of those feelings might subconsciously bias him, he did the right thing and asked his colleagues to screen those applicants instead.

Opt Out After an Interview

You might also notice that something about a candidate's appearance or style is bothering you during the interview, but you know deep down that this is not predictive of job performance. It can also be that you rate a candidate highly on the desire to work at your company, even if the candidate gave you a very similar response to a previous candidate that you gave a lower score to on that question.

At the end of the interview, think long and hard about whatever biases might have seeped in, positive or negative. If you find clues that this might have happened, you can rely on noninterview data to decontaminate your hiring decision or rely on other interviewers whom you think don't share the same bias.

Recruit from Diverse Pools

One of our clients that wanted to ensure diversity among its hires, which it defined as more female hires, brought us in to see how it could ensure that its interview practices were not biased. We discovered that it was not only the client's interview practices that were leading to an unintended lack of diversity. It was also the pools it was recruiting from. For its management ranks, the company was in theory open to "any background as long as the candidates were capable." However, the management team agreed that the ideal candidate would hold an MBA from a top-20 program or have a background in the military. We were able to show the members of the management team that none of their past 20 hires had fallen outside their ideal candidate profile, as much as they verbally repeated that they were open to any candidate background. And the pools they were actively recruiting from were male dominated. We showed them that only some 16 percent of the enlisted military forces were women[7] and that most of the MBA programs they were recruiting from had about a third women.[8] In light of these stats, the management team agreed to add two more "ideal candidate backgrounds" to the list which were from more female-dominated professions. You too can increase the diversity of your candidate pool by reviewing the channels from which you recruit. Are you consistently recruiting from the same job boards, colleges, geographies? Do any of these channels have less of a diverse pool? Can you increase the diversity of candidates by exploring any other channels?

Another common example of how the channels used to source candidates leads to unintended lower diversity in companies is overreliance on employee referrals. If your employees are mainly from one socioeconomic or ethnic background, they are likely to refer more candidates like themselves.

Increase Diversity of Your Interviewers

In a push to increase diversity at the executive rank, a Fortune 500 I work with is pioneering an initiative where it is not only tracking the firm's ability to produce a diverse slate of *candidates* for each role; it is also tracking how diverse its slate of *interviewers* are for each candidate to minimize the risk of interviewers sharing unconscious biases.

While it will slightly increase the administrative burden for the interviews, the approach of ensuring a diverse slate of interviewers reduces the chances that your interviewers all share a systematic bias due to their background.

Encourage Interviewers to Form Independent Views

Follow the steps under the section "Avoid Groupthink" in Chapter 4 to ensure that interviewers form their independent opinions and communicate them as openly as possible to the rest of the group.

Remove Veto Power of Interviewers

As discussed in Chapter 10, leading organizations like Amazon are removing the veto power of most interviewers. Candidates who are hired despite having one of five interviewers recommend the opposite have performed better than candidates receiving a unanimous vote. This supports the hypothesis that veto power among interviewers does more damage (turning down stellar candidates) than good (protecting the firm from bad hires).

If you still find that hard to believe, consider the following thought experiment. Imagine a candidate is interviewed by five hiring managers and each of these hiring managers has a one in six chance of having some sort of illogical bias that prompts them to reject a qualified candidate. The biases of the hiring managers are independent of each other. What are the chances of a qualified candidate being rejected for any illogical bias if:

- Any of the five hiring managers has veto power—that is, the candidate needs five votes to get hired?

- The candidate only needs four out of five votes to get hired—that is, two hiring managers must have an illogical bias in order for the firm to reject a qualified candidate?

- The candidate needs three votes to get hired?

The answers are:

- When any of the hiring managers has veto power, and therefore all five hiring managers need to agree, there is an approximately 60 percent chance the candidate gets vetoed illogically.

- When four of the five hiring managers need to agree, there is approximately a 20 percent chance the candidate gets vetoed illogically.

- When three of the five hiring managers need to agree, there is approximately a 4 percent chance the candidate gets vetoed illogically.

Standardize Interview Questions and Expected Responses

Eliminate loosely defined constructs and interview practices such as the beer test. In Patty McCord's words, "What if the job is not about drinking beer?" If you are screening for a candidate's "smarts," be clear on how you are defining that. Likewise, if you are screening for a candidate's EQ, be clear on how you intend to screen for EQ. Otherwise you'll risk giving high scores to candidates you like and vice versa, with little connection to the candidate's actual smarts or EQ.

Instead follow the guidelines for using structured interviews outlined in Chapter 5 and the advice around how to test for reliability of screening techniques in Chapter 9. One best practice when using structured interviews is to write out not only the questions you are expecting to ask, but also what answers will receive a high versus low rating. I have found this practice particularly helpful in disentangling the impression that candidates are giving off versus the substance of their responses. For instance, when asking a candidate why he or she is excited about an opportunity, the candidate's body language might be positive and excited, but if the candidate is not speaking to the core of why this role is a good fit, it's easier for me to remind myself that I need to probe further there and rate the person fairly on that dimension.

Rely More on Situational Interview Questions

Many interview questions start with "Tell me about a time when . . ." The logic behind these questions is that if someone has had the experience of dealing with a similar set of situations as the current job requirements, the person will be a good hire. There is nothing wrong with this hypothesis. However, as discussed in Chapter 5, the research by Van Iddekinge et al. shows that the assumption is highly dubious at best. This presents an argument against using experience when screening candidates. An additional argument against using experience as a screening tool is that it reinforces current biases in the marketplace. Imagine if tech companies would highly prefer to hire coders who have experience at other prestigious tech firms. Since most prestigious tech firms have an overrepresentation of male coders, the practice of screening for *experience* is likely to create a catch-22–type problem. To mitigate this problem, employers can focus more on screening for the *skills* needed for the job by asking more situational interview questions like, "How would you tackle a problem like . . . ?" This can be done through job assessments or interview questions. In doing so, candidates demonstrating the strongest skills in tackling an issue are given priority.

Don't Assume Your Interviewers Are on the Same Page

Take a step back and ensure that your interviewers are on the same page. This can be done by setting explicit guidelines for how you intend to reduce bias in hiring decisions and training your staff on these guidelines. Sure, internal training courses often have mixed results. However, the alternative is that you are assuming that everyone at your company knows what you are thinking and understands the common pitfalls and how to avoid these.

Use Independent Panels to Make Decisions

Google uses a separate hiring panel, not involved in interviewing the candidates, to make hiring decisions. This panel will review the questions asked by interviewers, read the responses, and decide if the interviewer rated the responses fairly. If not, the hiring panel will ignore part or all of the ratings of an interviewer.

Utilizing an interview panel reduces the risk that a candidate is rated highly across the board because of the person's charm as opposed to the substance of his or her responses.

Test the Possibility That You Are Wrong

The danger with having a strong hunch about what drives performance at your firm is that you never test it and that hunch is leading to biased decisions. For example, if you believe that you need candidates to have high SAT math scores, you are putting female applicants at a disadvantage since male test takers scored about 16 points above average and female test takers scored about 14 points below average for this portion of the SAT.[9] You might want to test your hypothesis that SAT math scores are predictive of success and hire a few candidates who don't have high SAT math scores to see how they fare. This approach requires a lot of patience and can also be costly, but the alternative is that you continue being wrong in your beliefs and practices for a very long time. You can read more about how to test your hiring practices under the discussion about validity in Chapter 9.

As Always, Track and Improve Your Practices

And at this point, it will not come as a surprise to you that I'm encouraging you to, as always, track your initiatives and the desired outcomes and improve your practices as you go along.

Chapter Summary and Conclusion

Context:

- Most people are more susceptible to making systematic errors than they like to admit when trying to remember the past, make sense of current events, and use these data points to make predictions.
- We're incredibly lucky to live in a time when most hiring managers pride themselves on not wanting to have negative biases against minorities or any disadvantaged groups. Just a generation or two ago, this was not the case.
- However, we're mistaken if we believe we are free of such biases when making hiring decisions.

What you can do about it:

- Willpower is not enough. The best interviewers don't simply rely on self-restraint and a belief that they have pure, unbiased intentions. They design the candidate vetting process in a way that reduces the chances of them being exposed to information that may bias them.

- Other methods used by interviewers and organizations that intend to reduce their interview bias and diversity are:
  - Actively identify and address sources of systematic biases.
  - Set the table, i.e., train themselves to notice cues that may bias them.
  - Opt out to decide on a candidate before an interview.
  - Opt out to make hiring decisions for a candidate after an interview.
  - Recruit from pools that are not biased to begin with.
  - Focus on not only increasing the diversity of the candidates, but also increasing the diversity of their interviewers.
  - Encourage interviewers to form independent views before being influenced by each other.
  - Remove the veto power of individual interviewers.
  - Standardize interview questions and expected responses.
  - Rely more on situational interview questions, testing more for capability rather than focusing on experience.
  - Don't assume the interviewers are on the same page.
  - Use independent panels to make hiring decisions.
  - Test the possibility that the interviewers are wrong.
  - Track and improve their practices over time.

CHAPTER 12

Bias Toward Action

Never mistake activity for achievement.

—John Wooden

BEING DECISIVE

"Bias toward action" is a well-known term in the business world. It favors active behavior over "analysis paralysis," which occurs when discussion and analysis of data dominate a team's work. In recruiting, it involves adding more complexity to the process without gaining new insights on a candidate's ability to be successful in the job.

This bias toward action is perfectly natural, though it can lead to trouble if it becomes extreme. I have stressed throughout this book that the decisive use of relevant data points gathered from a comprehensive interview process will add value.

"Resulting"

What you want to avoid is too strong a bias toward action that might seem rational but ends up destroying value. Two interesting historic examples of this are when unproven science coupled with bias toward action twice led to expensive failed efforts to induce rain in drought-stricken Southern California. The first time was in 1915 when "rainmaker" Charles Hatfield convinced the city of San Diego to agree on a payment of $10,000

($225,000 in today's dollars) to use "secret chemicals" to induce clouds to release rainwater over the region.[1] Hatfield seemed genuinely convinced his process would work. He used scientific terminology that sounded convincing and provided examples of his process allegedly triggering precipitation in Los Angeles, in Texas, and in several other regions. "I do not make rain," Hatfield explained. "That would be an absurd claim. I simply attract clouds, and they do the rest." Early the year after there was a downpour of about 30 inches of rain. The area was flooded. Farms, homes, bridges, and businesses were swept away. Two dams were damaged, and another one failed. A dozen to 50 people died. Causation? Correlation? Who cares, Hatfield had the "proof" he needed. He took what was most likely a random coincidence as a sign that his methods were working and went on to sell his services to region after region throughout the nation. But in town after town, his promises and elaborate processes for "inducing rain" were followed by more drought. After years of failed experiments, Hatfield went back to his career as a sewing machine salesman. Most likely people started seeing through the marketing facade he had set up. Anyone trying to induce rain in as many regions as he had, would get lucky at least a few times and have rain coincide a few days, weeks, or months after his experiments. But was it fair to give him the credit for the rain? No.

A hundred years later, cloud seeding was used by the municipal government in Los Angeles to end the severe five-year drought that was plaguing the City of Angels. Cloud seeding had come a long way since Hatfield's time, though the evidence of its effectiveness was less than overwhelming. Though the process was far from settled science, Los Angeles Public Works officials felt good about paying "only" $550,000 for a program they thought could produce water that would otherwise cost $3.2 million. Did it work? It's difficult to answer that question because meteorologists couldn't say with much confidence whether it would have rained anyway. Atmospheric scientist William Cotton remained skeptical, commenting that "a lot of it is just getting out there and doing something."

In poker the concept of judging the quality of a decision by its results, as opposed to judging if it was a good or bad decision at the time, is called "resulting." A poker player may make an awful call to go all in on a hand but be saved by the dealer. Should this player be proud of this play? No. As explained in Chapter 10, pros who make a series of decisions with a positive expected value, in poker called +EV wagers, can expect to win over time, while a series of negative expected value (−EV) decisions are likely to lead to going broke. In the movie *Flight*, Denzel Washington plays an alcoholic airline pilot, who after a traumatic mechanical failure, manages to save nearly all the passengers from certain death by maneuvering the airplane with extraordinary skill into a crash landing. He is hailed as a hero, and yet the authorities prosecute him as they correctly suspect him to have been drunk on the day of the flight. No reasonable person would argue that Washington's character made the right call to drink and fly. Even the pilot, who throughout the movie tries to evade prison by lying about his alcoholism, in the final scenes breaks down during a hearing and admits to being intoxicated while flying the plane, knowing that this was an irresponsible *decision*, regardless of the *outcome*.

In her book *Thinking in Bets: Making Smarter Decisions When You Don't Have All the Facts*, Annie Duke explains how she often asks executives about their best and worst decisions. She has yet to encounter an executive who provides an example where the decision was good but the outcome was bad or vice versa. Duke explains the case of a CEO who described his worst decision as firing the president of the company, stating that he had not been able to find anyone to replace him. When Duke asks why the president was fired, the CEO explains that the company had benchmarked its performance to competitors and had seen it could perform better, concluding that it most likely was a leadership issue. The company had worked with the president to identify his skill gap and had hired him an executive coach, and when that failed, it had considered splitting his responsibilities. The company had eventually decided against this last option, determining that it wouldn't be economical to split a position that should be handled by one person and that the staff would've seen it as a vote of no confidence. "It sounded like a bad result, not a bad decision," Duke concluded.

Too many hiring managers are celebrated when they get lucky and their illogical hiring decisions happen to be followed by a good outcome. Likewise, too many hiring managers are penalized for good hiring decisions that are followed by a poor outcome. Building a scalable hiring strategy with repeatable results requires organizations to counteract resulting, paying less attention to good and bad outcomes and more attention to good and bad decisions.

MISTAKING PRECISION FOR ACCURACY

Unlike the rainmaking experiments run by Los Angeles Public Works, few recruiting techniques have a direct cost of half a million dollars, and yet effective recruiters need to deploy best practices, those confirmed by the quantitative results of rigorous tests, instead of resorting to rainmaking rituals. In the quest to improve predictions of on-the-job success, recruiters often add complexity to their process. Does it help them get better at calculating who'll become on-the-job stars, or is it just a digitized beating of rain drums?

According to Glassdoor data, the average length of the interview process nearly doubled between 2010 and 2014 (see Figure 12.1). The share of companies using tools ranging from background checks to skills tests and personality tests has also increased (see Figure 12.2). What's often lacking in all the extra data are clear indications of greater predictive accuracy. The most evolved hiring managers will refuse to confuse precision with accuracy.

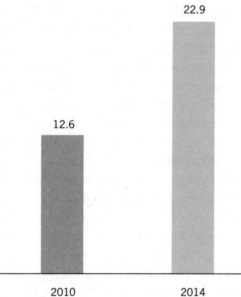

FIGURE 12.1 Average length of interview process (days).
Based on data from "Why Is Hiring Taking Longer?," Glassdoor.

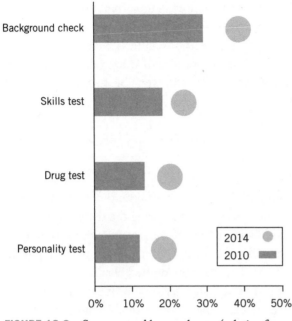

FIGURE 12.2 Screens used by employers (relative frequency).

Do Complex Hiring Processes Produce Better Results?

An event at the University of Texas Medical School provides a good example of the (lack of) value added by additional steps in the hiring process.[2] After the school had interviewed and admitted its regular class of students, the Texas legislature required it to increase its incoming class size by 50. The school decided to admit 50 students who had reached the interview phase of the application process but were ultimately rejected.

When these 50 students were later compared with their classmates in terms of attrition, academic performance, clinical performance, and honors earned, it was found that they did just as well as the other, earlier, admits. What about in terms of rapport with their patients and supervisors? Again, they did just as well as those who'd been admitted before them.

These 50 students had spent countless hours practicing the firmness of their handshakes, selecting their spiffiest outfit, plucking their eyebrows, smiling until their cheeks hurt, and preparing answers to questions about their strengths and weaknesses. Might it be that med school and other kinds of interviews often amount to meaningless prodding and posing?

Unfortunately, yes. It doesn't have to be, but all too often it is. Adding elaborate candidate vetting techniques and questions to your evaluation process will seldom yield better hiring decisions. Unless, that is, you go back and check to see whether adding complexity or more relevant interview questions actually revealed candidates who went on to succeed in your enterprise.

UTILIZE MORE EVIDENCE-BASED HIRING METHODS

Being action-oriented can be tempting. We all want to "just try something" instead of sitting around and hoping for better outcomes. However, improved recruiting outcomes start with measuring the *results* produced by techniques used, not by adding more tools to the process, hoping or praying that at least some of them will work. Feeling good about a recruiting technique does not mean that it will produce the desired results.

Does this mean that you should stop trying new ideas, or that all the recommendations in this book have been tested in double-blind studies and are 100 percent evidence-based? Of course not. Trying new ideas is a great way to learn. However, it's best to try new ideas using a hypothesis-driven approach.

While a number of the recommendations in this book have not been tested, I hope to collect more data on these hypotheses over time. I also hope that this book leads to more evidence-based practices in recruiting. Practicing what I preach, I will not be disappointed if some of my advice is disproved. I take more pride in following the evidence than thinking I have all the right answers to begin with. My ultimate hope is that this book will contribute to recruiters adopting more evidence-based methods, following a similar path to medicine, psychology, poker, stock investing, marketing, and numerous other fields that have adapted evidence-based methods. In the meantime, I'll take comfort from knowing that evidence-based methods are helping my firm enhance our understanding of how to drive success through talent acquisition.

Chapter Summary and Conclusion

Context:

- Action-oriented behavior is often valued over analysis paralysis in business.
- While this rule of thumb has been developed for a good reason, it can lead to overreliance on methods that seem to make sense in the moment but do not add much value.
- Just as in poker, many executives are tempted to measure success by the *outcomes* of their hiring decisions, not by the *quality of the decisions* themselves. This is a mistake.
- The average length of the interview process nearly doubled between 2010 and 2014, a consequence of companies adding steps to their interview process. What is often lacking in the statistics is how effective these methods have been in predicting candidates' on-the-job success.

What you can do about it:

- You want your bias toward action to be balanced by an accurate analysis of the data.
- Building a scalable hiring strategy with repeatable results requires organizations to counteract "resulting," paying less attention to good and bad outcomes and more attention to good and bad decisions.
- Adding complexity to your candidate evaluation process does not necessarily produce better outcomes. You have to go back and check to see if the added complexity is actually producing better outcomes.

Conclusion

This book addresses numerous methods you can utilize to improve your talent acquisition results. So where do you start? As in all areas of business, there are no one-step fixes. Maintaining your competitive edge requires continual improvements. All my recommendations should be tested in your setting, and if they don't improve your results, adjust them to better fit your company or stop using them altogether.

If there is one thing I would like you to take away from this book, it's that following an evidence-based approach, wherein you take pride in the process of establishing and updating best practices, will yield far better results than following the advice of others claiming to have all the right answers.

All of this being said, you have to start somewhere. My recommendation is to begin with the 10 steps listed below. As each organization will have a unique set of circumstances that determine which of these steps will be most effective for *it*, I highly recommend a bespoke approach, starting with the recommendations that will be most effective in your particular setting.

1. Understand how much it's worth to you to improve your recruiting results.

Before you decide that you will completely revamp your talent acquisition process, do a simple calculation. Understand how much it is worth to you to improve key metrics. Try to determine the value of more star performers and compare that with the value of more solid performers. Then calculate what you'd save by making fewer mis-hires or reducing attrition. How much would you profit from improving the productivity of your sourcing team or your interviewers?

Make these calculations realistic. You can set aspirational long-term goals, but unless you believe in your short-term goals, you'll soon get distracted by some other project and stop trying.

Determine how much time, energy, and resources you're willing to spend to achieve these new goals. A good litmus test is whether you're willing to make the investments needed to achieve the benefits to be gained. If not, it's a sign that you don't believe in the assumptions you have made. In that case, revisit the assumptions until you land at numbers you believe in.

If your own math shows that the benefits of improved talent acquisition are minimal, you can stop obsessing about this topic and focus your energy on different areas of your business. On the other hand, if you sincerely believe you can improve your business results through better talent acquisition, start investing the time, budget, energy, and other resources to achieve those results.

2. Assign one of your five best people to talent acquisition.

Putting one of your best employees in charge of talent acquisition is critical if you want to significantly improve your hiring results. As always, "the team with the best players wins." This is especially true in areas of your business that can't rely on already-established processes to maximize results.

3. Define what "good" means.

As tedious as this step might sound, you won't be able to improve your talent acquisition if your team doesn't know how to define "good" or "excellent" in terms of:

- Quality of hires

- Attrition rates

- Productivity metrics for the team

- Any other area that you want the team to improve in

Make your definition of "good' as quantitative and measurable as possible:

- "We want more star hires" is too vague.

- "We want 20 percent of new hires to be stars" is better, but still leaves a lot of room for interpretation, which can confuse and demotivate your team.

- "We want 20 percent of new hires to be stars, where stars are defined as employees who receive customer satisfaction scores of 4.5 or higher" is much more concrete and measurable and will set up your team to succeed.

Defining what "good" means also helps you to understand what activities you need to follow to achieve your desired results. Defining these activities is a critical step toward making your vision fully operational. It will be difficult for you to achieve meaningful results unless these activities become part of your organization's shared metrics to be tracked over time.

4. Articulate an explicit strategy.

Once you have defined what "good" or "excellent" means in your company, be explicit about your strategy for attracting those kinds of candidates. Will you try to win business battles by emulating *The Karate Kid*'s Mr. Miyagi or *Moneyball*'s Billy Beane? That is, will you try to increase the quality of your employees through training and development or by understanding better than others what winning teams need? Or both?

Prioritize and focus on the activities that create the highest value. A big part of this exercise is deciding what you *won't* focus on.

Does the way you allocate your time, budget, energy, and other resources reflect your explicit strategy? If not, revisit the question of how much it's worth to improve your recruiting results.

5. Next, define the talent acquisition team's role.

Determine the steps of the process through which your talent acquisition team can add the most value:

- Set the search strategy. Become a strategic thought partner to your hiring manager(s) by helping define:

- The mandate for a role

- The skills required to achieve that mandate

- The profile that is most likely to have those skills, which helps you prioritize which types of candidates you should target

- Improve candidate sourcing by improving methods you use to:

  - Identify the right candidates

  - Engage candidates to encourage them to apply for your openings

- Predict on-the-job success by having the members of the team:

  - Educate themselves and the rest of your company on screening techniques designed to predict on-the-job success

  - Help you to implement those techniques and processes

  - Help you to track the success of your initiatives

- Deploy your management skills to increase the chances of offers being accepted by:

  - Managing the candidate experience

  - Ensuring alignment with candidates early on in the process by setting mutual expectations and reducing chances of all parties wasting their time

  - Checking in with candidates to better understand whether their priorities have shifted during the process

  - Understanding and adopting best practices learned from experience that will increase offer acceptance rates

6. Never give up on tracking results and metrics.

What gets measured gets improved and, maybe more importantly, vice versa. How much have you been able to improve your talent acquisition without measuring key metrics and results? Can you really expect different outcomes if you don't clearly establish these metrics?

The key is not the desire to improve your talent acquisition results—everybody has that. What is important is the discipline to establish the right processes and then keep tracking the results and activity metrics to evaluate and ensure success.

7. Help your organization go from post and pray to systematic and repeatable success.

Establish and celebrate processes that lead to success based on repeatable and scalable methods, not on random events or luck. Demonstrate tangible wins through these processes. Your team members will lose their faith and patience unless you can demonstrate tangible results.

8. Prioritize and focus on testing a few candidate evaluation techniques at a time.

Pick one or two of the candidate evaluation techniques below and focus on implementing them before moving on to another one. Most organizations won't be able to improve in all these areas at once.

- Use structured interviews. Be explicit in what you are testing for when evaluating candidates. Use templates that match the criteria you want to test for. Have interviewers use numerical scores when rating candidates.

- Resist the temptation to evaluate candidates against your One Big Idea on what makes a good candidate.

- Use multiple indicators for each trait you evaluate.

- Don't try to read too much between the lines. Learn how to probe by clarifying the questions you ask about a candidate's experiences and traits.

- Become aware of your biases, and as often as possible, remind yourself of them.

- Establish processes that reduce interview bias.

- Use job skills tests.

- Avoid groupthink.

- Be truthful with candidates, and make it comfortable for them to opt out if they are not a good fit.

9. Have a specialized team that understands the fundamentals of evidence-based processes and helps you to implement them.

This team can help you to:

- Understand signals that can or can't be relied on.

- Set up procedures to improve the team's productivity.

- Apply best practices in predictions, but understand their limitations.

- Implement all these practices across your hiring process.

10. Don't overdo it!

Remind yourself about:

- The dilution effect. Don't confuse the *quality* of information with the *quantity* of information.

- The illusion of validity and modern rain dances. "Complex and sophisticated" does not mean "better" unless the results can be tracked.

And finally, I wish you good luck. As in playing poker, playing baseball, getting generally fit, getting into the right college, meeting the right significant other, landing a big client right before your start-up runs out of funding, and approaching nearly every other aspect of life, you need to be a little bit lucky, or at least not terribly unlucky, if you're going to land a few of your star hires. I hope the random forces in the universe, or at least your tiny corner of it, will align in your favor. But before you decide to take a seat back at the poker table of recruiting, remind yourself that in the market of talent, you are competing with hundreds of organizations—ranging from tech giants such as Google and Amazon to large corporates in other sectors such as Nestlé and Siemens to midsized companies across a multitude of industries—that are counting the odds of each hire turning into a star. It would be as unwise competing at this table purely relying on luck as it would be to count just on luck when playing in the World Series of Poker. Take a step back and think about how you intend to defend your market position, and the next time the barbarians—the new disruptive competitor in your industry—start pounding on the gate, ask yourself: Are you going to seek shelter behind the barriers to entry you have created to keep competition out, or will you welcome the fight knowing that your army of Spartans—your talent—is up for the challenge?

CHAPTER 6 ANSWER KEY

Answer Key to Table 6.1: How Good Is Your Gut Instinct?

TABLE 6.1 How Good Is Your Gut Instinct? Guess Which Headline Performed Better

	Headline A	Headline B	Winner
1	**Can the Snotbot drone save the whales?**	Can the drone help save the whales?	53% more clicks for A
2	Of course "deflated balls" is a top search term in Massachusetts	**This top Mass. Google search term is pretty embarrassing**	986% more clicks for B
3	Hookup contest at heart of St. Paul rape trial	**No charges in prep school sex scandal**	108% more clicks for B
4	**Woman makes bank off rare baseball card**	Woman makes $179,000 off rare baseball card	38% more clicks for A
5	MBTA projects annual operating deficit will double by 2020	**Get ready: the MBTA's deficit is about to double**	62% more clicks for B
6	How Massachusetts helped win you the right to birth control access	**How Boston University helped end "crimes against chastity"**	188% more clicks for B
7	**When the first subway opened in Boston**	Cartoons from when the first subway opened in Boston	33% more clicks for A
8	Victim and family in prep-school rape trial blame toxic culture	**Victim and family in prep-school rape trial releases statement**	76% more clicks for B
9	Guy in "Free Brady" hat is only one able to foil Miley Cyrus prank	**Pats fan gets an eyeful for recognizing an undercover Miley Cyrus**	67% more clicks for B

Source: Seth Stephens-Davidowitz, *Everybody Lies: Big Data, New Data, and What the Internet Can Tell Us About Who We Really Are* (HarperCollins, New York, 2017). Used with permission.

Acknowledgments

This book would not be possible without all the people who have helped me along the way. I'd like to thank the following thought leaders for freeing up their time and having insightful discussions with me on topics pertaining to this book:

- Patty McCord, Netflix, former Chief Talent Officer

- Mike Federle, Forbes, CEO

- Jim Williams, TPG Growth, Founding Partner

- Greg Hewitt, DHL, CEO

- Ron Williams, Aetna Inc., former Chairman and CEO

- David Kong, Best Western® Hotels & Resorts, President and CEO

- Marc Bitzer, Whirlpool, Chairman and CEO

- Craig Bouchard, Braidy Industries, Chairman, CEO, and Founder and bestselling author

- Denyelle Bruno, CEO, Tender Greens

- Professor James McManus, poker historian and bestselling author

- David Sklansky, three-time World Series of Poker champion and author of *The Theory of Poker*, considered by many to be the most influential book on poker

- Doug Dohring, Founder and CEO of unicorn start-up Age of Learning, Inc.

- Inanc Balci, Cofounder and former CEO of unicorn start-up Lazada

- Larry Kutscher, CEO, A Place for Mom (PE backed)

- David Ehrlich, Cofounder, President, and CEO, Aktana (VC backed)

- Stephane Vedie, President and CEO, Varroc Lighting Systems

- Kenneth Svendsen, CEO, Entertainment Cruises

- M-K O'Connell, Private Equity Investor, M2O, Inc.

- Brian Kelly, COO, National Veterinary Associates (PE backed)

- Rob Paulsson, President, Strategic Healthcare Programs

- John Kunysz, CEO, Intrepid USA (PE backed)

- Daniel Hamburger, former CEO, Renaissance (PE backed)

- Siddhartha Kadia, former President and CEO, EAG Laboratories

- Diego Imperio, President and CEO, RICOH Latin America

- Rachel Austin, VP HR, Best Western Hotels & Resorts

- Stan Telford, SVP Talent Acquisition, Cushman Wakefield

- Guillaume Herbette, CEO, MSL Group, A Publicis Groupe Company

- Professor Frank Schmidt, Gary C. Fethke Chair Leadership Professor, Emeritus, University of Iowa

- Tens of other CEOs and thought leaders who either wished to remain anonymous or for practical reasons cannot be mentioned

The list of friends and colleagues who have helped me turn my ideas into this book is too long for me to mention them all individually. I am, however, very thankful for all your help and support. I'd like to extend a special thank you to M-K O'Connell for particularly detailed and thoughtful edits, Tino Sanandaji for years of engaging and insightful discussions, Shane Frederick for continued thought partnership on this topic, and the team at McGraw-Hill Professional for helping me bring this idea to reality.

And finally, I'd like to thank my wonderful wife, Eli, to say that I would've not been able to write this book if it wasn't for your love and support would be an understatement.

Notes

INTRODUCTION

1. Jason D. Rowley, "Q4 2018 Closes Out a Record Year for the Global VC Market," *Crunchbase News*, Jan. 7, 2019, https://news.crunchbase.com/news/q4-2018-closes-out-a-record-year-for-the-global-vc-market/.

CHAPTER 1

1. Analysis based on available data collected in April 2019 from CB Insights.
2. Ernest O'Boyle and Herman Aguinis, "The Best and the Rest: Revisiting the Norm of Normality of Individual Performance," *Personnel Psychology* 65, no. 1 (March 2012): 79–119, doi:10.1111/j.1744-6570.2011.01239.x.
3. John E. Hunter, Frank L. Schmidt, and Michael K. Judiesch, "Individual Differences in Output Variability as a Function of Job Complexity," *Journal of Applied Psychology* 75, no. 1 (1990): 28–42, https://psycnet.apa.org/record/1990-15949-001.
4. O'Boyle and Aguinis, "The Best and the Rest."
5. Scott Keller and Mary Meaney, "Attracting and Retaining the Right Talent," *McKinsey & Company—Our Insights*, November 2017, https://www.mckinsey.com/business-functions/organization/our-insights/attracting-and-retaining-the-right-talent.
6. Nick Douglas, "I'm DoorDash CEO Tony Xu, and This Is How I Work," *lifehacker*, Dec. 27, 2017, https://lifehacker.com/im-doordash-ceo-tony-xu-and-this-is-how-i-work-1821196705.
7. "Tony Hsieh: 'Hiring Mistakes Cost Zappos.com $100 Million,'" *Inc. Video*, https://www.inc.com/allison-fass/tony-hsieh-hiring-mistakes-cost-zappos-100-million.html.

CHAPTER 2

1. https://hbr.org/2019/02/how-recruiters-can-stay-relevant-in-the-age-of -linkedin.
2. "Top Sources of Hire: The Definitive Report on Talent Acquisition Strategies," http://hr1.silkroad.com/source-of-hire-report-download.
3. Lynne Eldridge, "What Percentage of Smokers Get Lung Cancer?," verywell health, Mar. 15, 2019, https://www.verywellhealth.com/what-percentage-of -smokers-get-lung-cancer-2248868.
4 Sy Kraft, "New Study: Think You Need Bypass Surgery? Not So Fast!," *Medical News Today*, Apr. 5, 2011, https://www.medicalnewstoday.com/ articles/221380.php.
5. Frank J. Domino, "OTC Pain Control Best with Ibuprofen/Acetaminophen," Evidence Based Practice Updates, Feb. 22, 2019, http://www.ebpupdate.com/ 2019/02/title-non-prescription-otc-oral.html.

CHAPTER 3

1. David C. Court, Jonathan W. Gordon, and Jesko Perrey, "Boosting Returns on Marketing Investment," *McKinsey Quarterly*, May 2005, https:// www.mckinsey.com/business-functions/marketing-and-sales/our-insights/ boosting-returns-on-marketing-investment.

CHAPTER 4

1. Adam Bryant, "How to Hire the Right Person," *New York Times*, https://www.nytimes.com/guides/business/how-to-hire-the-right-person.
2. Brian Scudamore, "2 Easy Ways to Know Whether You're Hiring the Right Person," Inc.com, Oct. 24, 2016, https://www.inc.com/quora/2-easy-ways -to-know-whether-youre-hiring-the-right-person.html.
3. Frank L. Schmidt and John E. Hunter, "The Validity and Utility of Selection Methods in Personnel Psychology: Practical and Theoretical Implications of 85 Years of Research Findings," *Psychological Bulletin* 124, no. 2 (September 1998): 262–274, doi:10.1037/0033-2909.124.2.262.
4. Frank L. Schmidt, In-Sue Oh, and Jonathan Shaffer, "The Validity and Utility of Selection Methods in Personnel Psychology: Practical and

Theoretical Implications of 100 Years of Research Findings," *Psychological Bulletin* 124, no. 2 (October 2016): 262–274.

5. Albert Hastorf, "Lewis Terman's Longitudinal Study of the Intellectually Gifted: Early Research, Recent Investigations and the Future," *Gifted and Talented International,* June 2016, 3–7.

6. Kevin Grice, "Former Google Recruiter: This Is How to Improve Your Interviews," *Fast Company,* Mar. 13, 2018, accessed July 23, 2019, https://www.fastcompany.com/40540524/former-google-recruiter-this-is -how-to-improve-your-interviews.

7. Solomon Asch, "Effects of Group Pressure on the Modification and Distortion of Judgments," in H. Guetzkow (ed.), *Groups, Leadership and Men,* Pittsburgh, PA: Carnegie Press, 1951, 222–236.

8. https://hbr.org/2019/08/how-to-avoid-groupthink-when-hiring.

CHAPTER 5

1. Frank L. Schmidt and John E. Hunter, "The Validity and Utility of Selection Methods in Personnel Psychology: Practical and Theoretical Implications of 85 Years of Research Findings, *Psychological Bulletin* 124, no. 2 (September 1998): 262–274, doi:10.1037/0033-2909.124.2.262.

2. Frank L. Schmidt, In-Sue Oh, and Jonathan Shaffer, "The Validity and Utility of Selection Methods in Personnel Psychology: Practical and Theoretical Implications of 100 Years of Research Findings," *Psychological Bulletin* 124, no. 2 (October 2016): 262–274.

3. Mark A. Ciavarella, Ann K. Buchholtz, Christine Riordan, Robert D. Gatewood, and Garnett S. Stokes, "The Big Five and Venture Survival: Is There a Linkage?," *Journal of Business Venturing* 19, no. 4 (July 2004): 465–483, https://doi.org/10.1016/j.jbusvent.2003.03.001.

4. Laszlo Bock, "Here's Google's Secret to Hiring the Best People," *Wired,* Apr. 7, 2015, https://www.wired.com/2015/04/hire-like-google/.

5. https://hbr.org/2019/06/stop-lying-to-job-candidates-about-the-role.

6. Leslie John, "How to Negotiate with a Liar," *Harvard Business Review,* July–August 2016, https://hbr.org/2016/07/how-to-negotiate-with-a-liar.

7. Bradford Smart, "The TORC Technique, a Powerful, Free, Hiring Method," LinkedIn, June 21, 2016, https://www.linkedin.com/pulse/torc-technique -powerful-free-hiring-method-brad-smart/.

8. R. Persaud, "The Truth About Lying," *The New Scientist*, July 2005, https:// www.researchgate.net/publication/285664622.

9. Sonja Lyubomirsky, Laura A. King, and Ed Diener, "The Benefits of Frequent Positive Affect: Does Happiness Lead to Success?," *Psychological Bulletin* 131, no. 6 (December 2005): 803–855, doi:10.1037/0033-2909.131.6.803.

10. Chad H. Van Iddekinge, John D. Arnold, Rachel E. Frieder, and Philip L. Roth, "A Meta-analysis of the Criterion-Related Validity of Prehire Work Experience," *Personnel Psychology*, April 2019, doi:10.1111/peps.12335.

11. Chad H. Van Iddekinge, John D. Arnold, Rachel E. Frieder, and Philip L. Roth, "Companies Look at Job Candidates' Previous Experience, but Does It Predict Anything?," *LSE Business Review*, May 20, 2019, https://blogs.lse .ac.uk/businessreview/2019/05/20/companies-look-at-job-candidates -previous-experience-but-does-it-predict-anything/.

CHAPTER 7

1. Scott Thomas and Atta Tarki, "Attracting the Best Talent Starts with Defining Performance," LinkedIn, Sept. 5, 2018, https://www.linkedin.com/ pulse/attracting-best-talent-starts-defining-performance-atta-tarki/.

2. Patty McCord, "Stop Hiring for Culture Fit," *Harvard Business Review*, Dec. 21, 2017, https://hbr.org/2018/01/how-to-hire.

CHAPTER 8

1. Maria Renz, "Why I Work for Amazon: A Response," Vox, Sept. 25, 2015, https://www.vox.com/2015/9/25/11618868/why-i-work-for-amazon-a -response.

CHAPTER 9

1. https://www.usatoday.com/story/news/2017/07/17/easy-a-nearly-half-hs -seniors-graduate-average/485787001/.

2. David L. Rosenhan, "On Being Sane in Insane Places," *Science* 179, no. 4070 (Jan. 19, 1973): 250–258, doi:10.1126/science.179.4070.250.

3. María A. Ramos-Olazagasti, Francisco Xavier Castellanos, Salvatore Mannuzza, and Rachel G. Klein, "Predicting the Adult Functional Outcomes of Boys with ADHD 33 Years Later," *Journal of the American Academy of*

Child & Adolescent Psychiatry, June 18, 2018, doi:https://doi.org/10.1016/j .jaac.2018.04.015.

4. J. Edward Russo and Paul J. Schoemaker, "Managing Overconfidence," *Sloan Management Review* 33, no. 2 (January 1982): 7–17, https://sloanreview.mit .edu/article/managing-overconfidence/.

5. David Cesarini, Örjan Sandewall, and Magnus Johannesson, "Confidence Interval Estimation Tasks and the Economics of Overconfidence," *Journal of Economic Behavior & Organization* 61, no. 3 (November 2006): 453–470, doi:10.1016/j.jebo.2004.10.010.

CHAPTER 10

1. "Garbage in, Garbage out," *The Economist*, May 27, 2004, https://www .economist.com/leaders/2004/05/27/garbage-in-garbage-out.

2. Philip E. Tetlock, *Expert Political Judgment: How Good Is It? How Can We Know?*, Princeton University Press, Princeton, NJ, 2017.

3. Ashley N. D. Meyer, Velma L. Payne, Derek W. Meeks, Radha Ra, and Hardeep Singh, "Physicians' Diagnostic Accuracy, Confidence, and Resource Requests: A Vignette Study," *JAMA Internal Medicine* 173, no. 21 (November 2013): 1952–1958, doi:10.1001/jamainternmed.2013.10081.

4. Paul A. Samuelson, "Risk and Uncertainty: A Fallacy of Large Numbers," *Scientia* 98, no. 4 (1963): 108–113.

5. David S. Scharfstein and Jeremy C. Stein, "Herd Behavior and Investment," *American Economic Review* 80, no. 3 (June 1990): 465–479, http://www .people.hbs.edu/dscharfstein/articles/herd_behavior_and_investment.pdf.

CHAPTER 11

1. Lawrence Kushi and Edward Giovannucci, "Dietary Fat and Cancer," *American Journal of Medicine* 113, no. 9 (December 2002): 63–70, doi:https:// doi.org/10.1016/S0002-9343(01)00994-9.

2. https://www.td.org/magazines/ctdo-magazine/beware-the-lure-of-confidence.

3. Chun Siong Soon, Marcel Brass, Hans-Jochen Heinze, and John-Dylan Haynes, "Unconscious Determinants of Free Decisions in the Human Brain," *Nature Neuroscience* 11, no. 5 (2008): 543–545, https://www.nature.com/ articles/nn.2112.

4. Richard E. Kopelman and Dorothy Lang, "Alliteration in Mate Selection: Does Barbara Marry Barry?," *Psychological Reports* 56, no. 3 (June 1985), doi:10.2466/pr0.1985.56.3.791.

5. Wijnand A. P. Van Tilburg and Eric R. Igou, "The Impact of Middle Names: Middle Name Initials Enhance Evaluations of Intellectual Performance," *European Journal of Social Psychology* 44, no. 4 (April 2014): 400–411, doi:https://doi.org/10.1002/ejsp.2026.

6. Shai Danziger, Jonathan Levav, and Liora Avnaim-Pesso, "Extraneous Factors in Judicial Decisions," *Proceedings of the National Academy of Sciences of the United States of America* 108, no. 17 (April 26, 2011): 6889–6892, doi:https://doi.org/10.1073/pnas.1018033108.

7. George M. Reynolds and Amanda Shendruk, "Demographics of the U.S. Military," Council on Foreign Relations, Apr. 24, 2018, https://www.cfr.org/article/demographics-us-military.

8. Marc Ethier, "MBA Programs with the Most Women," Poets & Quants, Jan. 31, 2018, https://poetsandquants.com/2018/01/31/which-mba-programs-enroll-the-most-women/2/.

9. Mark J. Perry, "2016 SAT Test Results Confirm Pattern That's Persisted for 50 Years—High School Boys Are Better at Math Than Girls," *Carpe Diem*, Sept. 27, 2016, http://www.aei.org/publication/2016-sat-test-results-confirm-pattern-thats-persisted-for-45-years-high-school-boys-are-better-at-math-than-girls/.

CHAPTER 12

1. Gina Dimuro, "San Diego Hired a 'Rainmaker' in 1915 to End a Drought, but What They Got Was a Deadly Flood," All That's Interesting, Dec. 12, 2018, https://allthatsinteresting.com/charles-hatfield.

2. Richard A. DeVaul, "Medical School Performance of Initially Rejected Students," *Journal of the American Medical Association* 257, no. 1 (January 1987): 47–51, doi:10.1001/jama.257.1.47.

Index

About the Author

ATTA TARKI, CEO of ECA, a data-driven executive search firm. He leads the company's Private Equity and Venture Capital practice, where he supports PE-owned, VC-owned, and other high-growth companies by filling C-level positions with the very best people. Prior to founding ECA, Tarki served for six years as a management consultant at L.E.K. Consulting. He graduated with an MSc in Economics & Finance from the Stockholm School of Economics. Tarki regularly contributes to *Harvard Business Review* and *Forbes* on cutting-edge topics in recruiting.